'No matter what road my life ever took,
and there have been many, it always led back
to my local team, Manchester United.'
Nicky Welsh

MY UNITED ROAD

By a lad called NICKY WELSH
With JOHN LUDDEN

Typeset in Sabon by Sam Walton Studio

John Ludden

Manchester author and playwright John Ludden is an experienced football writer, with work published in three languages. His books include the acclaimed history of Manchester United *A Tale of Two Cities: Manchester United/Real Madrid 1957–1968*, and the now cult-classic *Once Upon a Time in Naples*, which formed the basis for the film *Diego Maradona*, released in 2019. He is currently working on a prequel.

John's other work includes a radio play about the bombing of Coventry during World War Two, broadcast on BBC Sounds in winter 2020, and a series of drama podcasts performed live at the Lowry Theatre, the NQL Salford, the *Hotel Football* and *FC United*.

John and Nicky worked closely together over many months to create *My United Road* and have since become good friends.

Dad and me

This book is dedicated to my dad 'Baza' – the best header of a football that I've ever seen, and believe me I've seen a few.

He sadly passed away in October 2020, the week my book was finally completed. I did manage to read him a few chapters by his bedside just days before he left us, although I knew unfortunately he wasn't really taking any of it in. You see Dad was in the final stages of Alzheimers, which he had been suffering with and fighting for the last fourteen years.

For me it can be no coincidence that many of the footballing greats are now being diagnosed with significant memory problems each passing year. Is it because they have all headed one ball too many?

My United Road will hopefully be successful in helping support the charity in a small way.

THE FIXTURE LIST

11   FOREWORD: BY BILLY GARTON

15   ODE TO BOBBY

23   RED, RED RAIN

31   STAIRWAY TO HEAVEN

39   YOU AIN'T SEEN NOTHING YET

51   KUNG FU FIGHTING

57   DON'T GO BREAKING MY HEART

61   PLANET OF THE APES

65   MAGIC DAY

77   OCTOBER 1974

81   GOODBYE TO TOMMY DOC

85   BIG RON'S AUDITION

91   SCARLET RIBBON

97   GOING UNDERGROUND

101   WILKIE

105   PASTURES NEW

109   THE RIGHT SHAPED BALL

113   CHANGES

117   NICK OF TIME

125   FEELS LIKE HEAVEN

137   THE BITTEREST PILL

143   ROAD TO NOWHERE (NOBBY)

151   MALAYSIA - MONEY FOR NOTHING

175   MOET MASON

181   UNCLE MATT (PART ONE)

187   SIT DOWN

203   ADVENTURES AT THE OLD FIRM

207   TWENTY-SIX YEARS

219   CHAMPIONS

227   UNCLE MATT (PART TWO)

233   THREE HAIL MARY'S AND A TREBLE

245   BARCELONA

257   THE WELSHY BABES

273   BILLY'S BOOTS

279   DARK SIDE OF THE ROAD

281   LEAR JET REDS

287   FROM RUSSIA WITH LOVE: MOSCOW 2008

297   BAZA! 'GET STUCK IN'

305   UNITED AGAINST ALZHEIMER'S

309   NICKY: MY BEAUTIFUL UNITED ROAD

'I want you to play different today Nick, yes. I want you to play well!'
Eric Harrison, Manchester United Youth Manager (1983)

Billy G
Man United 1981 - 1989

FOREWORD

BILLY GARTON

Nick's initial story as a young, aspiring footballer is no different than that of millions of others who kicked a ball around dreaming of being a professional player. I was one of them, attempting to replicate all that I saw on TV out on the streets and the small grassy areas of the then new Ordsall Estate. No coaching or guidance in that place. Those days it was down to how much you wanted it. How dedicated you were to getting better at the game that you loved. Similarly, Nick's 'surrogate' Old Trafford or Wembley were the roads and pavements of Little Hulton.

Our field of dreams...

Out of the millions who have this dream, only a tiny privileged percentage are given the opportunity to realise it and even fewer get to wear the shirt of the club they adore. Where Nick's story differs is that he did go a long way to finding the end of his rainbow. At one point it really was so agonisingly within reach that he could touch it.

Nick was able to pull on that famous red shirt of his beloved Manchester United, albeit only for a few years and in the ranks of the United Youth team.

What is great though, and what in many ways defined Nick, is that his love for United was a huge part of the adventure he found himself on. The best lads from Belfast, Dublin, Glasgow, London, Newcastle and other places up and down the country came to United on trials in search of their own dream. It wasn't ever easy to get noticed and impress, but Nick excelled to more than earn his place. Although a talented young player at that stage, Nick remained in awe of his surroundings. He'd still pinch himself every day as he walked past his heroes in the corridors of the Cliff training ground. Nick couldn't quite comprehend sitting at the same table, having lunch with England Captains Bryan Robson and Ray Wilkins. Or that Gordon McQueen and Lou Macari had just asked him how he played at the weekend. He was probably more excited as a United fan to be in and around his heroes, as competing against them to try and take their place in the team.

Myself, I couldn't have been more different. I wanted the star defenders to play poorly or get injured (nothing too serious), so that I might get elevated to the reserves, or, dare I say it, the first team. Even at sixteen I remember thinking like this. Totally driven, dog eat dog. Ruthless.

Whereas Nick, he wanted to talk, stare, listen, buy them a beer. Given half a chance he'd have trained with a United scarf tied on his arm. Old Trafford and the Cliff were fantasy land for my mate Nicky Welsh.

Nick just loved Manchester United and all it stood for. I honestly doubt if any footballer has ever played in any of the teams, in any levels at United, and been a bigger fan of the club than Nick. In truth, it was probably his Achilles' heel. Though undoubtedly wanting to succeed at United, maybe that essential extra fire in the belly wasn't there – because he was simply happy enough to be around the place. If you asked him, I'm sure he'd agree.

I've been blessed to share some great experiences with Nick. He's been a true friend for almost forty years and our friendship doesn't wane. In fact it's stronger today than ever. In our youth we were just two local lads – mad United fans, living the dream. So many special memories as we watched the Reds pull off great victories in the Fergie years especially. Often and unashamedly acting like big kids as we'd celebrate. Again, no shame in that for we just love our club and the passion that goes with it. Ultimately, as a player at United, Nick had some struggles along the way. Injuries that seriously hindered his progress. I'm convinced that during his time recovering from injury he'd sit and recite the words to every United song. In fact, I nicknamed him 'Rent a Fan' as Nick was so expert in knowing everything written or sung in association with Manchester United. He'd introduce me to a new song or chant on a weekly basis, and I'd be shocked at him knowing every word!

I wouldn't be surprised if Nick has been responsible for writing a few of them himself over the years.

I can't end these few words about my mate without mentioning his dad Baza. He was my worst critic and biggest supporter. Baza would always tell me that I wouldn't have been able to handle him in his prime and I'd disagree. Sometimes we got sparky, but it was all done in jest.

'You can't head it!'

'Well, you can't kick it!'

In fact, Baza made a point of coming to watch me play and was never short of advice. Little nuggets that I'd take on board. I loved the guy. Nick's Uncle Alan another one, an amazing character and, like Nick and

Baza, someone I class as family.

Finally.

I've always said that life isn't a destination, it's a journey. Nick's United Road has been filled with adventure, wonderful stories and glory. Although this is our type of glory, not the glory of medals and trophies, but that special prize of winning friends, respect and a fulfilled life.

Glory, Glory Nicko!

I love ya lad.

ODE TO BOBBY
CHAPTER ONE

It's Autumn 1987. I'm 20 years old. 11 stone wet through with a permed mullet and a bruised ego after my professional career had fizzled out in Malaysia (more about that later!).

Leeds, Leeds, Leeds.

As ever, I was running late and the traffic on the M62 across the Pennines to Yorkshire was much heavier than I had anticipated. It was a beautiful blue sky but a crocodile sun, and there was a chill in the air on this early autumn Sunday afternoon. As I drove past the farmhouse that sits defiantly between the eastbound and westbound carriageways, my mind began to drift back to the previous week when I'd played in a former players' match against Manchester City at Altrincham's Moss Lane ground. I played pretty well if I say so myself – mind you, I was half the average age of the players on the pitch so I guess I had the advantage! Always keenly fought both on the pitch and at the bar, post-match. Legs may have gone, but the skill, heart for battle and, it must be said, the ability to race to the bar and sink a few pints never left these old warriors. The match itself was memorable for me if not anyone else, except my dad, who cheered me on as though it was an important match, for late in the game I slotted a perfect through ball to the relatively new Manchester United Manager. A certain Alex Ferguson.

'To me now son,' he yelled across in his fierce Glasgow accent etched with that particular menacing Govan tone to ensure that I actually passed it to him. Would I freeze, imagining that maybe he might spot my hidden talent and sign me back on? Thank God I didn't. My sublime – again, if I say so myself – lay off was drilled home to perfection by Fergie, and we nodded to each other acknowledging his cool finish and my perfect set up. Whilst I tried to stay cool, calm and collected, I swear Fergie gave me another swift look to say, 'Who the bloody hell are you anyway son?'

As thirty years and more have passed, I think it's relatively safe to admit – even to Sir Alex – that after a tough start, me and my mates thought he wouldn't last long at United. Now, I'm so happy to report that we didn't have a clue and, to give him his due, let me go on record to say that Sir Alex Ferguson is the greatest football manager the world has ever seen and a true gentleman to boot. The best of that legendary clan of great Scots managers – Busby, Stein, Shankly, Ferguson and the rest – who have through the decades blessed us with their knowledge; their nous; their skill and their temperament; their respect for others, however important or 'small'; their love and passion; and most of all their steely determination to win. I acknowledge this – even if he never truly acknowledged my sublime part in his goal.

What a pass! Still time, boss.

Come the final whistle, I was tapped on the shoulder by one of our 1968 European-Cup-winning United legends, David Sadler. 'Nick, do you fancy turning out for us again next week against Leeds United at York City's Bootham Crescent?' Secretly, they must have been impressed after all with my set up for Fergie. 'Love to Dave, it would be my pleasure.' (I actually called him Dave?) It was obvious, at least in my head, that I was one of the boys now. 'The coach leaves Old Trafford next Sunday at 11am,' said my new mate Dave. 'Make sure you're not late, Nick.' Still shy amongst such prestigious company, true greats of the club who I and all my family so loved and adored – I thought it best to decline the lift.

'No, you're OK Dave, you don't have to trouble yourselves. I'll drive and make my own way to York in my car.'

To this day I don't have a clue why I rejected the offer of a trip with some of my all time heroes. Was I shy? Did I want to let him know that I had a car – or was it another case of Intermittent Welsh Tourette's syndrome?

To be fair, I would walk on my hands anywhere in the world to get the opportunity to represent United at any level and to pull on that famous red shirt just one more time. Dave didn't seem too bothered, simply shrugging his shoulders and walking off. I remember thinking that a little strange, but with me still grinning like a chimp who'd just been handed a basket of bananas, I thought nothing more of it.

So. Back to the M62 that Sunday afternoon. One week after 'that' pass! Kick-off was set for two fifteen and by quarter to two, with the team coach driver already on his second cuppa at Bootham Crescent, I was struggling to get anywhere near the ground in my much-loved, but sadly clapped-out Volkswagen Golf. I could just about make out the floodlights in the distance and also noticed that the crowds were drifting to the ground around me. A rowdy white sea of tatty Leeds scarves. All too late it dawned on me that this was enemy territory. Suddenly, there was fire in my belly and, what's more, the butterflies had begun to kick in.

The sixties and seventies had seen a re-run of The War of the Roses. Imagine Game of Thrones with flares and feather cuts, windjammers and platforms, Woodbines and Watneys Red Barrel. Every game saw punch-ups and head-butts and people getting booted six feet in the air – and that was just on the pitch. Off the pitch it was equally brutal, both at Elland Road and Old Trafford. The Pennines had always been a natural barrier between two warring tribes, as well as one of the north's most splendid natural landscapes. The animosity between the red rose of Lancaster (we won) and the white rose of York (they lost) has remained in the blood centuries after the last battle of that war at Bosworth Field. After our hatred of Liverpool I reckon Leeds is next – even 15 years after they got relegated to the Championship in 2004. It remained in the blood long after those warriors had hung up their boots, and today promised to be no different.

It was two o'clock by now and I still hadn't moved for a quarter of an hour. I checked my watch. It was getting close and I was starting to panic.

'Make sure you're not late, Nick' echoed in my head – which by now felt as hollow as the Etihad on any average match day. The traffic crept along at a snail's pace as the coach driver probably started on his pie, chips, peas and gravy – which by now I was desperate to tuck into – not unusual for players in those days. Nothing was ever rushed on this side of the Pennines. All around me the half-witted, grey-faced, grim-browed Yorkshire orcs were shouting their vile, humourless chants about my club – but I thought it best simply to seethe in scornful, furious silence. The odds of winning a scrap if I stopped the car and jumped out to defend my club against that throng of imbeciles were terrible – also, I wasn't actually driving the bat mobile.

At an upcoming junction I spotted a side road leading to the ground. This was my chance, but as I signalled to turn, a policeman came knocking on the window of my car. 'Oi, who do you think you are, Don bloody Revie? That road is off limits to the public. Back you go.' Ah, I thought, this is where I play my top trump card.

'You don't understand officer, I'm playing for Manchester United today and I'm already late. I need to get to the ground urgently.' PC Don was probably close to retirement and was still on the beat – not good. He stared at me with the kind of look you have on your face after walking into dog shit with no shoes on – and this was a squelchy, slimy, modern one, not a good old fashioned white one at that! Definitely not impressed.

'I'm sure you are son, and I was in bloody Starsky and Hutch. Now, sod off and park away from the ground back with the others before I lose my temper and book you for something.'

'Come on mate,' I shouted back, really worried by now about my team starting short – without its new top midfielder at that – and having to use the typical 'Traffic was bad' lame excuse. 'Do you really think I'm sad enough to try and blag my way into a charity football game? I'm here to help you lot raise money.'

'Are you on Coronation Street or something?' he asks. 'My Mrs watches that. I like Emmerdale Farm myself.'

'Yeah,' I replied. By now I was desperate and close to losing it. 'I was a barman in The Rovers Return. I actually won a Bafta.' The policeman smiled wide. More a grimace to be honest. 'Right OK, well why didn't you say so in the first place. Off you go then, like a proper little superstar.' With that I smiled and muttered 'Up yours' in my head as he motioned for me to drive on. Thank God I wasn't going to be late. George Best may have got away with stuff like this but not me. Even if my new best mate was Dave Sadler.

On reaching the car park I pulled up next to the Manchester United coach, grabbed my boots, shin-pads and lucky Stimarol chewing gum from the back seat – I hadn't even had chance to pack a bag that morning – and raced over to the main entrance already imagining myself tearing through the midfield and leathering the ball into the top corner of their net.

Then, I headed straight into yet another jobsworth. Otherwise known as a steward.

'Who are you then?'

'You don't recognise me? I was in Albion Market on ITV mate. Had the fruit and veg stall. Done loads of pantomime as well.'

He smiled widely, 'The Mancs that desperate eh? In you go then. Hope you get hammered.' Give me strength!

I burst through the battered door into the reeking, decrepit dressing room only to be met by former Manchester United player and manager Wilf McGuiness. A true Manc, Wilf had only missed being on the plane to Munich because he had been injured.

'Oh, Nicky. Brilliant. Glad you could make it!' I'm sure I detected a hint of sarcasm. My sudden anxiety and slight deflation increased when 1977 FA-Cup-winning Captain Martin Buchan added, with his legendary, dry and sometimes cruel wit: 'Yeah, we've only got ten players. You'll have to do 'til someone half decent shows up.'

As an aside – as an example of his type of wit, once, after a game at Old

Trafford when he was asked by a journalist for a quick word, Martin simply replied 'Velocity.' At least it didn't look like he had his guitar with him.

Small mercies when, to my rescue, in walked my mate David Sadler. 'Hello Mick.' (Mick!) 'Get your kit on now, you're playing in centre midfield with Bobby.' Bobby? Bobby who I thought? Still red faced 'cause of my late arrival and smarting from Martin Buchan's taunt, I at least had something to get on with as I was thrown my kit. I started to get changed. I kept my eyes glued to the floor in case he caught my eye again and ripped me with another one-liner. Then, as I was shoving my shin-pads down my black United socks, I glanced up to my left and suddenly realised that the great Sir Bobby Charlton was now sitting next to me. Yep, that Bobby! I'm only playing centre midfield with Bobby bleedin' Charlton! Now my embarrassment evaporated – instead I was immediately nervous. My head began to spin and my breath quickened as I thought to myself – am I dreaming this?

The former players' team was mainly made up of players from the sixties and seventies including my mate Dave, Martin Buchan, Sir Bobby, Brian Kidd, Carlos Sartori and Alan Gowling, etc. For younger legs, myself and Wilf's son, Paul, who had played in United's youth team, were brought in to bring a little energy to support the talented golden oldies. The legends were still as passionate as ever and undoubtedly still possessed ability by the bagful, but they no longer had the legs anymore to match their Red devil hearts.

By now we were all kitted up and the smell of wintergreen filled the small away dressing room. Two of the Busby Babes stepped into the centre and I felt a chill go down my spine. Wilf McGuiness, with Salford's own John Doherty alongside him, began not so much a team talk as a call to arms. Wilf starts and his words are spat out like bullets or spears. Churchill in The Battle of Britain and Henry V at Agincourt would both have been proud of him.

'Come on lads, we hate this lot. You know there's no such thing as a friendly against dirty Leeds United. Keep the ball on the ground and do your best to try and keep the tempo up. We've got Nicky and Paul here with the young, fresh legs so let them do the work. You do the rest.'

I'd played in a few of these games before, but I'd never seen the players so fired up. Wilf carried on with a snarl. 'So, let's go out there, get stuck in and show this Leeds mob that there's only one United. That's Manchester United!'

I'm not sure how the others felt, but at that moment my heart was racing. I was back in the shirt I loved, playing against a deadly rival who we hated – and they us.

In the tunnel, I glanced across at our opponents. The intense concentration on their faces. They all looked like they'd been fed red meat in the changing rooms. The things you do for bloody charity on a Sunday afternoon eh, I thought. We exchanged words and jokes and Wilf started to try and lighten the mood. He walked along past both teams, carrying his raincoat over one arm. 'Afternoon lads, come to get another football lesson from us, have we?' I stared across, bollocks to 'em, I had a devil on my shirt and felt ten feet tall. I was doing something I had dreamt about from being a young lad – playing for Manchester United.

Ever since I can remember, that just meant absolutely everything.

The Leeds line-up was amazing. I couldn't believe my eyes. Gary Sprake, Peter Lorimer, Paul Madeley, Johnny Giles, Jackie Charlton, Terry Yorath, Arthur Graham, Joe Jordan, etc. Something told me this lot on the wrong side of the Pennines were taking it seriously. Off we went, the clatter of studs on the concrete floor. God, how I'd missed that sound. As we approached the pitch I looked around and the ground was virtually full to capacity. A hail of boos, and the odd traditional cry of 'Manc scum,' greeted our arrival. Not quite the spirit of Live Aid. Bootham Crescent had been transformed into Elland Road for the day. All this only helped to fire our lads up even more. It may have been just for charity, but for those of us blessed to be of the Red persuasion, nothing mattered more than shutting this lot up.

The game kicked off at a ferocious pace. Even the legends were charging around like twenty-five-year-olds, although that wouldn't last. Not long into the game I took the ball in midfield and got whacked hard on the calf by Joe Jordan. His front teeth were out, showing that big Joe meant business. As I got back to my feet, this one-time United hero of mine flashed his famous toothless grin. I felt almost honoured that he had felt it worthwhile to foul me, but I forced myself to stop short of thanking him. We took an early lead with Leeds equalising a short time afterwards to send Bootham Crescent wild with delight! It was a cracking game. End to end, with flashes of wonderful skill from the greats, and comedy moments from others who weren't so great.

Five minutes remained of the first half when the ball was passed inside to me, about ten yards outside the Leeds box. I could hear Bobby Charlton shouting 'Pass, pass it!'

Sir Bobby was unmarked to my left and racing through. That elegant, legendary dashing style. Now he stopped and waited, waving his hand in the air. World Cup and European Cup winner.

Yep, that Sir Bobby… unmarked and in front of goal.

Now then, here's the question.

What's the best way to react when such an opportunity is placed in front of you? Do you (a) pass to the best striker of a football that England and possibly the world has ever seen, or (b) carry on doing what you've done all your life since playing in the street, back garden and school playground. Slick measured pass and a shared celebration – or go for glory, have a dig and break the back of the net? What do you think? So, yes, I'm afraid to say that, head throbbing with overexcitement I elected for option b. I took aim and let fly with my right foot, and my shot (if you can call it that) was met by huge cheers – well, more like jeers – and donkey noises, and the utter joy of the rabid home crowd. Oh, how the home crowd loved it; pity Bobby didn't! The ball dipped groundwards, swerved to the right, away from goal, along the turf and spluttered out for a goal kick – fifteen yards wide. I was lucky not to give away a throw in! I stared downwards, hands on hips. Gutted. A hole gaped in the pitch in front of me – well, it felt that way. Then, what seemed an age later as my gaze lifted upwards, arms wide open, pointing to his feet at where the ball should have obviously been slid, I heard a very particular, familiar voice screaming loudly, 'What you doing? Who do you think you are?'

Bollocks, I thought. Welshy, you've done it again.

'Soz Bobby,' I muttered, and as the legend glared at me with disdain, for some unknown reason I thought back to an incident that some might say was even slightly more embarrassing, many years earlier.

Down my United Road.

RED, RED RAIN
CHAPTER TWO

So where did my United Road begin?

Contrary to what I've told people over the years – and still do to be honest – in the odd (well, not really so odd) drunken tale, I wasn't actually born on the United scoreboard paddock, but rather in more humdrum, if slightly exciting circumstances, at home in Glynrene Drive, Swinton. As my mum Eileen prepared to give birth, my dad, Barry, my hero and best friend, raced to the nearby pub, The Morning Star, to use their phone to call a midwife. Unfortunately, it was out of order, so Dad set off at a pace to the next boozer – not very far away, as there seemed to be a pub on every corner in those days. The Red Lion, next to Moorside railway station. Again, broken but luckily the kind landlady allowed him to make the emergency call from her own home phone line in the living quarters. Now panicking, Dad sprinted back home. He made it just in time and with my two-year-old sister Jane given the shock of her young life on entering the room, before being told to 'scarper,' I made my way into this world. Luckily, by this time a midwife was on the scene and with the help of dad I popped out.

Stephen Nicholas Welsh made his first ever appearance off the bench.

'I was always gonna be a Red, no question about that.'

Grandad Harry Welsh and my dad were born and bred in Newton Heath, just off Briscoe Lane, a stone's throw to the old railway depot where Newton Heath – who later changed their name to Manchester United – had been formed in 1878.

In our family, on both sides, the club is in our blood, pumping around every capillary, vein and artery. It's our inheritance. Our backbone. Our pride. Our DNA. Our joy. The history of the club is taught to you, imprinted on you, from an early age. 'United' is one of the first words you learn and you will come to use that word millions of times during your lifetime. It will be inconceivable to even contemplate wavering towards another club. It's part of every cell in your body.

The sickening disaster at just after 3pm on February 6, 1958 on the slushy runway in Munich and the names of those greats we lost are etched onto our collective psyche – as are the heroic efforts of the great Jimmy Murphy and Sir Matt and their quest to rebuild the club and make it even greater. The greatest. The triumvirate of Best, Law and Charlton helped us, finally, to win the European Cup after our first attempt ten years earlier had cost us so much. How bittersweet. How magnificent. How much the start and end of that decade means to us all.

My grandad Harry and my nana Welsh always had a fantastic work ethic. Dad often told me about Harry's entrepreneurial approach to life. A third eye; a vision for the future. He would tell my dad and his brothers Tony, Barry and Steven, that in years to come everyone would own their own motorcar and go on holidays abroad to the Mediterranean. Trips to Blackpool or North Wales for your holiday would be old hat. He used to encourage his three lads to work for themselves, which was still rare in those days, as most working class people aspired to little more than scraping a living and raising their families as best they could.

'Start your own business and work as hard as you can. The sky's the limit but you'll also reap the benefits – hard work has never hurt anyone.'

Harry's only time off from his daily graft would be his visits to Old Trafford to watch the Reds every other week or sometimes, if he was going to really treat himself, a trip to the cinema in town late at night to watch the major world title bouts in another sport he loved – boxing.

Grandad Harry used his work ethic to great effect when he took over a run-down, seemingly broken, Wilson's House pub called The George Hotel that was set right in the heart of Cheetham Hill Village. In no time Harry turned The George into the best drinking house around. Business thrived. The beer was always top notch and every inch of the boozer, including the cellar, was kept immaculately clean. As for food, Nana ensured that the punters never went hungry, toiling away in the pub's kitchen.

On entering The George, you walked onto a spick and span black and white tiled floor. To the left was an Irish vault. The right, an English. Harry had it sussed. As you carried on past the vaults into the main lounge, people from all walks of life mixed together. The George Hotel developed a reputation for a fantastic landlord and landlady, a friendly environment and a crackin' pint. But it was also a pub that never stood for any trouble. As ever, thinking ahead, Harry had chosen the pub due to its location and catchment areas from the large nearby estates of Hightown,

Crumpsall and Broughton. There were characters aplenty. You can only imagine some of the clientele it attracted. Life was never boring. One time, a Timpson's shoe shop across the road had been 'visited' and there were all sorts of people in the pub trying on shoes out of brand-new boxes. Everybody loved a bargain. My dad vividly recalls a big Irish navvy in their vault explaining to one of the thieves in his heavy brogue: 'The right foot is just a little bit tight on me big toe, Murphy, you couldn't just go back in and swap it for a 12 could you?' Minutes later Murphy returned, after going back through the front window of the shop to swap it, and the navvy was smiling wide as the replacement pair fitted like a pair of gloves! Sometimes, though, it simply couldn't be helped and with Cheetham Hill such a melting pot of humanity, trouble inevitably erupted.

On one particular Saturday evening The George was getting revved up for the usual boisterous craic. During weekends in those days my dad and his two brothers used to help out, as it could get a bit 'lively'. The punters drank hard, played hard and fought hard. They were hard times. On one occasion all hell broke loose and there was actually a death from a fight which had spilled out of the pub onto the croft at the back. Later in life, Dad told me that one of the scrappers had picked up a brick and cracked the other bloke over the head, killing him. This apart, Harry and his three lads could more than handle themselves running as tight a ship as they possibly could, always alert to any potential flash points and nipping it in the bud before the demon booze could take a hold and fuel many a confrontation – but somehow managing to achieve this whilst keeping up a friendly atmosphere. Hospitality and security. Thus, the punters kept coming and the George Hotel's reputation remained high.

Come 1968, me, Mum, Dad and older sister Jane were actually living full-time at the pub as we waited for our new house in Little Hulton to be finished. It was the weekend of my second birthday and even at such a tender age, I was decked out in United red and white. These days this would hardly be unusual, but you have to remember back then there was no JJB, Sports Direct or United Megastore. The chances of a kid having a full kit were virtually zero. Well, not in our family, for my dad's uncle, Steve Newton from Wythenshawe, was a shirt maker by trade. As a present for me, with expert and loving care he designed a red shirt with white cuffs and collar that also had a crisp white number nine stitched neatly onto the back. The number of the United and England Captain. Guess who?

The day of my birthday, our kid and me, dressed in my new birthday present, were upstairs, settled in the lounge, watching telly. As ever, you could hear the noise, the chatting and music from below, but we'd simply grown to ignore it. As the afternoon wore on my dad came up and said that there were a lot of people downstairs who all wanted to see the little Bobby Charlton in his new United kit. He carried me downstairs and we went through the door at the bottom of the stairs leading into the main lounge. It was packed, mostly with United fans. Seeing me appear, some started to sing, 'Aye, aye, aye, Charlton is better than Pelé, coz Pelé is a no-good bum, and so is Eusebio'. This, a song that had been sung at the World Cup and European Cup Finals – both at Wembley – in which a certain number nine had been instrumental in helping both club and country achieve their then greatest triumphs. I looked around, a little startled to see so many people all staring at me, waving their drinks in the air, singing and laughing. The whole pub was singing at me. I was fully the centre of attention and I remember to this day the feeling of embarrassment and fear, seeing all those red faces and open mouths. A small group even came out of the vaults to join in. 'Charlton!' clap, clap, clap. 'Charlton!' clap, clap, clap. Everywhere there were hordes of wide-eyed, drunken adults singing and pointing. My proud dad was still holding me up round his shoulders. 'Wave Nick,' he shouted above the hubbub, smiling widely. 'Come on Nicky – wave at everyone son!' Then, without any warning, Dad frowned. Something was 'up'. Hmmmm. He could tell – well, in fact smell – that something was wrong. He lifted me down from his shoulders and I looked into his eyes. We stared at each other. Then we both looked down. My sparkling white shorts had suddenly become a slightly beigey, brown colour... my first memory! I looked like I'd played a match on a soggy afternoon and had done a sliding tackle at that! Not quite as immaculate as the real number nine!

'Soz Bobby.' And that's where my mind drifted back to that afternoon at Bootham Crescent. Sir Bobby couldn't have imagined what was going through my mind at that moment as he berated my selfish lack of skill.

* * * * * * * * * * * * * * * * *

Back to my childhood.

For those who don't know, Little Hulton is a large Salford overspill up past Swinton and Walkden in the north west corner of Manchester. A last outpost on the outskirts of civilisation before you get to the wilds of Bolton. As a piece of social engineering Little Hulton would in time go to the wall, but in those days it was home and I loved it. Our house had by now been built. It was situated just off Hilton Lane, on the edge of one of the largest council estates you could ever imagine. A vast human sea of iniquity; a mish mash of all sorts of folk: good, bad, evil and downright mad. Gangsters, poets, actors, singers, priests, bank robbers and footballers. We lived on Derwent Close which was a cul de sac and perfect for playing out as a youngster. It also backed onto a railway line, on the other side of which sat a number of football pitches and old mining slag heaps which hold many fond memories from my early years, particularly in terms of getting up to mischief. It was a kid's playground paradise. I was never an angel; more a troublesome imp with a good heart. Or so I tell myself. I found out some years later that Shaun Ryder from the Happy Mondays lived on the next street whilst Bez was on Hilton Lane. Doctor Who himself, Christopher Eccleston, was another, living not a stone's throw away on Coniston Avenue, as was Peter Hook of Joy Division and later New Order. But, at the time, all of us were just little rags, out playing footy, marbles, on our Raleigh bikes, having adventures and trying to get up to no good. Later on, the area grew intolerably worse with gang crime and drugs. I read recently about Ryder recalling a period when every criminal moved to Little Hulton because the police had simply stopped going up there.

My older sister Jane went to school at St Raphael's (later to change its name to St Edmund's). It was located at the top of Hilton Lane across Manchester Road on Bridgewater Street. I'd go with Mum sometimes to drop off or collect her and the time couldn't come quick enough for when it was my turn. Not to pick wits against other kids in the classroom with silly, unimportant stuff like maths and English, but to get playing in the playground with a ball and meet new mates. As far back as I can remember, I loved playing with the ball. It didn't matter how big or small or whose it was. Leather, plastic or rubber. Mitre, Frodo or tennis ball even, anything that was round and would bounce. So long as I had a ball to kick, I was happy. The cul de sac was perfect for playing games as there was no through traffic and many of the kids from the surrounding streets headed to outside ours to set up footy games, or play kerby or wall-ee. I'd join in with the older kids when they let me, loving the challenge. Looking back, even then I felt some kind of love towards a ball. I was one-eyed, Red-eyed and as far as I was concerned I was already at the start of my United Road. The road to being a United player.

As for school, luckily I was there before I knew it.

I loved St Raphael's. It was well run by the headmaster, Mr Delaney, who was strict but always fair. Obviously, there were many rum kids from families that made the Corleone's look like the Walton's, but this all added to its special character. Hardly surprising given where we lived, it had the usual free meal tables and some kids were, for want of better words, on their arse and poverty stricken. Sometimes their arses could literally be seen through the rips in their pants. One girl in my class I remember always stunk of piss and no one ever wanted to sit next to her. Someone would touch her, then chase after the others trying to tig them, pretending to pass on the disease we cruelly imagined she had. 'Tig! You've got the mange!' we'd cry with glee. Nowadays we know this as bullying but attitudes were different back then and it was thought of as just a part of growing up. I'm mortified to think back about how cruel we all were. This wasn't just for one day by the way, but an entire year. Thankfully, the Welsh's were never that poor, although we weren't allowed bottles of pop from the Alpine lorry that came around our way. I used to watch it and think those kids from families who got pop must be dead rich to be able to afford the fizzy that was dropped off on your doorstep. I could almost taste the Dandelion and Burdock and Sarsaparilla – even the exotic, bright green American Cream Soda! This apart, we never really wanted for anything and all the essential things were provided for thanks to my hard-working parents. Mum worked at Lewis's as a sales assistant, whilst dad toiled every hour attempting to follow Harry's advice and get various businesses off the ground. I remember chatting with a couple of my mates from Ordsall, talking about how poor they were growing up. Forced to water down the milk for it to go around and having to put cardboard on the inside of shoes they'd worn through, probably already worn by older brothers and passed down. In comparison I was more fortunate and privileged, but there were many of the other kids, including friends around me at my new school, that had these issues. Wealth is relative, and as being deprived of pop was the only thing I remember missing out on, I know that I felt comfortable – even well off.

※※※※※※※※※※※※※※※※※

I met Peter Dunne on my first ever day at school. He was mixed race and adopted – a great lad for sure and we'd go on to be best mates in our early school years, along with David Baker, who was the biggest and hardest lad in our year. The three of us had a common bond. One more important than life itself. We were massive Reds!

It was by now the 1972/3 season, the early Tommy Docherty era after Frank O'Farrell's disastrous short-term reign. United were going through a transition (sound familiar?) after Sir Matt Busby's retirement. United needed major surgery. The club was rotting from the inside. The greats like Bobby Charlton and Denis Law were becoming weary and old, Georgie Best was off his trolley on the top shelf and working his way through Miss Worlds. Most of the others in the club who were left to carry the red flag were simply not good enough to wear the shirt. The Doc was given full rein by Sir Matt and the board to freshen things up – out with the old and in with the new, so to speak. I think they expected surgery with a scalpel, but he chose to use a machine gun!

It was the start for me though of the Doc's Red Army years. I now realised how passionately I felt about my local team. I was part of it with my close mates who were exactly the same. At school the three of us would sing and teach each other the United songs we'd heard; mine mainly from The George pub, which I would regularly go back to at the weekend (but not in my kit, I might add). The other lads had older brothers who regularly went to the match, so they would pass on the songs.

'We had joy, we had fun, we had City on the run – but the joy didn't last, 'cos the bastards ran too fast' was one I vividly remember learning around this time. It was relevant to the Denis Law back heel and United's relegation to Division Two – let's leave it at that eh, although it did mean that I'd be going to see my first ever live Manchester United game in the old Second Division with my Uncle Alan. More about that later. Not only did we know all the songs but our conversations would turn to what the main lads were wearing at the match. You see, you simply had to look the part!

I owned a little denim jacket with three United badges already stitched on the back. My aim was to fill it with more over the three months before the start of the next season. The look was finished off with a mullet/feather haircut, 36-inch, eight-button Oxford bags and three-star jumpers, with Dr Marten boots or wedges, which were all the rage. It was the time of the Bay City Rollers and United had developed a strong Scottish link with the manager. The Doc had a deeply felt desire to add a huge tartan blood transfusion of players and breathe much needed new life into the team. Tartan became the colour of the day. We also had our own version of the Rollers' Bye Bye Baby song which all the lads in the area would sing at the time.

'You're the one girl in town I'd marry. Big tits and a hairy fanny...'

I remember getting a right belt off Mum for singing that one in front of our Jane!

Then came some great news. For the first time in our young lives we'd get the chance to stand up in the flesh for Manchester United. For our team. A huge new supermarket had just been built at the top of the precinct in Walkden, up behind the Pembroke Hall, called Scan. It had been announced that United centre-forward Stuart 'Pancho' Pearson was coming to open it and me and my mates were ecstatic – a United player coming 'round our way? It just never happened. Oh, they'd open shops and stores in South Manchester or the leafy, rich Cheshire suburbs, but here? This was a heartland of support for the club. Little Hulton and parts of Walkden were mostly made up of Salford people, therefore mostly Reds. There was the odd City supporter (odd being the right word), but you could probably fit them all on the top of a double decker bus – which you could then drive into a bridge! Also, because we were further out from Salford, moving up more towards Farnworth and Atherton, there were probably as many Bolton Wanderers fans. Now, they were a different breed altogether. To be fair though, they had a decent team back then with the likes of a young Sam Allardyce and Peter Reid. I remember them beating us a couple of times. Frank Worthington in particular was a real thorn in our side.

Anyway, keen to get close to Pancho Pearson, our little posse got to Scan early. There were loads of kids present – a hundred plus – and we could see Pancho sitting at a table, signing autographs for all that had shown up. As we edged further and further towards him, we suddenly heard some lads, about five or six of them, one with a Bolton scarf tied round his neck, start shouting from the back, 'Pearson you're crap, United shite.'

Another, 'I've got some toilet roll here for you to sign on.' Peter Dunne had his older brother Vinnie with him and there were a few other older lads also from the estate with us. We all looked at each other in disgust and without saying anything turned to walk towards these idiots. I remember David Baker, who always had a bit of a gob on him, shouting over and hiding behind his even bigger brother, 'Piss off, you bunch of inbreds'. We always used to joke that anyone from Bolton or Blackburn when celebrating would give each other a high six!

Someone else shouted, 'Get outside. We'll show you what's what – knob heads!' There were about ten in our group, us three being much younger than the rest, and before I knew it, we were on the Scan car park. 'Come on then!' went the call. The Bolton lads started to panic and turned to run as a couple of punches and kicks rained down on them. Before long we were legging after them, up the hill of the car park, towards the Unit 4 cinema and out onto Bolton Road, our flares flapping in the wind! As they disappeared in the distance, the cries of 'United, United!' went up and we laughed our heads off walking back to the new superstore. Unfortunately, by this time Pancho had gone and our chances of meeting him vanished along with those Bolton fans. Deep down we weren't that bothered though, for the little Red posse from Little Hulton had done ourselves and our team proud. We'd been blessed with being born under a Red, Red rain and it felt boss! Soon, for me, the time was drawing near to visit heaven itself. Old Trafford.

STAIRWAY TO HEAVEN
CHAPTER THREE

As if I didn't get lucky enough with my dad, I also happened to inherit one of the best uncles in the world. A United fanatic going back to the early fifties. The chameleon. A man equally comfortable in the presence of Manchester's highest fliers and downright scoundrels, but most of all a family man. One of us. Wise, honest, smart, lightning fast with a joke and a heart the size of the Stretford End. That's my Uncle Alan. Born in higher Crumpsall, not lower (he'll always remind you), where the biscuit works resided. When he was younger he was offered a scholarship at RADA. Whilst his mum could not be happier, dad was a different story. 'Place will be full of turd burglars,' he told him. 'You're not bloody going lad.' This, the same Alan whom in 1968 proposed to his girlfriend Anne at the end of the European Cup Final on the terraces. His dad, also a huge Red, had won big that same day on the Epsom Derby, with a bet on Sir Ivor, and had travelled onto Wembley to watch United. Before the game began, he gave Alan a wad of money from the winnings and told him to put it under his carpet. 'Don't let your mum see it son!' Come the final whistle and overcome with emotion, Alan went down on one knee, proposing to a shocked Anne and to great cheers and probably much relief from the surrounding jubilant United supporters, and Alan, she said yes! Whether he would've proposed if Eusebio had scored at the end, when Alex Stepney pulled off a magnificent save, we will never know! Three months later they were husband and wife. A match made in heaven – or heaven made at a match, more like! Uncle Alan got the ring on a deal and today remains happily married. Though he does like to remind people that Anne won The Nobel Prize for nagging. Three times! Once a big smoker, I remember him telling me of going to watch United at Villa Park. Thinking nothing of buying twenty fags for his nerves and smoking them during the game, on hearing the teams being announced over the tannoy, and the dreadful news that Paddy Roache (United's dodgy reserve keeper) was playing, Al turned to his mate and said, 'I should've bought forty!'

I remember Alan used to nickname Paddy Roache Dracula. I once asked him 'Why Dracula, Uncle Al?' to which he replied, 'Well, they are both obviously terrified of crosses, Nicky.'

Also, incredibly, in the early 1980s Uncle Al had his car wheels stolen and replaced by bricks two years on the run when going to watch United at the Hawthorns against West Brom. I've been told the look on his face the second time around was priceless! This is the man who, on 30th November 1974, made a seven-year-old's dreams come true.

My other grandparents, on Mum's side, were grandad Pop and Nana Toal, whom both originated from Ireland. They lived on Bent Street, close to Strangeways prison, but then got moved to a brand new maisonette in Collyhurst. With Mum and Dad still working all hours, we'd spend weekends there. Every single Friday after school we'd get the number 90 bus through Walkden, Swinton, down past The Crescent into town and it would stop under the arches near Victoria Station. The route from there was on foot, either the River Irk footpath that ran along the back of Collyhurst police station. Or, if me and our Jane could talk Mum into it, up towards Thomson House to Tib Street, past the pet shops that seemed to line the street and into the legendary joke shop that sold all the United badges and scarves. I'd stare at them for ages through the window, whilst our kid would do the same at the pet shop next door but one. From there we'd walk onto Oldham Road to Nana and Pop's for Friday fish & chips. The smell made all the better with loads of salt and vinegar and all wrapped in pages from the newspaper. Delicious! Later they'd move to Bothwell Road in Collyhurst where I loved playing football with all the local lads. Although there was a NO BALL GAMES sign by every piece of grassed area no one took a blind bit of notice. Pop's best mate was a man called Nobby White from Cheetham Hill, whose son Bernard worked at United's ticket office. What a stroke of luck that was! Sadly, at that time Mum, Nana and Pop would never let me actually go to the match with mates because of the hooliganism, much to my dismay.

There's a good friend of mine, 'Big Malc' Reynolds, who's a little older than me. His United Road began earlier and took in Manchester United's now legendary opening match in the Second Division, along with his mate, Paul Foster. Leyton Orient away. Then, only fourteen, Malc remembers that when you got on the train to take you to a United away game, there were some rituals to perform before you'd settle down to have a drink and sing your songs. These involved ripping the seats to pieces, taking out all of the light bulbs, smashing them, and, of course, throwing every toilet roll on the train out of the windows. (In fact, I had a mate, Gez Ford, whose party trick involved eating light bulbs on the United away football specials in the early 80s!)

The talk all summer in the newspapers and amongst fans had been 'Would the United fans stand by their team after the ignominy of relegation?' The doubting Thomases claimed Old Trafford would be barely half full and, as for the away matches, why should fans waste their weekends and hard-earned money going to the likes of Bristol, York and Hull. Leyton Orient even? Well, on Saturday 17th August 1974, those same people got their answer, as an estimated 17,000 Manchester United supporters decked out in their red, white and black clobber descended on the quiet, homely, and totally unsuspecting Brisbane Road. It all began at Euston station. As the first train pulled in, United fans were jumping off before it even came to a halt. A Red sea of raised hands, scarves tied to their arms, punching the air. The clapping, the chant went up, more a war cry, "United!" The first five hundred, an advance party of the Red Army, had arrived in London town. The waiting police with their dogs and horses watched on open-mouthed! So began what was, for outsiders, a season of hooliganism and infamy. For those on the inside, however, such as Malc, with the tassels on their scarves and the ironed-on badges, these were the greatest days of their young lives. Amidst scenes of utter crowd mayhem with lumps of concrete being torn from the terraces and used as weapons, United won the match 2-0, but that was almost immaterial in comparison to what was happening before, after and around the match! Beforehand, with United fans ensconced in crazy, mad hordes seething through every orifice of the ground, bulging onto the pitch, Sir Matt Busby appealed over the tannoy for calm.

'I appeal to all Manchester United supporters, please behave yourselves for the sake of the game and the club.'

It had little effect and the United fans even attacked ITV's Television gantry box trying to rock a terrified Brian Moore out of it! Finally, a semblance of normality was momentarily restored and the game began, but, as Malc recalls, getting back home remains the real memory. Coming out of a creaking, traumatised Brisbane Road, they hurried along with a crowd of excitable Reds, heading for the tube station. Now, this was London late on a Saturday afternoon and most of the capital's teams had been playing that day – every match would have started at 3pm. The first stop on the tube saw a rabid bunch of Chelsea fans trying to get at Malc and his pals; happily they were unsuccessful. Next along the line were the police – with truncheons and snarling dogs. The police herded the fans off the tube train like cattle and corralled them up a single escalator. The police knew very well that waiting up at the top was a tooled-up Spurs mob raging in wait for the United fans as they reached them, two at a time. Bang! Next bang! Finally, the Met's fun was over. Malc and the remaining battered and bruised Reds were led under an escort of sorts to a connecting tube. At the next two stops a furious crowd of West Ham and Millwall supporters lay in wait and the madness continued unabated as the cockneys' vicious and booze-fuelled hunt for northern scalps went on. At last, they reached Euston Square and the few remaining United supporters left from the original crowd who had boarded at Brisbane Road came across their fellow Reds. 'Thank God,' Malc remembers. 'These lads were older; clued up and we were safe.' He and his battered band finally relaxed. As they headed across to Euston station on London's jam-packed streets, Malc and his pals, bloodied and bruised but by now thinking they were 'Jack the lads' after the day's adventures, began singing 'United!'.

'Shut up for fuck's sake!' shouted their rescuers. 'We've still got 200 yards to go!' Duly admonished, they did as they were ordered and made it onto the train and back north. Hardly unscathed, but laughing, joking and proud! Ten o'clock that evening, Malc arrived home to his mum asking why he was so late and moaning that his tea had been in the oven for hours and was now ruined!

It was only seven days to the next match and Malc was already counting down the hours.

As for me, my own United journey was set to begin.

Step forward Uncle Al, who to my absolute joy volunteered to take me to Old Trafford. 'I'll take him in the cantilever stand,' he told Mum. 'Let him sit on my knee.' So, one cold November, Saturday afternoon, Sunderland at home, Al picked up a 7-year-old football-mad urchin from Bothwell Road, Collyhurst in his beloved silver Capri (or the dream machine as he used to call it). A chain smoker, there were always dimps and fag ash scattered around his car. Excited beyond words, I put my scarf out of the window as I'd seen so many fans do since I could remember and off we went, first turning onto Rochdale Road heading towards town. I remember us stopping close to May's Pawnbrokers – just where the Electric Circus, an early home of 'Punk', would spring up years later. Walking on the pavement, pushing a pram, was an attractive young blonde bird. 'Cor, look at the headlamps on her.' shouted out Uncle Al! Now, you have to remember I was only seven years old. But, on a second good look, I quickly realised what he meant. A pair of headlamps!

Taking a drag from a newly lit Benson and Hedges ciggie, Uncle Al smiled wide. 'We're gonna win today anyway Nicko. Nothing more certain.' On we went, waving our way through the back of town round near Victoria station and through the rat run, down past the side of Salford train station, onto East Ordsall Lane. Al always drove religiously on this route to Old Trafford. I looked over towards him.

'What makes you so certain we're gonna win then, Uncle Al?'

'Cos Auntie Anne has only gone and found my lucky red United undies,' he replied. 'They must've fell down the back of the radiator in the spare room.' I wasn't sure really what he was going on about to be honest. 'Never lost a home game since I starting wearing 'em this season.' Suddenly, like Uncle Al, I was filled with even more confidence. Sunderland didn't have a prayer!

This went on, not just for weeks but for seasons! I swear to God; those undies must've got in a right state over the following years. I remember the '77 journey down to Wembley and him moaning on about his left bollock getting strangled in them. Dad just looked at him like he was mad. 'Change em you daft sod!' But, no. Never happened. Uncle Al and his lucky red underpants were for him an integral part of following Manchester United. Whatever the discomfort!

Edging closer to the ground, the butterflies started fluttering in my stomach – they felt more like dragons. Could this really be happening? After parking up at White City, which was still a greyhound track back then in '74, we stepped out and joined the red throng walking up Warwick Road. It was an army, a huge and troublesome one, kitted out in our colours with flares and denim jackets covered in badges, scarves tied to our arms. The chant began. 'United, United!' At first one lone voice would chime up with a song or a chant and then, in no time, it became louder – like thunder crashing across the sky. Onto the forecourt we pressed, the smell of onions from the burger stalls, Double Diamond beer and the inevitable fag smoke. The police horses lined up with their handlers watching like hawks from above us. 'Is that your girlfriend?' a voice from the crowd shouts towards one. The copper glared back, trying not to smile. 'Behave or else!' All the time I'm staying close to Uncle Al, who seems to know everyone! 'Stay close Nicky,' he says once, if not a hundred times! I look up to the floodlights, so close now. Al ruffles my hair. 'C'mon, we'll go in.' Through the turnstiles, they checked his ticket, it was time to move, for the gates were being shut early. The attendance of over 60,000 turned out to be the highest at any league game in England 1974–75. For a Second Division match!? 'This is us lad,' smiles Al, pointing up a small flight of stairs with a dash of sunlight at the top. 'Up you go Nicky.' I stepped slowly and gingerly onto the first, then excitement took over and I flew up the rest and out into the stadium, surrounding the glorious, green – and pretty muddy – field of my dreams!

My stairway to heaven.

Words don't come easily as I try to describe what my wide-open, seven-year-old eyes witnessed at the top of those stairs. Needless to say, I was dumbstruck. To the right, the Stretford End was already in full cry. Thousands upon thousands of the Doc's Red Army. A living, breathing, seething mass of passion. One love. Mixed in with the United red were plenty of yellow and red Scottish emblems. Banners and scarves being waved high. At its very heart an enormous Union flag draped over the tunnel with 'Manchester United Red Army' written across it. The songs were in full flow. A choir whose lyrics could make a docker blush. Five minutes to three and the teams came into view. Everyone was on their feet: I couldn't hear myself think. Uncle Al picked me up to get a better view. I watched my heroes warming up. This, the closest I'd been to Stuart Pearson since we chased those Bolton fans off from the Scan! Don't let me down Pancho.

The game began: it was a top-of-the-table clash and incredibly the noise grew even louder and more frantic. The passion and furore from around the ground, including the travelling Sunderland fans, only added to the crackling, electric atmosphere. I could hardly breathe! United went forward: waves of red shirts charging over the halfway line. Then, eleven minutes gone and 'Goal!' A beauty of a pass from Lou Macari and Pancho smashes one in with his left foot from outside the box, right into the bottom corner – and I'm certain it's for me! Old Trafford erupts! Uncle Al grabs me tight: this is United. 'Super Reds,' we sang. My team. No, no, no, no! Straight from the kick off Sunderland have only gone straight down to the Stretford End and equalised. The cheek of it! Billy Hughes you mop-haired git. United appear rocked as the visitors come at them again. 'Get stuck into 'em, for fuck's sake!' shouts my Uncle Al. Too late, Billy Hughes once more with a blinding goal that he started off with a weighted pass to Robson, then a locomotive burst toward goal and a thundering shot. Now it's 2-1 to them. My heart has nearly stopped. The game goes on and I watch with my heart in my mouth – pumping and beating quickly. Excitement blended with fear. Him again, that Billy bleedin' Hughes should've made it 3-1, only for Stepney to pull off a great save. The referee blows his whistle to end the first half and everyone takes a deep breath. 'Don't worry Nicky,' says Uncle Al, as he lights up yet another ciggie. 'We always make it hard for ourselves.'

Words that would resonate with me many times over the next four decades and more on my United Road. I look around at the disappointed faces. It's clear that everyone is taking a breather.

'Where you off out tonight?'

'You meetin' that bird again?'

Whereas all I could think about was what'd happen next? This was life and death. Finally, the teams reappear and with the tannoy announcer still reading out the half time scores from elsewhere, no one was listening, for Old Trafford had ignited once more! We were now attacking the Stretford End like we almost always do in the second half. It was a siege. United roared forward. Pancho Pearson crosses for 'Wee' Willie Morgan who slides in and scores! Utter mayhem breaks out. Then, the mad hysteria around me suddenly ceases. What the...? The referee had gone across to his linesman. Don't you dare ref, don't you bleedin' dare! The Stretford End had been simmering but now it was about to boil over and explode. The police were watching anxiously, ready for an invasion. Truncheons in hand, helmets fastened tight, horses – massive, shiny, snorting horses – primed outside the ground. Uncle Al had been prodding me throughout the first half because I had constantly been watching the crowd as well as the match. Something I still do. The songs, the sights – even the smells – fascinated me.

'Watch the bloody game, Nicky!'

We wait – standing on tip toes I hold my breath while the ref and the linesman discuss what had just happened – then the whistle goes to his lips and the referee gives the goal and now we are level and with the momentum!

What a comeback! In no time, smelling blood, the Doc brings on our new signing as a swap for 'The Stroller' George Graham. Ron Davies. A centre-forward from Portsmouth, comes on to replace an out-of-sorts Brian Greenhoff. Still the Reds attack and finally the ball falls to Sammy McIlroy on the penalty spot, the last of the Busby Babes. Sammy shoots low and into the net. 3-2 and the ground shakes! I'm jumping up and down like a mad, bad, good' un. Screaming 'Yes, yes, yes!' Uncle Al hugs me. 'Welcome to Old Trafford, Nicky lad!' From that day forward, like my grandads, my dad and Uncle Al – already lighting up another ciggie alongside me, smiling wide – I knew I'd come home. I will never forget that feeling – heart as big as a ball, pumping madly, a smile from ear to ear and a dizziness like you feel at altitude. I was at the top of the world and I still get that feeling every time we score a vital goal, every time we win and whenever I stop to think about Old Trafford.

Just magical...

YOU AIN'T SEEN NOTHING YET

CHAPTER FOUR

From then on, I lived for Manchester United. Saturdays (always at 3pm), mid-week games and the few minutes on Match of the Day when highlights of our games were shown. But also, I just loved playing footy myself. Mornings, noon and night. Against a wall, in the playground, on fields or street corners, in the lounge when Mum wasn't looking. Anywhere there was a flat surface – horizontal or vertical – plus a ball of any size or condition. Alone, with my mates or school pals or my dad, or even with a dog. I had caught the bug and I had caught it badly. I was obsessed. I was Bobby, George, Dennis, Willie, Pancho or anyone in a red shirt. Never Charlie George, Malcolm McDonald, Colin Bell, Kevin Keegan, Peter Osgood, Bob Latchford or Trevor Brooking – no way. Only Reds – or maybe Pelé or Johan Cruyff I suppose, if they were lucky, that is!

There was obviously other stuff too – like hanging out on Eastham Way in the playground next to The Pied Piper pub. I had my first kiss there. Joanne Molloy, a pretty brunette. She was at my primary and was a year older than me, a cougar you'd call her nowadays, and I can still smell her perfume now – probably Avon! I was wearing my dad's Brut of course – 'Splash it all over!'

I also loved going to Walkden baths by way of the banking, a disused railway line, with my mates. Knitted trunks and towels rolled up under our arms. David Baker lost his cherry there at the age of eleven! Early starter was our Dave. You'd be given a metal contraption of a basket welded to a coat hanger that you were supposed to arrange your clothes on somehow and a coloured wrist band. I remember that the baths were always so packed you never got room to actually swim – never mind 'heavy petting' or dive bombs. After you'd outdone your allocated time the call went out. 'Would the blue/red/green bands leave the pool please.' Then it was beans on toast, or 'skin heads on a raft' as we called them, with wet hair and the long walk back home.

Not all our antics were so innocent and whilst we were hardly bad kids, we could be rascals. There were the false fire alarm phone calls. My mate Peter Dunne just loved fire engines so I used to ring 999 now and again from the phone box near to his house so he could see them drive past. I got caught once when they traced the call and I got a right rollicking. I never did it again! Down near the railway line we would regularly build a den or play chicken with the trains. Who would be the last to run in front of the train? Putting stones on the tracks or throwing them at the train windows even. In the end they actually deployed transport police trains to stop these antics.

At school it was always footy at break time. Some days though there'd be a United day. About eight of us, standing against the wall singing the match songs. Raising scarves, pretending it was the Stretty, giving it absolutely everything! Loud and proud. Wearing our badges.

'Pancho Pearson.'
'MUFC Rule OK.'
'MUFC Stretford Rule.'
'MUFC Stretford End magic Kippax Street Tragic!'

The teachers watched on shaking their heads, as did our Jane and her mates. But did we care? Did we 'eck as like, cos we were the Doc's Red Army. We were United!

'MU-MUF-MUFC-OK!'

'Who's that team we call United?
Who's that team we all adore.
They are the lads in red and white,
And they play with all their might,
And they're off to show the world that they can score.'

'Five foot eight,
Not much weight.
Gerry Daly's fuckin' great!'

'Hello! Hello!
We are the busby boys.
Hello! Hello!
We are the busby boys.

And if you are a City fan surrender or you'll die,
We all follow United!'

It was an addiction.

Our school was Roman Catholic – well, just Catholic actually – we
never heard the Roman bit until we grew up. Just Catholic. There was also
a Protestant school, Bridgewater, directly opposite and the 'Celtic,
Rangers' chant was often heard when the lads came together. Back then,
growing up, religion was still a huge issue and it often kicked off. Our
priests and our teachers would warn us gravely never to play with a
'Proddie' in case they tried to convert us. And NEVER stray into a
Protestant church – as if!!!!! What we were fighting for, none of us ever
really knew. Happily, in the end it always came back to the football. God
didn't seem to care what we were so long as we were good with a ball.

After Sunderland, getting to Old Trafford on match days became all
consuming – a drug. When Uncle Al couldn't take me, I'd go with Pop's
next door neighbour Keith on Bothwell Road. Another United fanatic
who went everywhere with the Reds, home and away. We'd catch the bus
to Oxford Road railway station and travel to Old Trafford from there. I
adored that short rail journey, those fans on the train were 'proper'
United. Older lads. Hardcore. I'd listen avidly, all ears, fascinated with the
stories of their wild 'adventures' across the country. The ransacking and
pillaging of some poor, sleepy outpost such as Norwich, or the battles
that raged out of control in Cardiff or London against the likes of
Millwall. Dreaming one day I'd be on one of those legendary 'away days',
following the Reds as we sang 'From Rome to Mandalay, I'll be there...'
Finally, after endless pestering, I was allowed to go to Old Trafford with
my mates. One new lad in our gang had supposedly been expelled from
his last school for trying to burn it down. But we got on like a 'house on
fire' and he was a Red. That's all that really mattered. One of us. Besides,
anyone is entitled to make a mistake. A good lad – we just never let him
near a box of matches!

It was the Junior Stretford End for us. The smell of Bovril. Wagon
Wheels, crisps and sealed, corrugated plastic tumblers of orange juice
passed through the iron fences after being bought off basket-carrying
sellers at the ground. An unlikely paradise on earth – but ours nonetheless.

I have so many great memories of that all-conquering season in the
Second Division.

With Coppell and Wee Willie Morgan tearing down the wings, Sammy
McIlroy, 'Skip to the Lou' Macari and Gerry Daly (I loved his penalties!)

careering through the midfield we were invincible. Then, last but never least Pancho Pearson. That clenched fist salute to the Stretford End and we'd go crazy: a tidal wave of emotion that swept around the ground. A crowd as one with the team. No 4-5-1, five at the back or defensive wingers, it was a simple 4-2-4. The Manchester United players were described by the Doc as like 'flies around a sugar bowl' whenever an opponent had the ball in their ability to win it back. Rapid. Imagine Guardiola's great Barca side on speed! Well that was my United back then. Not one touch, but two touch football – and we'd not so much beat as blow teams away. Emotionally, blood-boiling to watch, laced with flair, brimming with skill and when necessary, like the fans who'd follow their Red Devils into the pits of hell, always ready for a scrap!

I was now off and running and had my pass-out to the match every other Saturday at Old Trafford. We were also getting pretty decent at blagging and we spent most journeys into town clinging on the back of the buses and hiding from the conductor to 'jib it' and avoid paying, or 'decking on' as we used to call it. Once at the ground you'd queue for hours to ensure getting in before they closed the gates, which would often be well over an hour before the three o'clock kick off. As far as we were concerned, United rocked and ruled the roost both on and off the pitch. However, on 9th March 1974, the Red Army had a taste of our own medicine.

When playing out in Collyhurst, at my nan and grandad's, I always remember walking around the corner past St Patrick's church on Livesey Street and round onto Bothwell Road. There stood an old red-brick wall on the croft next to Oldham Road. Sprayed in white paint in huge letters was the scrawl:

' ...KILL RANGERS...'

This always fascinated me. Why kill them? Though I sang the 'Celtic-Rangers' chant at the match and school, as I wrote earlier, I was innocent to its religious connotations. At that age I knew nothing of sectarianism and even less of the sheer hatred it evoked between 'Catholic Celtic' and 'Protestant Rangers' in Glasgow. United were perceived up in Scotland as having Catholic leanings, mainly due to Sir Matt Busby who was a fervent left-footer. A powder keg was set to explode and on Saturday 9th March 1974, it erupted in all its bile and bigotry at Old Trafford and on the surrounding streets of Manchester. After being knocked out of the FA Cup at Walsall, United had arranged, on just two weeks' notice, a 'friendly' match against Glasgow Rangers to cover the spare Saturday afternoon. This was one game my parents banned me from going to because of the prospect of trouble, so I need to refer back, once more, to

'Big Malc.'

In Manchester, late that morning, again with his mate, Paul Foster, they took shelter from the ever-present Manc rain in Lewis's doorway on Market Street to eat their chips. This was a favourite spot for a soaked Malc and Paul because of the warm air that blew down from the pipes, thus helping the lads dry out. Suddenly, a clapped out, battered Austin Cambridge pulled up facing them. Inside were four men who, noticing the lads in their United gear, yelled over at them: 'United bastards, we're gonna kill ya!' before driving off.

Malc still vividly recalls their 'Mad, crazy eyes.'

Thinking it was simply a one-off encounter with some nutters, they thought nothing more of it, shrugged their shoulders and jumped on a bus heading towards Old Trafford. Now, these were the old diesel buses that chugged along at a snail's pace. Never get on one if you're in a rush. Not being smokers, they sat downstairs at the back behind a bus full of old ladies laden down with shopping bags and busy gossiping. As the bus got to Hulme, the lads watched through the window as a large mob of Rangers supporters appeared around the corner. One of them pointed over towards the bus. 'Look, United! Get em!' As if watching in slow motion, Malc and Paul suddenly snapped out of it, realising they were the target of the Rangers supporters' wrath! Matters turned infinitely for the worse when the bus came to a halt at a stop to allow a passenger to get off. Their attackers ran ever closer. 'Oi, mister, drive yer bleedin' bus away will yer!' screamed Malc, as a seemingly unconcerned driver lit up a cigarette, without a care in the world. Meanwhile, the Rangers fans howling and screaming abuse were closing in and just as they reached the back of the bus and started banging on the rear window, the bus began to chug off towards the ground. Not before the lads watched in horror as one of the mob pulled a fireman's axe from under his coat and, with visceral hatred in his eyes, launched it at the bus, only for the axe to land short. It was like a battle scene from Braveheart and Malc and Paul had no plan to face the Picts! 'Put your fuckin' foot down mate, pronto!' screamed Malc in panic, much to the annoyance of a gaggle of old ladies, still unaware of the raging horde of pissed up and very hostile visitors from Scotland, intent on disembowelling the two young lads quaking in fear at the back of the bus, their scrawny necks wrapped in their red and white hooped Manchester United scarves.

'Mind your language young man. Where do you think you are?' Although both only fourteen years of age, Malc and Paul had already got plenty of experience of the different levels of football hooliganism and violence, and both knew a thing or two about what might happen when it kicked off. The livid violent rage they witnessed in the eyes of the Rangers supporters was unlike anything they'd ever experienced. Even now Malc winces. 'They seriously wanted to kill us,' he said. 'It was nothing to do with football. It was all about religion and in their eyes our scarves turned us into the papist enemy!' Finally, as the bus picked up a bit of speed, the Rangers fans disappeared back into the distance, still roaring out their bile, trying in vain to catch up. Malc and Paul prayed there'd be no more of them waiting to get on or off at the next bus stop! Frightened but relieved, their heart rates returned to normal and with false bravado and nervous laughter they spoke of these same maniacs getting their 'heads kicked in' later on when the Red Army got hold of them!

Their relief was short lived, however, because on arrival at Old Trafford at the top of Warwick Road (now Sir Matt Busby way), looking out of the windows all they saw was a swaying ocean of Rangers blue stretching from Lou Macari's chippy on the corner down onto the forecourt of the ground. It was incredible, an invasion! Bannockburn come to Stretford! The overwhelming stench of whiskey mixed with adrenaline in the air, the chants and jeers echoing loudly. 'Up to our necks in Fenian blood!' Not a United fan in sight. Not being lemmings and not exactly desperate to commit suicide in honour of the absent Red Army, the lads made a wise decision to stay onboard with the old ladies, skulking out of sight below the back window of the bus. A close escape. They didn't get off until they reached Stretford Precinct, a mile or so further on. By that time, they'd removed their scarves, badges and any other tribal memorabilia that could get them lynched and they stuffed it all under their budgie jackets. Malc even considered taking his lucky United socks off! In shock, they sat down on a sheltered bench in the railway station. Looking anxiously around, they were dismayed that there was no sign of any fellow Reds. They were alone in enemy territory! Surely the lads couldn't be the only United supporters going to the match that day?

Around 2pm the cavalry finally arrived. The familiar war cry of 'United' boomed and, to Malc and Paul's great relief, around three hundred of the Red Army, all suited and booted, turned up ready for battle. These weren't kids, it was a mob fuelled by alcohol, intent on recapturing Old Trafford from the throng from beyond Hadrian's wall and currently camped in their backyard. It was like a modern day scene from Game of Thrones and the Scots were the white walkers! Mixing amongst the cavalry, our two new heroes joined in the familiar chants as they headed back over the bridge from Stretford. The Reds set eyes on the Blues and without hesitation, despite being heavily outnumbered, the Red Army charged down into thousands of Rangers fans at the back of the Stretford End, and all hell let loose! Carnage.

Contrary to Rangers' folklore, despite swamping over three quarters of the ground in a 22,000 crowd that day, the visitors never took the Stretford End in scenes resembling the Alamo and Rorke's Drift combined. It wasn't for the want of trying, but the United fans, brains and muscles pumped up with territorial pride, fought them off in pitched battles throughout the afternoon. This was so much more than a football game for the Rangers. It was an outrageous scene – a toxic mix of booze, football hooliganism and religious hatred – or Hate Red! A full-scale battle broke out. With this being a match that had nothing really at stake for United, many of the out of town fan supporters and even locals had stayed at home, so the odds numerically lay with the massive Rangers travelling support.

In those days there would usually be entertainment on the pitch before the game and on this day there was to be a show put on by an RAF display team that was set to perform a dogs through burning hoops routine. They had appeared on the pitch momentarily, only to swiftly abandon the performance and help the police try and restore law and order. The grass was turning red and the air was filled with everything from launched pies, coins, tins and bottles, as the Stretford End fell under siege. From the lads' vantage point to the left of the tunnel, between ducking from incoming objects, Malc distinctly remembers a rabid solitary Rangers fan charging into the Stretford End and receiving an absolute pummelling, before retreating/staggering back onto the pitch, where a St John's ambulance-man bandaged his badly bleeding head. Then, to the utter astonishment of Malc and those others around him watching, the same Rangers fan, rather than slipping away quietly to mend his wounds, instead roared out 'Rangers!' and charged once more headfirst into the Streford End, determined to wreak revenge, only to be handed another vicious beating. It was fanatical: another of the travelling horde picked up a flag pole – back in the day they were also on the centre line, not just the corners – and began playing the sash with it before hurling it into a band of United supporters who swiftly scattered. Luckily, it missed all of them.

Still it raged on.

A Rangers fan laid a Union Jack on the centre circle, only to be swiftly dealt with by two United supporters who'd followed him on! The Manc lads themselves then swarmed into a revengeful Blue mass screaming for blood. Those of the Red Army who travelled to away games must have been given an inkling that day of just how it felt when they went rampaging, after rolling en masse into unsuspecting towns and cities. Nothing on this scale has ever been seen since at Old Trafford, and probably never will be. It was quite simply a war zone.

The Rangers fans finally made it into the Stretford End, but were fought off as they tried coming up the tunnel. This was sectarianism in all its unholy glory, and the only game Malc and Paul ever left early. After racing through the skirmishing, trampling police horses, a flurry of batons and stand-offs on the forecourt, they finally made it onto a bus on Trafford Road. Once upstairs, the lads looked back down Warwick Road to the chaotic scenes. By now, United fans in the ground had been reinforced, as the word spread around Manchester and the battle the Rangers had come looking for turned into a war of Red v Blue, Manc v Scot with unbelievable scenes of bludgeoning, kicking, punching, bedlam and mayhem.

A brutal afternoon at Old Trafford. One that went down in folklore for supporters of both sides of that vintage. Incidentally, the game was won on the pitch 3-2 by Rangers, whilst off it, by a miracle, nobody was killed. On a happy post-note, Malc and Paul arrived safely home that night with wild tales to tell, and more importantly, Malc still had his lucky United socks on! A crazy day where football simply never mattered. It was all about something much more…

****

'Come on you Reds!'

On Saturday 5th April 1975, at the Dell against Southampton, promotion back to Division 1 was clinched with a Lou Macari goal, and to celebrate at the end of the game 7000 Reds invaded the pitch dancing like maniacs. Two weeks later a 2-2 draw away to Notts County meant Manchester United would go back up as champions. Goals from Stewart Houston and Brian Greenhoff sent the vast travelling Red Army ecstatic. This time, around 10,000 Reds poured over the hoardings to celebrate the fact that, after a short spell in the wilderness, United were back where we belonged!

All we needed now was the presentation of the Second Division trophy and, on Saturday 25th April 1975, Old Trafford would rock to the sound of the Bay City Rollers as the party got under way!

Our match-day routine was by now set in stone: meet up at the top of Hilton Lane by The Albion pub, then buses to our Red Mecca. Just after one o'clock that day we stepped off the bus and all the pavements near to the ground were absolutely jammed to the hilt. This wasn't normal, even for Old Trafford. Heading down, crammed shoulder to shoulder towards the forecourt the crowds gathering were off the scale. Down near United Road, the queue for the Stretford End was actually stretching way past J stand. Left with no choice but to join the thousands already in front of us, we stopped at the back of the crowd, edging forward at a snail's pace. Panic began to set in. Our set drill every other week was to know exactly where to be by one-thirty, then ten-to-two and so on to ensure a safe entrance – but that day nothing was moving and it was starting to sink in that we were actually facing being locked out of our own ground. United had announced the previous day that they were going to be presented with the trophy before the game, which was why all the extra punters had suddenly appeared. Everybody wanted to be there when our Captain lifted that Second Division trophy high.

We thought it wasn't fair for us to be locked out – by now it was our right to step onto the terraces and stand there with the rocking, raucous crowd, but United were champions and it was party time after all! So, we forgot our disappointment at probably not being able to see the game and danced away in the endless swirling mass of fans, singing our songs, until news finally filtered down that the gates were officially shut at just touching one-thirty. It later transpired nearly 20,000 were locked out that day – us among them. I watched as some older lads tried to climb up the floodlights, scarves swinging on their arms, and some actually succeeded. Quite a few others got onto the top of the main stand somehow, but were eventually coaxed off by the police, undoubtedly getting a good slap for their antics when they came down.

Three o'clock came and went and we milled about for the afternoon. These were obviously the days before mobiles, so we had to guess at what was happening from the roar of the lucky lot standing and cheering and jumping for joy inside. We were gutted to miss out on the trophy presentation. The noise from the joyous crowd thundered over the grandstands and onto the forecourt and the surrounding streets where we hung around, counting down the minutes. With 60,000 squeezed inside the ground, half watching and half just singing their heads off, goals from Pancho (2), Macari and Greenhoff handed United a 4-0 victory. The clock ticked down: our plan was to sneak into the ground when they reopened the gates with ten minutes left. Then, at least we'd see the final whistle and be able to cheer the team off... We'd be there... That's what it really was all about. Eventually, after a few close shaves with stewards and police we managed to get in via the Stretford End United Road paddock corner. Totally crammed, it was a matter of weaving your way down towards the front and getting into position to run onto the pitch. The atmosphere was beyond electric: a fiesta. A Red carnival of sorts. Unadulterated, wonderful madness!

The final whistle blew and Old Trafford erupted in a cacophony of noise and glorious euphoria! 'United are back, United are back!' roared out from all corners of the ground. Onto the field we raced and, within moments, hundreds turned into thousands. 'C'mon on!' we all shouted, as we ran across the pitch towards the cantilever stand. Here I was sprinting through the centre-circle wearing my six-holer cherry docs and my white silk 'Doc's Red Army' scarf (a Christmas present from Uncle Al) tied around the left wrist, and my lucky red three-bar one on the right. I noticed a group of lads kicking their boot heels into the hallowed turf, scooping up large sods of turf for mementos. No way were the Welsh's missing out, so I decided to get some for our back garden.

Only twelve months previous, the scenario had been totally different. End of the world in fact. Denis' backheel and down we went. I love the story my mate and former United defender Billy Garton tells of that afternoon. Some of his mates were not content to have away with just the turf, they went one better and got away with the home team bench! It was with great pride that they carried this, their own trophy, where their heroes' backsides had rested so many times, back across the water to Salford, where undoubtedly it still sits in somebody's backyard or garden, pride of place!

Noticing that the police were across at the main stand stopping the celebrating massed throngs of supporters reaching up the tunnel to the players, I made my way towards the far corner near the scoreboard where the turf was at its thickest and dug out my own piece of heaven. As this precious grass was going to be transported back to Little Hulton and Derwent Close, to where I could practice my dribbling like Bestie and my thunderous net breaking strikes like Bobby Charlton, I decided it had to be the finest piece I could find. I looked around and up at the cantilever stand hovering high above me and took a moment to imagine what it must be like to play on here. I felt butterflies deep within, took a deep breath then proceeded to pick up the largest sod of turf I could manage and wrapped it tightly within my red scarf – no one's having this off me. Not for all the money in the world! Division Two had been a rollercoaster of a ride, but after one season in strange territory, against weird sounding teams and towns, the Doc's Army were coming for City, Liverpool, Leeds and all. We were back and the red flag was flyin' once more. You ain't seen nothing yet!

'Division One can kiss my arse,
We're in Division Two at last.
We don't mind and we don't care.
We'll keep the red flag flying there!

City fans, just out from school,
Manchester is yours to rule.
But with the Doc and Sammy Mac,
Division One we're coming back!'

KUNG FU FIGHTING
CHAPTER FIVE

By this time, everybody was Kung-Fu fighting and more!

I was eight years old in the glorious summer of 1975 and by now, for me and my mates, Manchester United was our lives. We'd wiped the Second Division out in all respects. Our style of play, attendances were without peer – and not forgetting our triumphant hooliganism. This latter 'skill' was seen as a scar on the good name of our club, but it wasn't going anywhere fast. The establishment was up in arms. Newspaper headlines aghast.

'String 'em up!'
'Birch 'em!'
'Bring back National Service!'

The chaos theory had erupted into red, white and black. We were the biggest and most feared fans in the land – in all the world. A Red Army gathered every match day from across the country. Everything was sparking. The pendulum had begun to swing. United were on the march again – on and off the pitch – and I was marching with them, head held high and totally committed to the players, team, the club and the Red Army. 'Tommy Doc's red and white army,' we sang. There was absolute belief, a love affair – one we celebrated every Saturday in our faded denim jackets, sewn on badges, tassels on our scarves and songs of love, devotion and war that we roared out loud at Old Trafford and far beyond. Impatient and excited for what was to come, I counted down the days for the start of the season, in that long-ago glorious summer of 1975, not for a moment suspecting that this would be the first time United would break my heart.

'Tommy Docherty walks on water!
  Na, na, na, na, na, na!'

****

'We're gonna burn ya bonnie!'

Bonnie Night… Guy Fawkes, for any southerner reading this. It started around the end of the school summer holidays. When we headed back to school in September, the talk was always of 'Who's gonna have the biggest bonnie in Salford?' Although we actually lived in the Walkden area of Little Hulton, considered by some to be virtually in the countryside, most of the people around us in the various streets were Salfordians. For them, and us – their kids, building and protecting the biggest bonnie was a favourite backbone-building annual challenge. You would spend the whole time running up to 5th November determined to achieve the pride that could only come from building and protecting 'the best bonfire in Salford.' Inside, I'm still the same kid at heart as back then. Guy Fawkes was and remains Bonnie Night for me. As Catholics, maybe it meant more to us than it did for Proddies? We never knew much about what had happened back in 1605 – it was just Bonnie Night. Of course, the wood never came to us easily. We'd go hunting for it day after day for weeks, usually in wet and windy weather, wearing clothes that weren't made for this challenge. Nothing was safe. Fences were fair game, although it'd start with pallets and old wood from the brook or off people happy to be rid of it. Then, when all avenues for fresh wood were exhausted, the time came for the hunt. This meant your gang going and fronting up against the nearest bonnie to you. Usually it'd be on the next croft or a spot of spare land nearby where a fire could be safely lit. Never though more than a five- to ten-minute walk away.

By the time the half term school holidays came around, it really felt like you had to up your game, because Bonnie Night was drawing near. I remember going to an opposition site one night, and they knew why we were there. Our numbers were equal. Six in each group. They taunted us, 'Right, let's pair lads up for the scrap.' I was one of the youngest and smallest in our group and, sadly, I was put up against a right desperate Dan twice my size. He proceeded to give me a real good hiding and an early lesson in life, which was 'There's plenty of dead heroes!' We finished that night bruised, battered and returned to camp empty-handed. Of course, your gang could never all go because one or two would have to stay to guard your own, in case it got raided. Some kids would even hide inside the ever-growing bonnie. These were exciting times; a game of cat and mouse or England v Germany, cowboys and indians, and I miss those days so much.

The closer 5th November dawned, the bigger the bonnie became and the pressure grew ever more to be the best. Some bastards burnt ours down one year, just two nights before Bonnie Night, and everyone was gutted. It must've been done quite late on by some older lads, for we always stayed on guard as long as possible. But you just had go home sometime. School called. Some lads had earlier curfews than others. Luckily, our bonnie was at the end of the road, and my cousin Guy would keep a look out until everyone was definitely in bed from his bedroom window. Always on patrol! Once Guy did admit to nodding off, much to our annoyance!

Come the day we'd trudge to school – on edge for fear of a last-minute raid from another gang or – worse still – rain. All day we would pray for a dry day and night. 'Please God, don't let it piss down! Amen.' It was nothing to do with starting the fire – you could always just throw petrol on it. Job done! More because you simply wanted to enjoy the evening. Be proud of your bonnie that for weeks, months even, your gang had worked so hard to build, topped off by a guy who you'd also traipsed round in an old pram for weeks, scrounging for money to buy fireworks with. When I think back, it never occurred to me when we were out begging on the streets for money for bangers with our guy made from old clothes and rags, that my cousin Guy was actually called the same as our stuffed begging prop.

Now, you just wanted everyone to enjoy it. Watch the flames reach high, feel the heat on your face. There were no organised firework displays like today and the Catherine wheels would just be nailed to the nearest fence and ignited and we'd leg it back, death defying. Anyone would light up a Roman candle, a rocket or an air bomb, with loads of kids of all ages running round like lunatics, bumping into each other in the pitch black night. Health and safety hadn't been invented back then. Bangers and rip raps were simply tossed at each other. I remember once on Derwent Close, one being thrown in our Guy's direction when he wasn't looking and landing in his hood. We were all screaming at him, 'Throw your hood up!' Luckily, he acted fast and just managed to throw the hood up and the banger exploded in the air two feet above his head. Close shave!

Finally, the bonnie would burn through and the smell of gunpowder filled the foggy air, and the time came to roast your potatoes on it and start to plan for the following year! To ensure it'd be even bigger and better. The next day at school everyone always claimed they'd had the best, the one that'd lit up the Salford sky! Turning it MUFC red of course! Once upon a time on Bonnie Night. Loved it...

****

On the 23rd August 1975, I paid my 25p and took my place along with 56,000 others for the first home game of the season against Sheffield United, back in Division One where we belonged. Doc's United team had already played twice – away to Wolves and Birmingham – and won both games 2-0. The run continued as we took the Blades apart 5-1. It was football from the gods and took us top of the table! Old Trafford rocked and swayed: the Stretford End erupted like a perfect storm at sea. A lone ball being thrown around by the waves: an ebb and flow of thousands. A tidal wave of scarves swaying above our heads, the noise like a jet plane – not that we'd ever been close enough to one to know! A chanting din so loud it could wake the dead. You could taste the optimism in the air. 'United are back,' we sang. I was still fascinated, watching and listening to the crowd. The spectacle mesmerised me. It was a perfect stage for the football on display. Tommy Docherty had promised United would attack and show no fear, and as the goals flew in, Pancho Pearson (2), Daly, McIlroy and an own goal, we all felt that the Doc was being true to his word. We were fantastic. Before the game, Sheffield United's classy Tony Currie had been mouthing off in the newspapers. 'United have no flair,' he claimed. 'They're two years away from being anything special.' Well, with the goal tally steadily mounting, the Stretford End remembered these words and 'Currie, Currie, what's the score?' thundered out! As the venom rained down on his head, Currie looked a broken man.

After being shunted off the top by Liverpool, who beat us in November, we finished 1975 joint top with them. We jostled with them and QPR for top spot but, ultimately, United would finish a more than respectable third behind champions and runners-up QPR. We played electrifying football throughout, but it was in the FA Cup where the story truly lay that season. Also, in November my soon-to-be-new-hero (sorry Pancho), Gordon Hill arrived from Millwall for a bargain £70,000. Hill was a gobby, flash cockney, a practical joker and decent Norman Wisdom impressionist, but more importantly he was a magical left-winger and, with Steve Coppell wreaking mayhem on the other side, we now had perfect marauding balance. No-one epitomised the carefree all-out attacking spirit of the Doc's team more than our two wingers. To be honest, I love it when we are blessed with a matching pair of great wingers. Hill was always on his toes with a devastating left foot that could open any defence. Any early concerns about this forever-smiling Londoner swiftly evaporated on the terraces as he captured Red hearts, and none more than mine. I worshipped him. The manager handed Hill our number eleven shirt, one that came laced with a history impossible to live up to, as it once belonged to Georgie Best. Whoever was chosen to wear it could only ever tread carefully and try their all to do George's memory justice. Our new favourite cockney would succeed in this, though I suspect that no-one can ever match George's genius. Sadly, I never saw George play, but I love hearing people tell tales of his skills – and others like Duncan Edwards.

When I think back, I just have so many memories of Gordon Hill that make me break into a smile. I was so fortunate to be able to attend the semi-final with Grandad Harry and my cousin, Guy. Grandad Harry had bought three tickets off a tout, but at that time he was suffering from cancer. I knew he hadn't been well, but never knew the full extent until he died the following year. A lovely man and definitely my father's father in so many ways...

United were viewed as huge underdogs for the semi-final and, in the Hillsborough tunnel beforehand, our players were taunted by some members of Derby's squad. Several of the Derby team were handing out tickets to friends and family. One of them, Leighton James, turned to Gordon Hill as he walked past and shouted across, 'It's really not worth you guys turning up today. You've no chance!' This was a team filled with experienced top-class international footballers, but so what? Talk about tugging the tail of a Red Devil! Manchester United were on the up; a tidal wave of youthful, boundless enthusiasm. A Mancunian cavalry charge, undoubtedly a coming force, there were few that gave us much hope, but did we care? Did we 'eck. On Saturday 3rd April 1976, the Red Army arrived in Sheffield by train, coach, van, car and anything else with wheels. Come kick-off, it was the red, white and black of United supporters that dominated the terraces. The vast majority of the 55,000 roaring their heads off were cheering for the Mancunians. An incredible show of support. Both ends of the ground were drenched in United banners, flags, and scarves swirling. A following loyal to the point of fanatical, all demanding: a love supreme, but don't you dare let us down. So much for a 50/50 ticket allocation, it was more like a home game. In the dressing room, Tommy Doc simply walked in with the Derby team sheet and screwed it up in front of the United players. 'Don't worry about them,' he said. 'Let them worry about us. You do what you always do!'

'Attack!'

As in every Manchester United pre-match warm-up, the Red Army sang in turn the various players' names until they acknowledged the singing, receiving in return a massive cheer. Pancho Pearson's was always a proper wave back. Like your mum did on seeing you off to school, until you were out of sight! We'd then sing his song. It was fantastic to watch. Five thousand hands with scarves tied on wrist waving every couple of seconds: 'I'd walk a million miles for one of your goals, ohhh, Stuart, oh, oh, ohhh, Stuart, Stuart!'

From the off, United tore into Derby with Stevie Coppell fluffing a shot from three yards over the bar from an early corner. We were after them – not letting them breathe. On twelve minutes, Brian Greenhoff broke out to find Gordon Hill who swept it on to the darting Gerry Daly. Moving forward Daly again sought out Hill, who looked up and from outside the Derby penalty area, curled the ball so sweetly with his left foot into the top corner past Graham Moseley. 1-0! Hillsborough exploded! A great game unfurled with both sides going hell for leather at a frantic pace. Derby had chances, but six minutes from time Stevie Coppell was brought down on the edge of their box, and up stepped Hill once more to beat Moseley and send United to Wembley! We went mad!

'That's bloody it now lad,' said Grandad Harry, hugging me tight. 'That's it now!' I couldn't take my eyes off the joyful sight of thousands upon thousands of Reds going absolutely berserk! Come the final whistle the old stadium simply erupted and I noticed one of our supporters head straight for Derby's Bruce Rioch in the corner, whose last action in the game, borne surely out of frustration, had been to scythe down Sammy McIlroy. Luckily for Rioch, the fan was grabbed by police and stewards just before wreaking his revenge! Soon the pitch was swarming – a jumping, jubilant sea of red. 'Wemberley, Wemberley!' rang out loud from the massed Mancunian choirs! 'We're the famous Man United and we're going to Wemberley!' Our opponents in the final were to be lowly Southampton and although Tommy Docherty preached loudly to both supporters and his players not to underestimate them, who was the Doc trying to kid? For we were his famous Red Army and the FA Cup was all but ours. We just had to show up... Show up.

'We all agree Manchester United are magic!'

DON'T GO BREAKING MY HEART
CHAPTER SIX

Twelve quid for a standing ticket? That's what the Manchester touts wanted. No way could I afford that, so on Saturday 1st May 1976, our house in Derwent Close was transformed into Wembley!

In those days, this was the biggest day of the year on the telly by a country mile! After Christmas Day it was the biggest day full stop. We'd get crisps and beers and soft drinks in and spend all day glued to the telly watching both sets of fans being interviewed and getting up to silly pranks – there was even an FA Cup 'It's a Cup Final Knockout' in those days.

I wrapped my Union Jack/MUFC flag around myself and sat down on the settee in front of the television to watch the build-up from early in the morning. All the time, without my knowing, Mum kept half an eye on me. I dreamt about watching Martin Buchan lift that famous cup above his head at about five o'clock. The thought of losing the game never entered my eight-year-old head. How could it?

Southampton had finished sixth in the Second Division. They had good players, but we were United, the Doc's Red Army. No way could anything go wrong. The day unfolded, twelve o'clock came and went, my eyes were glued to the television. The boys looked confident with Gordon Hill clowning around. He won't let me down. None of them will, I remember thinking. The players on the pitch, the band playing all brass, braid, pomp and colour. The crowd singing 'Abide with Me' and suddenly the teams are walking out the tunnel and Wembley stadium explodes with excitement. As does Derwent Close! Again, it looks like United fans had taken over the terraces. The most magical ocean spray of red, white and black.

'Gordon Hill Sells More Dummies Than Mothercare,' read one banner. The following ninety minutes are like a blur. It's history now that on eighty-three minutes, Southampton's Bobby Stokes broke clear to shoot low past Alex Stepney to cause one of the greatest FA Cup upsets of all time. A controversial goal to this day, one that looked and was without doubt offside, but given by Welsh referee Clive Thomas. United simply never performed. A couple of half chances were all they managed that terrible afternoon and, as I fidgeted nervously under my flag, becoming increasingly fraught as the clock ticked ever down, it was with sheer horror that I watched Stokes' effort skim past Stepney's fingertips before hitting the back of our net. Bog off Southampton. You and your yellow shirts. Stuff you Lawrie McMenemy and Jimmy Hill, I hate the lot of ya. The final whistle blew and, like Brian Greenhoff and the rest of our lads, I shed buckets of tears. I was inconsolable and nothing Mum could say helped. This wasn't supposed to happen. It just wasn't. No Starsky and Hutch that night, and definitely no Cup Final Match of the Day. I sat on the bed and I just cried myself to sleep, still wrapped in my United Union Jack flag...

The next morning, still red-eyed and miserable, Mum made me go to church. It was the ten o'clock mass at St Edmunds, and the sombre atmosphere suited this little Red's heartbroken mood as I sniffled and rubbed my bloodshot eyes. I was holding my own until the priest declared that our next hymn would be 'The saints were high with glory'. That's all it took, I was off and raced out of the church trying hard to keep myself together. It was still so very raw....

What brought my mojo back was going to the homecoming along with tens of thousands of other Reds. Manchester welcomed back the Doc and his team with so much love that, despite losing, it actually felt like we'd won the cup! Albert Square was transformed in its own way into a place of worship, but to Manchester United. All vantage points were taken: up statues, trees, the fountain, window ledges, every orifice – hanging onto lamp posts for dear life! The Red Army had turned out in full to salute their team. Scarves still waving defiantly. Songs sung, chants in tribute to every player, and of course the manager. Pride in defeat because our team had given everything that season and it was our team – our heroes. We were at one with the team. We had won, drawn and lost together.

I was lucky enough to grab a decent view by climbing onto a bus shelter. Below me was a sea of heads with arms attached, punching the air. 'United!' went the roar. When our heroes appeared on the Town Hall balcony, Albert Square and the surrounding streets erupted into a cacophony of noise! The Doc came to the mic' and declared, 'We'll be back!' Again, we roared, for the Red Army to a man, boy and girl believed him. Tommy Doc walked on water. If he said that next year, we'd win the

FA Cup, then so be it. Slowly, in time, I learnt to smile again, but there's no doubt when I look back now on that long-gone early May summer's day of 1976: this was the first time that Manchester United broke my heart, and despite a lifelong love affair, it wouldn't be the last.

PLANET OF THE APES
CHAPTER SEVEN

'We'll be back, we'll be back, we'll be back, back, back!'

1976–1977. Tommy Docherty had promised us in Albert Square at the end of the previous season that we'd be back at Wembley the following year, and he kept his word! This time around, I promised myself by hook, luck or crook, I'd have to be there. We were starting as huge underdogs against the 'bag snatchers', the all-conquering red machine from up the East Lancs road.

It was all set to be a northern thing. Two clubs only twenty-eight miles apart, but in terms of football rivalry, an unbreachable, hateful chasm.

A miracle occurred that same season which convinced me, as if I needed it after Tommy Docherty's words, that this was definitely going to be our year. I'd been unable to make the Bristol City, Wednesday night home match and was missing the programme and, much more importantly, the token. I had tried to swop or scrounge one from everywhere I could – but no such luck. This meant that if – or when, as the Doc had said – we got back to Wembley, I wouldn't be able to apply for a Cup Final ticket. It was one of my first tragedies. The following school day, a Thursday, it was a heartbroken kid who sulked around the St Edmunds playing fields at dinner time, who, amazingly for once, couldn't even be bothered joining in with the footy. I just watched on. As the bell sounded to return to class, still feeling ever so sorry for myself, I headed back in. Then it happened, whether a gift from the gods or someone else's terrible bad luck – to be honest I didn't care. There it was, lying on the grass. Soaked, as it had been drizzling, but just waiting for me to pick it up: the Bristol City match programme from the previous evening. I looked around. No one was close or watching and it was swiftly tucked into my pocket out of sight. That night, as soon as I got home, I started to dry it out. The token was undamaged and I glued it firmly, but with tender loving care, to my token sheet. A miracle sent from God to cheer a little Red up? No idea, but what I did know was that if the big fella upstairs was on my side, 1977 would be United's year.

First though, a semi-final against one of our greatest enemies again at Sheffield Wednesday's Hillsborough. Leeds, Leeds, Leeds awaited. This was a game I travelled to with Dad. Beeping and waving at fellow Reds as a convoy of cars, vans and coaches once more headed over the Pennines, with scarves hanging out windows and songs blaring. Defeat was unthinkable. Amazingly, we again swamped the terraces to outnumber the Leeds United supporters. It later emerged that a load of Manchester touts had been travelling over to Elland Road to buy up huge amounts of Leeds' allocation of tickets. This meant that before kick-off the Leeds End erupted into all-out savagery, before the police charged in to separate this incendiary War of the Roses: part two. Incidentally, there were even some of West Yorkshire's finest selling tickets to Manchester United supporters earlier on that day. Everyone was looking to cash in on the Red Army's desperation to make sure they made it into the ground, including well-known figures from my own club, who I suppose will have to remain nameless. In reality and with hindsight everyone now knows, but this was going on everywhere. Who wasn't at it in those days? Stan (how many do you need) Flashman: every chairman's, manager's, director's and player's best friend, back then.

Planet of the Apes. My abiding memory of the day aside from the game is undoubtedly the now-legendary United ape. A gang of Gorton lads had got pissed in the morning and one of them, Alfie, had kitted himself out for a bet in an ape suit from a fancy-dress shop. They set off for Sheffield in a rented Salford Van Hire minibus. All sixteen of them. Singing their United war songs, still drinking, none more or louder than Alfie the ape. I had to look twice from where me and Dad were looking down onto the massed Leppings Lane terraces, as this ape surfed the cheering, laughing United crowd. Its arms in the air, joining with the chants.

'Dad, what's that?' I asked.

'A bloody ape Nicky, what do you think it is?'

It was a very stupid question I suppose, even for me.

Before the game they'd struggled to find a parking spot in the crammed United area, so decided to risk all in the Leeds end. With the minibus having both a Manchester and Leeds office number plastered on the side, the lads felt confident enough to get away with it. They hid their scarves, while Alfie the ape went quiet with the singing. It was a tense walk through enemy territory, with the ape getting more than a few stares as a pissed-up

Alfie glared back at them. 'Don't say owt Alfie,' was a gentle warning from his mate. 'You're a pissed up Manc ape, not bleedin' King Kong.' Finally, they reached safety amongst fellow Reds and the scarves reappeared. Alfie the ape took a bow and a legend was born.

Afterwards, there was no such luck, for as the lads headed back to the minibus with scarves once more hidden, they had a problem. Alfie was a sitting duck with nowhere to hide! All through the match he'd been the centre of attention giving 'V' signs and making all manner of despicable ape-like gestures towards the Leeds end! You can only imagine!

Quickly and hardly surprisingly, Alfie was clocked.

'There's that United ape!' went up the cry from the huge seething Leeds mob. 'Are you Man U?' they screamed, a familiar war cry as it erupted between the two gangs of supporters. Well, there were no other apes in Sheffield that day and poor Alfie, sweating buckets in his suit, was legged all around Hillsborough, before finally being tripped up and receiving a kicking. The ape suit was ripped, bloodied and ruined but luckily Alfie the ape survived to tell the tale on returning to his natural habitat of Gorton.

A few years ago, I was having an extension done on the house and took some teas out to the lads doing the work. They were all Reds, and the conversation obviously centred around current events at Old Trafford. It was all doom and gloom until one of them said, 'Do you remember the 1977 FA Cup Semi-Final at Hillsborough against Leeds, Nick?'

'Yeah,' I replied. 'I was there with my dad.'

'Do you remember the ape in the United end?'

'Of course, I do,' I replied, smiling wide. 'How could I forget?'

'Well, that was me, the name's Alfie!' He beamed at me and let out a chuckle. I was so chuffed. One of life's great mysteries finally solved.

Of all the people I've met in my life. Legends, heroes, villains, etc., finally meeting Manchester United's Alfie the ape is up there with them!

Now, for the game…

Saturday 23rd April 1977: Hillsborough had once more turned United red, white and black. A wildfire of Mancunian support. Even the hanging trees at the back of the grandstands lay decorated with members of the Red Army holding on precariously for life, but still singing their heads off and with scarves twirling.

A nice 2-1 win thanks to goals from Jimmy Greenough and Steve Coppell. Get in there!

'Wemberley, Wemberley, we're the famous Man United and we're going to Wemberley!' Again! Thank you, Tommy Doc, thank you God for dropping the Bristol city programme from the heavens. Thank you, Reds, thank you Dad and Grandad for making me a fan of the greatest football club in the world!

Now, all we had to do was beat... Liverpool...

MAGIC DAY
CHAPTER EIGHT

The FA Cup Final: Manchester United v Liverpool.

Surprisingly, perhaps it was the first time our two teams would meet in a Cup Final.

Saturday 21st May 1977: Magic Day. I couldn't sleep all night. I just watched the clock. Finally, daylight broke and, as always seemed to be the case on Cup Final day, the sun broke the flags on a beautiful May morning. I had butterflies in my stomach, for I was off to Wembley to see the Reds! Excited and nervous, there was a good luck hug off Mum, no doubt dreading a repeat of the previous year's meltdown. Although confident, I tried desperately hard not to think that anything might go wrong. For this was my magic day, so don't you dare Scousers. Don't you bleedin' well dare.

Around eight o'clock in the morning we set off for London, travelling by car with Dad, Uncle Al and his brother-in-law Peter, who was over from Canada. Originally from Middlesbrough, he loved United, which meant Peter was OK by me! What fun we had in that car and at the motorway services on the way down! Such precious times: the songs, stories, scarves out the window. The tickets, apart from mine, again came from Bernard White, our contact at the Old Trafford ticket office. The problem was that because we got them at face value, they were random tickets and never together. All that mattered to me though was that I'd be there with Dad and Uncle Al to witness, with our own eyes, Manchester United's attempt to lift the FA Cup for the first time since 1963.

It was a decent run down in Dad's yellow Cortina Estate, travelling on the M6 and M1 and arriving in London quite early. I'm not sure why, but on first impressions, I was a little disappointed. I'd imagined the streets in the big smoke to be like scenes from Oliver Twist or Peter Pan. I couldn't see Big Ben either. Not like when you got near to Blackpool and start to see the tower. First to spot it got 5p. But, here? Nothing. A right let down. Around Wembley, you might as well have been back in Little Hulton. Just endless rows of average houses and council flats. Even the shops were the same. Newsagents, bookies, laundrettes and chippies. Where was the magic dust? Dick Whittington and his cat came to London thinking the streets were paved with gold, and they were disappointed.

And people claimed it was just a fairytale.

This young kid felt Dick's pain.

Dad parked up and we headed to a local pub near Wembley Way, where Uncle Al had arranged to meet a load of Manchester lads he played football with on a Sunday, from the Village Barbers in town. Georgie Best's mob. The place was heaving and full of United. I loved it in there, as I still do now before a big game, and they didn't come much bigger than United v Liverpool in a Cup Final. The pre-match build-up, the anticipation, the excitement mixed with nerves and nowhere better for this than inside a pub. It's like there's electricity in the air. Obviously, I wasn't drinking, but I still got the buzz. 'We're just one of those teams that you see now and then,' someone slowly started off. The new 'Manchester Boys' song, which I knew off by heart. 'We often score six, but we seldom score ten.' I joined in the second line onwards, loving every single second of it. Dad came back from the bar, somehow balancing three pints and a small bottle of coke with a straw in it for me, and a packet of crisps wedged between his teeth. I was in Red heaven. Everyone was talking about how they got down on their pilgrimage. Quite a few had come by train, some the night before making a weekend of it. And their predictions for the game itself. Next minute, a porno mag gets passed across into our group, the older ones all having a look as it's spread open on the centre page. I quickly tugged on Al's jacket and as he looked down I raised my eyebrows, saying to him smiling, 'Nice headlamps eh?' We both laughed. Dad didn't get it… or at least pretended not to anyway!

They were calling it the Jubilee Cup Final and the flags and banners amongst the United fans were works of Manc magic. A city's poetic, dry comedic soul on show for the world to witness.

'BUCHAN does 70mph on the Heighway'
'UNITED we are, United we stand
The greatest by far, the best in the land'
'UNITED strike faster than Leyland'
'YOU'RE the kop, we're the robbers'

'OUR Lou is flushed with success'
'MUPPET REDS: doing the treble: you've no hope
we'll reduce the roar: to a croak'
'JESUS saves, but Pancho nets the rebound'
And on and on…

Bob Paisley's – I hate to say it – all-conquering Liverpool had already secured another First Division title, whilst we'd slumped to an ultimately disappointing sixth place finish. In just four days they were also due in Rome for the European Cup Final against Borussia Monchengladbach, with the real possibility of becoming the first English club to win a unique treble. Manchester United simply could not allow that to happen. It wasn't a question of just shutting them up, more a case of breaking their Scouse hearts. Liverpool had a magnificent team, which couldn't be denied. They were a footballing machine: brilliant, ultra-efficient and deadly, but if anyone was going to stop them achieve their dream it was the Doc's Red Army.

As the military band marched and played, splendid in black uniforms, braid and white helmets, the poignant words of the hymn 'Abide with Me' brought a tear to all around me as we sang our heads off, hearts pounding, temples pumping and pulsing. This drunken, boisterous Red Army spread out across one half of our rickety national stadium, but back then it was still a truly special place. An atmosphere built since that famous white horse final in 1923. The older members of the crowd would never forget the World Cup Final or Best, Charlton and Kiddo knocking four past Eusebio. The clashes with the Scots and so on. This wasn't a place for semi finals and play offs. This was it. This was the single biggest game of the year. Every year. And I was there for my first time. Magical. In the middle lay a lavish carpet of lush, green turf in this place we Mancs call London town. The greenest pitch I had ever seen. Dazzling. Up for the cup we were and not going home without it. A Mancunian serenade of songs, a cascade of banners and flags, scarves raised above heads. Cheers and shouts, banter and chatter. A buzz of excitement.

Finally, the teams came into sight, walking side by side, led by captains Emlyn Hughes and our own Martin Buchan. I imagined myself striding out with the ball in my hand. Team captain. Club captain. God! A bit different to the first time I'd worn a United kit back in The George! And the rest? Well, from that moment on it was in the lap of the gods. The big fella had ensured I made it here by sending me the Bristol City programme from the sky. Of him, I could ask no more. It all came down now to the first love of my life – Manchester United. My palpitations were intense.

I was breathless and joyous and excited and ready to cheer our winning team at full time – now only 90 minutes of football away. 'Come on you re-eds!'

As the sun beat down on us, the game began. United had won the toss and obviously chose to play in red; Liverpool, a changed strip of white shirts. The greatest football stadium in the world, Wembley stadium, the home of football, shivered with excitement. 100,000 fans, mostly standing, crowded into that loud and clamorous space. The Twin Towers guarding our battlefield at the end of Wembley Way. Football heaven.

Ten years had passed since we'd last won any silverware. The European Cup at this same venue. I'd always tried to imagine what it must've been like on that sweltering May evening back in 1968 after we'd beaten the great Real Madrid in the semis. Our first of many such nights. The night that Uncle Al went down on one knee and asked his wife Anne to marry him. Bobby's two goals and tears, George's magical dribble, Kiddo from Collyhurst scoring a cracker on his nineteenth birthday. A true cornerstone of United's scarlet legacy. Now we were back trying to win the FA Cup again, and it was time to put the right kind of scarlet ribbon back on that famous old trophy. Time for my future taunter, Martin Buchan, to hold the trophy aloft and shake it at the Red Army – and in the faces of the Scousers. Time to ruin their chance of a treble. Time to piss on their bonfire – a Bonnie night of all Bonnie nights. I realise now just how building, protecting and jumping around our Bonnie on Bonfire Night was all a huge part of preparing me for a life of supporting United. The other Bonnies were Leeds, Liverpool, City, Rangers – and we had the best one! United.

The first half, played on a pitch drenched in shadows, was a nervous, tight affair, and you could sense it both in the stands and amongst the players. There was little in terms of goalmouth action as the tension and heat combined to stifle any kind of open contest. Come half time it remained 0-0.

All would be decided in the second half! We were 45 minutes from glory! I just knew it!

Five minutes after the restart, the game exploded into life and the destination of the FA Cup was decided. A slack pass from Liverpool's permed, mulletted superstar and England Captain Kevin Keegan, who'd already announced he was leaving to go and play for SV Hamburg in Germany (good riddance), was intercepted. Jimmy Greenhoff took the ball and went past England captain Emlyn Hughes, to flick the ball through to Pancho Pearson. Off he raced to burn off two white shirts and fire a low shot past England's keeper, Ray Clemence, at his near post to send the Red Army dancing with delight! Pancho celebrated with a typical raised fist salute. Game on, you Scouse muppets!

Around me, wonderful carnage and cavorting broke out. Hugging, jumping, pushing and swaying. Screaming and singing, grinning and laughing. I knew it was written in the stars, I just knew it!

Liverpool kicked off again and still we sang. Louder than ever.

'Forever and ever! We'll follow the boys.'

'United!' roared like thunder from our bouncing end. A swarming human hive. A Red Army. Our Red Army. With half an eye now back on the pitch I despaired as Jimmy Case, with back to goal, chested the ball down and, with the United fans still celebrating, smashed a thunderous shot past a stranded Stepney into the top corner: 1-1. Short-lived ecstasy. This time it was the Scousers' turn to go mad as their end exploded and we suddenly stood in silent bemusement, as if witnessing a car crash in slow motion. Fuckin' Nora!

'United! United! United! United!'

It was a typical Liverpool equaliser. That's why Paisley's brilliant team had won the title. A typical Case goal too. A ferocious, furious, vicious right-footed half-volley into the top corner and once more it was 'game on'.

My emotions were wrecked: why did United do this to me? Now, their flags were flying. 'You'll Never Walk Alone' – their famous anthem – rang out and we had to suck it up. It was United's turn to restart, the Reds still buzzed like flies over their local rivals. Undoubtedly, Liverpool were the better team in that period, although I hate to admit it, but as has been the case over decades, that usually meant nothing when the two mighty clubs clashed.

A long ball forward into their penalty area was flicked on by Lou Macari. Their grizzled hard man Tommy Smith struggled to clear and, as Macari took a swipe, it rebounded off Jimmy Greenhoff and, incredibly, scuffed past a stranded Ray Clemence into the net! 2-1! Again, we went crazy! I didn't know whether to laugh, cry or scream, so I did all three! I nearly passed out with the thrill and could have cried for joy for the first time in my life. Three goals in as many minutes and the Cup Final wasn't just alive, it'd caught fire!

Now, they came at us, cascading waves of white shirts. The ball moved smoothly amongst them like clockwork. The longest afternoon of my young life was underway. Time was slowing to a standstill. Alex Stepney was certainly the busier goalkeeper in the closing stages as Liverpool threw everything they had at us. Stepney denied Case a second equaliser as he let fly from the edge of our box, but this time Alex pushed the ball away, before Keegan could snap it up to try to poke home the rebound. Moments later we watched on in horror as Ray Kennedy's rising shot beat Stepney, only to clip the angle of post and bar. I closed my eyes: this was torture. 'Come on you Reds!' Voice now almost gone, around me grown men close to a collective heart attack. Hands behind heads. Hands over mouths. Some hands even over eyes. This was now torture. Why do we do it to ourselves?

Then, as the late-afternoon London sun cast ever more dancing shadows through the clouds onto the pitch, the referee finally blew his whistle to end the match. Delirium broke out in our end of Wembley. Sheer joy. The best moment of my life up until then and still in my top ten. 'United!!!' We'd done it! Manchester United, as Tommy Docherty promised, had gone to Wembley to win the FA Cup! 'Wemberley. Wemberley! We're the greatest Man United and we're going to Wemberley! United!'

And we'd blocked their chances of the treble to boot! Unbelievable.

As we danced and embraced the Scousers lay quietly, stunned, on that green carpet which, for 90 minutes, had been fought over like 100 yards in the Somme. Their dream of the treble dead. Their fans speechless and in shock – which made it even more sweet for us. Schadenfreude – well in those days we didn't have a word for it. I think the English definition of that word is 'The smugness you feel when United have just beaten Liverpool'.

We watched from afar as Martin Buchan lifted the trophy high. I cheered till I could cheer no more as my United heroes made a swamping, joy-filled, scarf and hat-wearing, exuberant, if seemingly never-ending lap of honour. All taking turns to raise the cup in front of an ecstatic Red Army: the Greenhoff brothers together, now so iconic. RIP Brian.

We all joined in clapping the Liverpool team as they walked past us, looking exhausted on their losers' lap of 'honour', with United supporters chanting en masse 'Liverpool!' This was to be almost our last peaceful act of a rivalry that virtually overnight morphed from fierce rivalry tinged with respect, to a mutual sheer hatred. What began on that long-gone, golden Wembley afternoon resonates an unholy rivalry to this day, for the following season, undoubtedly still sore that we had ruined their treble bid (they did beat Monchengladbach the following week), the Scousers invented Munich songs and banners which then made their first rancid appearance. Unforgivable!

As for me, that afternoon there was still a last fearful moment when I was caught up in a bottle-neck crush leaving the stadium. I'd found Peter, and we were off to meet Dad and Uncle Al. Suddenly, the jostling crowd felt like a collapsing wall as everyone went left and wormed down a massive bank. People began to trip, stumble, fall and be trampled on. It was absolutely terrifying. I felt my feet leaving the floor and the breath going out of me. Luckily, it began to ease and both of us, to our great and red-faced relief, managed to break free and scuffle into random bits of space. To this day Peter still talks about those moments of panic and fear, and when the Hillsborough disaster occurred twelve years later, I'd a small inkling of what those poor people caught at the front, tragically pressed against the iron railings by their fellow fans who had been let down by the police, went through. Ultimately, for me, I've tried not to think too much about it, instead lingering more on the bear hugs that were awaiting from Dad and Uncle Al when we finally met up again and the wonderful feeling of Manchester United beating Liverpool to win the FA Cup. I could only imagine what Mum went through that day watching on the television, probably praying I wouldn't return with a face longer and even more foul than the Irwell. Instead, I was the happiest kid in the world going home up that motorway!

These are, and will always be among my happiest memories. Moments that have shaped me and helped me become an optimist, a dreamer, a believer. Moments that have given me a joyous place to retreat to at sad and tragic times. Healing moments – my panacea. Tommy Docherty had kept his promise and made the Red Army's and a nine-year-old boy's dream come true. 'Cheers Tommy, a magic day – I'll be there on that bus shelter in Albert Square tomorrow to welcome you all back!'

'We promised you last year we would bring the cup back, and we have brought it back to the finest supporters in the world!'
Tommy Docherty

A

B

C

D

E

F   G

H

A   Back of the pub with sister Jane centre and her mate
B   Christmas Cardies 1974 - From left; me, cousin Simon, our Guy
C   Nana Toal's Bothwell Road, Collyhurst with Dad and Jane
D   Grandad Harry with his three lads - Baza left
E   The George Pub, Cheetham
F   Queueing for the Stretford End - Coco RIP centre
G   On the pitch! - skipper Martin Buchan with Second Division trophy 1975
H   The Stretford End cage

A

B

C

D

E

F

G

A   St Edmunds with Cup - David Baker with ball, Peter Dunne top right
B   Scoring for Parkside v Barr Hill - Stott Lane, Salford 1976
C   The Gorton gorilla - Hillsborough 1977
D   Derwent Close 7.30am ready to set off to London for 1977 Cup Final - From left; Dad, me, Uncle Al, Jane in nighty and Peter from Canada
E   Market Street, Manchester - early 80s
F   The best thing to come out of Liverpool after the Beatles!
G   On Anfield Road - away 1981

OCTOBER 1974
CHAPTER NINE

At school, every spare minute was dedicated to playing the beautiful game with anything spherical we could lay our hands – and feet – on. I vaguely remember one normal Monday afternoon break when, as I was about to pass through the double-doors back into school, sweating with effort, our sports-teacher Mr Connolly, who'd been leaning against the wall watching our lunchtime 20-a-side, jumpers-for-goalpost match game on the playground, called me over.

'Nicky, we have a trial tomorrow lunchtime. Why don't you come along?'

'Thanks Sir,' I replied. Any excuse for a game was always welcome and I didn't actually take in what he had meant. The so-called trial was just a normal, small-sided match on the grass pitch at the back of the school building. It's all a bit hazy now. Lost in the mists of time. Unbeknown to me it was a trial for the selection of the school team to play in the school's next match. What I do remember though is the following afternoon, when, I can still clearly recall now, David Baker ran excitedly into our classroom shouting, 'Nicky, Nicky, you've been picked to play in the team against St Andrews East on Thursday!' The unusual thing was that I was only in the top infants, whilst the rest of the team was made up of lads four or five years older. It was the first time in the school's history that someone still in the infants had been picked to play for the school team. I wasn't aware of this at the time but I'm sure that, even if I had been, I wouldn't have cared. Again, it was all just about doing what I loved. Playing footy!

As the bell sounded to end school, instead of racing like hell for the gate as normal, I headed straight for Mr Connolly's classroom. Earlier that day, my own teacher Mrs Chandler had reminded me to do so. 'Don't forget to pick up your team kit for tomorrow Nicky Welsh.' As if? I knocked at the door and Mr Connolly waved through the glass for me to enter. 'You up for it then Nick?' he asked with a huge smile on his face.

'Yes sir, I can't wait.'

'Good lad, you'll be fine. You're quick enough to stay out of trouble, so I'm playing you on the right-wing.'

Fine – I'm Willie Morgan, I thought immediately. Willie... Willie Morgan...

Willie Morgan on the wi-ing!

He handed me the neatly pressed, green and white kit and I quickly shoved it into my satchel. As if not giving Mr Connolly any time to change his mind!

'I won't let you down sir.' Off I shot like a whippet! I couldn't wait to get home and tell everyone. I'd never run as fast in my life as that journey home, dodging and dummying past lamp posts and kicking any loose stones in my path. In my mind the match had already begun, and we were going to murder St Andrews East!

The next day in school (Match day!). I was a waste of time in class, unable to concentrate or think straight. All I could think about was the game against our local rivals. The game was at home and our pitch had a slight slope to it. The first half we played downhill and I'd done OK nothing special, but nothing wrong in a 1-1 half-time draw. It was the second half however, that I'd always remember, as we played uphill towards Manchester Road East. There were around ten minutes left to play and by now we were winning 2-1. One of our lads fired the ball in from the left-wing. The orange leather size-four casey came across the area and out of reach for their keeper. As I ran into the box, I managed to launch myself at full speed to make a connection, and as I skidded across the rain-soaked grass in my oversized kit and now clodden boots, I watched as the heavy ball crashed against the inside of the post and skittled into the net. I swear it's a feeling I'll never forget. I can relive it now as if I'm still there. Getting on for fifty years later, it still brings a smile to my face and fills me with a glow of happiness. To this day, it's my favourite ever goal.

'GOAL!'

I remember one of the older lads lifting me up off the ground and screaming, 'Nicky, you've scored. Yeah!' What a feeling...

Happy days... By the way, we won 3-1.

So, my St Raphael/St Edmunds football career was off and running. That night I ran the game over and over in my head as many, if not all footballers tend to do. Although you do think more of the good moments than the bad, just in order to finally drift off. Since then I've had more than a few sleepless match replay nights in my life. Next day I couldn't wait to get to school, not so much to talk about the match and my goal, but to find out when the next game was – if selected of course. It was the following Wednesday away at St Mark's and I was told by Mr Connolly that I'd be playing again. 'Well done last night Nick,' he said. 'Keep it up lad.' The smile on my face could've lit up Old Trafford.

Sat behind St Mark's church near the Worsley junction of the M62, the school was known for its sporting excellence and their football teams were no exception. Since our last game, the rain had lashed down every day, typical Manchester. I remember, years later, in my late teens, jumping into a cab in town after a night out, being absolutely soaked and moaning to the driver how I was sick of it always raining. A pleasant old man, we soon got chatting with him telling me he was doing a bit of part time work in his retirement. As for the rain? 'Don't knock it son,' he said smiling. 'This town of ours would be nothing without the damp wet climate.' Before going on to educate me how the cotton industry flourished here. 'It made the cotton fibres less likely to snap during spinning.' Also, I got a history lesson on how the ship canal bypassed Liverpool and we built the docks right here in Salford to supply demand from across the globe. Ha! Nothing wrong with that I thought. Anything to annoy the Scousers was fine by me... I digress.

The St Mark's pitch was piss wet through. A mud splattered quagmire: today, no way would they have gone ahead and played, but this was the mid-seventies and hardly any game, be it school, amateur or professional even, ever got called off. I was struggling to keep my laces properly tied and, on such a treacherous surface, I was all over the place. Onto the field came a man called Bill Hardman who worked nights at BOC in Wardley and whose son Darren played for us. He leant down, sorted out my laces, then patted me on the head saying, 'Right lad, show 'em what you can do.' Immediately I started to play better. Afterwards, seemingly impressed, Bill pulled me and asked if I fancied turning out for his Sunday team, Parkside Athletic, who played in the Worsley Junior League at Harriet Street. In years to come my dad would help Bill run this when he finally got the business up and running and got some staff in.

This was no easy league for it contained the likes of Mancunians who were United's unofficial junior team and played in red United shirts. Just to let all the other teams know! Whitehill from Cheadle acted as City's junior team, later Blue Star, and the Marauders who were Bury's. I'm not really one to blow my own trumpet, but I was decent. More than decent actually. To the point that Bill always played me two years above my age group. This happened all the way through my Parkside years until

Manchester United came calling. At Saint Edmunds against the other Catholic schools we practically cleaned up. I could take teams apart. I had electric pace, like lightning. Playing lads of my own age I never really felt it challenging.

One particular moment stands out from back then. We were playing against Salford Lads' club. Before the match, on the car park, both sides were gathering their gear together when a car pulled up and all their lads started cheering when this lad stepped out. They were patting him on the back, shaking his hand.

'Who's that?' I asked our manager.

'That's Billy Garton, Nicky. He's just been signed up by Manchester United.'

I couldn't stop staring. This boy had already achieved my dream. Today, Billy is one of my closest lifelong friends but neither of us truly remember playing each other, or what the score ended up that long-gone Walkden morning at Harriett Street. I like to think he's blocked it out!

GOODBYE TO TOMMY DOC
CHAPTER TEN

It was the sweet summer of 1977 and all was grand in the world. The six-week school holidays had begun; United had won the cup, and then came Monday 4th July. That evening I was sat at home having tea when Granada Reports came on the television. Normally, I ignored the programme apart from the footy pieces, but not this time. The words hit me like a hammer on the head. 'The Manchester United manager Tommy Docherty has sensationally been sacked for what has been described as a serious breach of club discipline.' Suddenly, my summer paradise was over. What had he done for this to happen? Everyone knew the Doc was a character, but for United to get rid of him now, when all was starting to take off?

The rumour mill went into overdrive.

In no time the newspapers got the story that Tommy had been having an affair with Mary Brown, wife of the club physio, Laurie Brown. The Doc claimed he'd been sacked for falling in love, but Willie Morgan, who'd become a sworn enemy of Docherty like so many others at Old Trafford, claimed he had got the bullet for making Laurie Brown the reserve team coach, then sending him on scouting missions, whilst in his words 'Going around to Laurie's house and giving his wife one.' It turned out that on the evening of the Cup Final win, Tommy had confided about the affair with the chairman's son Martin Edwards during the post-match banquet at the Royal Lancaster hotel. With everyone at the club basking in the glory of the day's events, Edwards told him not to worry. 'Stuff like this has been going on since Adam and Eve, Tommy.' Sadly for the Doc, Edwards' positive words proved utterly misleading, for within a short time he was gone. It was simply too much for the club to stomach. Busby gave the final word to sack him, with the Chairman Louis Edwards taking his counsel. The fact that Tommy and Mary are still together after forty years means Docherty was telling the truth about being in love, but it would later turn out to be one of the few times back then that he did so. The word Machiavellian apparently didn't do his style of footballing management justice, which was proved shortly afterwards in a court of law. Within days of Docherty's dismissal, he appeared in public with a black eye, courtesy of jilted Laurie Brown. Adding fuel to the fire, the Doc had also decided to sue former player Willie Morgan, who'd retired from the game and was working at Granada TV. Morgan had declared in an interview on Kick Off with Gerald Sinstadt that Docherty was the 'Worst manager of all time.'

The Doc took serious offence at Willie's remarks and decided to go legal. It turned out to be a horrendous error on his part, for the Old Bailey court case (which he duly lost) saw Docherty's darker way of doing business fully exposed, particularly his techniques for getting rid of players from the club, a bitter Willie Morgan foremost amongst them. Armed with evidence from Manchester United stalwarts such as Denis Law, Paddy Crerand, Lou Macari and Jim Holton, the Doc was humiliated in the witness box, lucky to escape charges of perjury and forced to lick his wounds and try to salvage what appeared left of a shattered reputation. Football, however, forgives all and soon chairmen were queuing up, for here was a man who had only recently won the FA Cup, beating the mighty Liverpool, and who had built one of the finest young teams of the previous twenty years.

After initial approaches from clubs in the Middle-East and Norway, Docherty eventually took over at Derby County in September 1977, but he hadn't yet finished with Manchester United. What's more, we hadn't done with him, and to the tune of 'Knees Up Mother Brown' we sang:

'Who's up Mary Brown? Who's up Mary Brown? Tommy, Tommy Docherty!'

When Tommy returned to Old Trafford as manager of Derby, it was one of the season's few highlights. We destroyed them 4-0, playing with all the panache and style normally associated with a Docherty team. A full house stood to applaud him before kick-off. The Stretford End as one sang his name for old times past. The Doc's Red Army: whatever his faults, for all United fans of a certain vintage, me included, Tommy Docherty will always have a special place in our hearts.

At the time, though shocked and saddened, for me it wasn't the end of the world. I'd miss the Doc, but we still had all our players and there was the added excitement of who United would appoint next. In came Dave Sexton from QPR, and in a very short time we'd be pining desperately to have Tommy Docherty back in the dugout. The Manchester United board with their much-publicised, strong catholic morals, Sir Matt Busby prominent amongst them, were desperate to appoint a manager who was seemingly the antithesis of everything the Doc stood for. Sadly, this also applied on the pitch, for little did we know but the days of swashbuckling football careering forward in wave after red wave would soon be over. Our wings had been clipped by Sexton's preferred 'functional' style of play.

On the terraces, little changed as the passion, furore and support remained firmly behind the team. 'Onward Sexton's soldiers,' we sang. Despite most of the time being bored to death. The press soon dubbed him 'Whispering Dave'. Sexton's measured, studious, some might say downright tedious approach to managing the greatest club in the world meant our patience would be severely tested.

BIG RON'S AUDITION
CHAPTER ELEVEN

Dave Sexton was slowly draining the life out of us. After an opening three wins and a draw, an embarrassing 3-1 loss on 10th September at home to Manchester City, when Kiddo returned to score twice against us, showed us that the rabbits weren't just refusing to come out of the hat, they'd done one. Murmurings were already starting on the terraces. Come November, I was already hearing 'Sexton out!' chants in the crowd. United raised their game to something like their old selves for the visit of Liverpool to beat them 2-0 with a performance full of skill and energy. Injuries, lack of form and players unhappy behind the scenes (none more than my hero Gordon Hill, branded 'work shy' by Sexton) saw us slip alarmingly into mid-table mediocrity. Rumours of Hill being sold horrified me. They'll sort it out, I told myself. Gordon was simply too good to let go. The malaise continued unabated when on 17th December, Brian Clough's recently promoted Nottingham Forest turned up at Old Trafford to destroy us 4-0 and all but ruin my Christmas. The result was no fluke, and showed how far we'd fallen. In an all-yellow smart Adidas kit, Forest were stunning to watch, none more so than John Robertson. An old-fashioned, Scottish left-winger jinking, leaving our defenders on the floor and in his wake as we watched on glumly, but ultimately sufficiently impressed that come the final whistle we clapped them off the pitch. Cloughie's team would finish champions that season, and deservedly so.

A schizophrenic 6-2 win at Goodison on Boxing Day brought great relief as we struggled to figure out just what was happening to our club. More drops into the footballing abyss with horrific performances.

On hearing the news, it hit me like a thunderbolt. Had United gone mad, selling our top scorer? They'd only gone and sold my Gordon Hill to Derby for £250,000. He left the club for the Midlands in tears. It'd been festering with Sexton, whose public persona hid a man who, though quiet, was steely strong and not afraid of making big decisions. As always appears the case in such situations, the manager won out. Hill was a free spirit on the field and a spontaneous and undisciplined player like him could never perform to his best in Sextons's new model army. This new defensive, disciplined and dour United was being put together bolt by bolt by dreary Dave. This was a team badly lacking the magic dust that the Doc had sprinkled liberally over Old Trafford. No flair or real character. Strange really, because the clubs Sexton had managed previously, Chelsea and QPR, had played open, expansive football and not the dirge we were being made to watch. On a Warwick Road wall, somebody had scrawled in huge letters 'HILL IN –SEXTON OUT'. I felt sick to my stomach and, like so many others, as if a crime had been committed.

Dave Sexton was on very thin ice with the Stretford End, and the anger fuelled the double signing of two legends, Gordon McQueen and Joe Jordan from Leeds United for £350,000 and £495,000, respectively. McQueen's transfer in particular outraged the Leeds fans, as just a couple of weeks before in Shoot Magazine, he'd spoken about wanting to stay at Elland Road for the rest of his career. He also said on signing for the Reds something that's now gone down in United folklore:

'Ninety-nine per cent of players want to play for Manchester United and the rest are liars.'

Good lad Go-Go!

These two signings helped ease the distress caused by Hill's move, but for the rest of the season the football was turgid. The few flashes of inspiration shown by red shirts were merely moments of déjà vu of happier times and the team swiftly reverted to Sexton's rigid type. Corner kicks at this time meant we would have to watch Sexton's morbidly mesmerising, strange hand signals for our lads to move into position. These seemed to be a ploy by Sexton to confuse the opposition – but his own team seemed just as bemused. The Sexton semaphore never, ever worked and was something I never managed to get my young head around back then. Many years later, I asked a couple of the players of that time just what was going on. I remember Jimmy Nicholl filling me in when we were both playing at West Brom and travelling down together by car: 'We just belted the ball over to big Gordon at the far post and hoped he'd head it in!' After slow and at times painful starts to their United careers, both McQueen and Jordan would become terrace idols, but come the summer of 1978, as the footy ended, we'd finished tenth.

I missed my old United though.

Saturday 30th December 1978: West Bromwich Albion. 'The Game of the Century.'

By the time Ron Atkinson's buccaneering, eye-catching team arrived in Manchester on the day before New Year's Eve, Dave Sexton's popularity amongst United fans had dipped to that of the Yorkshire Ripper. Since the start of the season events had turned for the worse. The atmosphere and the football had both turned rancid. The worst moment was easily back in November, when a 5-1 thrashing at Birmingham City saw United fans snap. A day to forget: Brian Greenhoff was knocked flat out by Argentinian nutcase Alberto Tarantini and goalkeeper Paddy Roache was finally put out of his misery – and our lives. On the plus side, this would save Uncle Al a fortune in fags! By this time, United had truly metamorphosised from the Doc's team. Following in the legendary wake of the tragi-farcical Roache and side-lined, soon-to-be-gone Alex Stepney, we now had a young South African keeper, Gary Bailey. Tall, handsome and blonde, originally from Ipswich, Bailey had grown up abroad but paid his own air fare to return home for a trial at United. He impressed enough to become, in just a short period, United's new number one. Also incoming, the Welsh midfielder Mickey Thomas was signed from Wrexham for £330,000 as a straight replacement for Gordon Hill. Both on the pitch and off, they couldn't have been more different, and Thomas was struggling badly to adapt. Though to be fair, how do you take the place of such a Stretford End legend as Merlin?

The week previous, a tedious and lethargic 1-1 draw at home to Southampton was bad enough to see members of the Red Army travel to the Midlands for the Birmingham match wearing 'Sexton Out' badges. What happened at Saint Andrews meant he was on borrowed time.

It'd become desperate.

Slow handclaps and boos at Old Trafford were akin to a Roman emperor preparing a thumbs down to an arena baying for blood, and it was happening in front of our eyes. We were bleeding to death, white faced with boredom. When the crowds start to stay away and write angry letters to the chairman, that's when the penny, as well as the thumb, drops and the axe is wielded. 'Whispering Dave' – as he'd been nicknamed by the press – was whistling close to the wind.

Then came West Brom. 30th December.

Wrapping my hands tight around a polystyrene cup of piping-hot Bovril, looking over at the travelling Baggies I noticed they'd filled only two of the away pens.

Merry bleedin' Christmas.

It was a bitterly cold Mancunian winter's afternoon, with darkness approaching and snowflakes gently swirling. The weather matched my mood. United had already done their best to ruin Christmas again for me with two ghastly defeats and performances. Losing 3-0 at Bolton was bad enough, but then getting turned over by the same score on Boxing Day, to of all teams, Liverpool? I'd convinced myself turkeys were having a better festive time than me. Surely it couldn't get any worse? Little did I know we were about to get burnt once more by the Three Degrees.

It was a match that would enter the annals of English football as amongst the greatest ever played. An Old Trafford crowd of 45,091 (I was the one) were lucky enough to be present as Ron Atkinson's side lit up this grand old footballing arena. The visitors arrived sitting loftily at the top of the league whilst we lay marooned in a miserable tenth position, though still displaying an annoying trait of raising our game when the mood arose. Manchester United's disastrous Christmas period surely had to end somewhere, and even though that day we truly were given a good hiding, the Reds' performance was one more than worthy of the shirt. United were simply taken apart by a very special team playing at their peak. That West Brom's black players were subjected to incessant monkey chants and boos as they wove their magic was an odious sign of the times. Back then such racism was rife on the football terraces, although rarely heard at Old Trafford. Sadly, that day it was captured in all its monstrosity by the Granada television cameras and commented upon by Gerard Sinstadt. A disturbingly sad soundtrack to what was, at times, the equivalent of a footballing ballet, and dragging our proud name through the gutter.

In the first half, United went toe to toe with the league leaders. It was an electrifying opening by both sides, and Brendan Batson went close with a header from a free kick by a mop-haired young midfielder called Bryan Robson, who appeared half-decent. Then it was United's turn, as young United-bred Andy Ritchie crossed for Sammy McIlroy, only to see his low shot blocked. In the following scramble the referee called for a drop ball, eight yards from goal. Mickey Thomas jokingly went to form a scrum, before the ball fell loose for Brian Greenhoff to hammer in an effort tipped over the bar by Tony Godden. From the following McIlroy corner, it again fell to Greenhoff, who this time aimed lower and smashed an outrageous, arced twenty-five-yard volley past Godden, into the top left-hand corner! 1-0. Old Trafford erupted! West Brom stormed back: with the abuse ringing loud towards him, Laurie Cunningham soon set up an equaliser when he teased a wonderful pass for Robson to dummy and an on-running Tony Brown fired in low past a diving Bailey. 1-1.

Immediately, the sky turned white. The snow began to fall harder, but we didn't care, for this was a proper game of football. As if determined to ram the chants back down supporter's throats, Cunningham exploded again, roaring in-field, beating one, then two. Skating-dancing through the mud, ice and snow. Facing off more red shirts before finding Cyril Regis – his backflick perfect for Len Cantello, who finished ferociously past Bailey into the roof of the net from fifteen yards. 1-2. A blizzard had now blown in and the snow was sticking across the pitch. Refusing to lie down, United hit back in style and a Gordon McQueen header levelled the game from a Sammy McIlroy free kick! 2-2! Two minutes later, McIlroy's snake-like dribble through a pile of West Brom defenders into the penalty area ended with a thunderous shot into the far corner, past a despairing Godden. 3-2 the Reds! It was like the old days. 'United are back,' we sang. Hopes of keeping our lead until half-time collapsed when, seconds before the interval, Brown bundled home his second, and West Brom's third, from close range. 3-3. The whistle blew and Old Trafford as one applauded and wondered what riches awaited in the next forty-five minutes?

It began worryingly as West Brom appeared to shift effortlessly up a gear or two and run us ragged. No-one destroyed us more than Laurie Cunningham: the kid with diamonds in his feet. Lightning fast, impossible to stop when in full flow and blessed with the ability to wreak havoc. The great Laurie Cunningham was a footballer fit to grace any stadium in the world. He and Cyril Regis plainly planned to devastate, humiliate and wreak havoc on us. Victory wasn't enough – they sought humiliation! Two momentous saves from Gary Bailey, as he dived goal-length through the air to deny Regis both times from twenty-five and thirty-yard screamers. Regis also had a header cleared off the line by Brian Greenhoff. It'd turned into a siege: that man mountain, Regis, making us look like boys, took possession to put Cunningham clear to race away and make it 4-3. This goal showed the true gulf in class between the two sides, for as the winger ignited into the United penalty area, Stewart Houston tried desperately to hack him down, only to swipe wildly and miss as the astute Cunningham, easily rode it and shot low past Bailey into the left-hand corner. All done in one sweet movement to leave our defence looking second rate and thrashing around in the snow. It was murder on the dance floor. Still, the best was to come, a fifth to nail us to the cross. Again, it was the rapier-like figure of Cunningham flying down the right-hand side, the ball loved, tended like a newborn baby, his feet hardly touching the ground. Now there was a player who deserved kangaroo-leather boots! Magnificent and not honoured enough in my opinion for the amazing breath of fresh air that he was. He left Stewart Houston huffing and puffing like a breathless old drunk racing to Yates's before it closes. Pacey and graceful, Cunningham accelerated across the halfway line to feed Brown, his swift move inside and pass onto a barnstorming, sprinting Regis, who unleashed an unstoppable first-time shot past Bailey. 5-3, and a legend was born…

The full-time whistle blew to end the masterclass and I was speechless. 'Least we scored three,' I remember one of my mates saying. What do you say after experiencing that? United had given their all and simply been outclassed. Despite it being shocking, it was exhilarating too as we gained an insight into how we should be playing. Amazing. As Old Trafford rose to applaud both sides back down the tunnel, something seldom seen here, it was a case of what next? West Bromwich Albion were everything and more I wanted my United to be. Their manager Ron Atkinson, larger than life; the players Cunningham and Regis, out of this world; and the curly-haired midfield engine controlling half the pitch with his perpetual motion! Bryan Robson. Full of skill and heart, always urging, demanding more from his teammates. A real winner. We could only dream of having such a player as that. Looking back now, if Big Ron had wanted to lay down a marker to United for his managerial talents, his masterclass of 30th December 1978 was the perfect CV.

As for Dave Sexton, redemption (at least for a while) arrived in the form of a most unlikely ally.

Liverpool. The litmus test. Live or die – death before dishonour!!!

SCARLET RIBBON
CHAPTER TWELVE

Though it hurts me to say it, the Liverpool team of the late seventies was head and shoulders above Manchester United and, though it's become popular these days to say we had their number in one-off games, that certainly wasn't the case in the 1978–79 season. Twice they battered us, first at Old Trafford on Boxing Day with an emphatic 3-0 drubbing and then later, in April, a 2-0 defeat at Anfield. On both occasions we were comprehensively stuffed by Bob Paisley's team, a well-oiled machine full of sadly brilliant footballers such as Graeme Souness, Jimmy Case, Terry McDermott and Kenny Dalglish. That season Liverpool were at their arrogant, stunning best and they would go on to claim the league title back from Nottingham Forest with sumptuous ease by eight points. Then why was it that when United drew our deadliest rival in the FA Cup Semi-Final, I felt so confident of beating them? Easy, I was eleven years old, full of it and secondly, I'd be going to the game – to be played at Maine Road – with my dad, meaning the Scousers wouldn't just be up against Sexton's misfiring soldiers, but also Baza shouting instructions for the Reds every time they had the ball. Uncle Al would also be in the crowd. Liverpool would have no chance. Our cup run had seen us knock out Fulham, Colchester and Spurs who had all proved difficult, awkward opponents, but nothing like we'd face at City's ground in Moss Side.

As Maine Road hissed, sizzled and buzzed with sheer mutual hatred, you could almost taste the vitriol, the simmering, adrenaline-pumped violence in the air. The thin Blue line around the ground appearing more up for a ruck than the supporters. Dogs fed on red meat, batons sharpened. 'Just try it you bastards' appeared to be the mood of the twitchy Mancunian constabulary. Three o'clock on a Saturday afternoon, 52,843 packed in tight, every vantage point taken. The songs, the abuse.

'Munich' ringing loud. A war, without guns or bullets, declared by a single whistle, the first battle set to play out – with rules – on a football pitch, but the second to follow later on the streets and crofts of Moss Side. There'd be no rules. Just fists, kicks, headbutts, bricks and your regulatory Scouse Stanley knives. Shouting, charges, scuffles and attacks.

The game began: United in a changed strip of white shirts and black shorts, Liverpool, all yellow. Ninety minutes of sheer unyielding torture was in store for both sets of supporters, whilst the neutrals casually labelled it a 'classic'.

After an opening quarter of an hour in which United began well, on the front foot, it was Liverpool, courtesy of a typical piece of magic from Kenny Dalglish, who drew first blood. Twisting and turning like a yellow eel past a host of our defenders, before shooting low past Gary Bailey. Suddenly, as the Scousers erupted in celebration, old doubts resurfaced. Would we fold again? Another good hiding – three on the run. I needn't have worried because, in the cup, Manchester United were a different animal to what we'd been forced to endure in the league. Two minutes later, from a lofted Brian Greenhoff cross, Joe Jordan came charging in to terrify Bruce Grobbelaar and smash a glorious header into the corner of the net. 1-1! Maine Road exploded again, this time with a Manc flavour. So much sweeter.

The tumult was deafening: tempers flared, Graeme Souness squared up first to Brian Greenhoff, then rather unwisely to his international teammate Jordan. As we roared for big Joe to 'Knock his Scouse head off,' matters settled down a little and the football, albeit frantic, pinball-like, continued unabated. Every tackle a last resort, neither side giving an inch, the ball fought over, lost, won back with a tenacity verging on lives depending on it.

Stevie Coppell was in fine form, raiding constantly and almost setting up Jimmy Greenhoff, whose shot flew just wide. There was nothing between us. Where had this United team been hiding? Then, seven minutes before half time, Liverpool were awarded a ridiculous penalty when Martin Buchan was alleged to have fouled Dalglish, as they both challenged for a header! An absolute joke of a decision. This lot didn't need any help from referees, they were good enough without it. Gordon McQueen was booked for protesting and though we howled in derision, the decision stood. It was now just a case of praying they'd miss it.

Against a venomous backdrop of three quarters of Maine Road whistling and raining down abuse upon his head, up came Terry McDermott, cool as a cucumber to smack the ball against the post! Yessss! Still, Liverpool won the ball back and the return cross from Dalglish fell to Souness, whose thunderous shot was brilliantly saved by Bailey! It was heart-stopping, 'call me an ambulance' football and I loved it! 'United, United!' we roared out. We ain't rolling over today. Half time came and went and still United were going toe for toe. By now we were looking the more likely to score. On fifty-six minutes a cross from Arthur Albiston saw Coppell go in on Grobbelaar, the ball dropped loose falling for Brian Greenhoff, who hooked the ball into the net from eight yards. 2-1! A cacophony of ecstatic joy; massed red choirs jumping, punching the air. Wembley beckoned once more. Thirty-four minutes remained and nothing was more certain now than Liverpool going for our throats. Moving up a gear, Paisley's men rallied and very swiftly we were pinned right back. Oh, they went close, none more so than McDermott, but luckily for us, Albiston got in the way and the ball deflected wide. We breathed again. By this time, Jimmy Nicholl and Gordon McQueen were playing injured. It was a brave but ragged rearguard holding off this yellow tempest, and it felt like the clock had stopped.

Fifteen minutes remained when our little Welsh, perpetual-motion man Mickey Thomas almost put the result beyond doubt, but his free kick was brilliantly turned over by keeper Ray Clemence. Thomas had been brilliant all game and was finally showing just how effective he could be. No Gordon Hill obviously, but there remained more than one way to skin a Scouse cat. From the resulting corner an unmarked Gordon McQueen with socks down by his ankles headed wide. It was torture and when Stevie Coppell broke clear with just the keeper to beat and screwed his shot wide, we feared the worst. All was now Liverpool, relentless, moving over the halfway line, a machine-wave after yellow wave. Dalglish's sheer look of astonishment, as he chipped over the bar with only Gary Bailey to beat. The substitute Steve Heighway wreaking havoc, bursting into the United box to set up Ray Kennedy, only for Bailey to save once more. It was a siege, we were boxed in, couldn't get out, and it felt like just a matter of time.

Martin Buchan off the line from Souness, scrambles, close shaves and countless 'Hail Mary' moments, until... Seven minutes remained when the incessant pressure finally paid off. Dalglish's cross shot was saved by Bailey, only to fall at the feet of their calm and collected centre-half Alan Hansen, who coolly slotted the ball home from close in – then proceeded to race all the way back down the pitch with both arms raised. Absolutely gut-wrenching. Now, we feared the worst. Liverpool almost got a late winner, but Heighway's fierce effort was denied once more by the brilliant Bailey, who'd kept us in the cup with a host of fantastic saves. Come the end, our lads appeared exhausted walking off and I wondered if they'd anything left for the replay, against what had to be said was a magnificent team. Ye of little faith, Welsh. Afterwards, feelings remained high in the tunnel on leaving the pitch, when Emlyn Hughes declared loudly that United had wasted their chance.

'We'll fuckin' batter you on Wednesday at Goodison.' Only to be sparked flat out by a seething Gordon Go-Go McQueen, who was in no mood for Hughes' bullshit. This was Manchester United v Liverpool, it wasn't over and remained to be settled...

Not surprisingly, the match was followed by scenes of savagery in the surrounding streets of Moss Side, as police battled hard to keep supporters apart. The United–Liverpool rivalry was by now etched with hatred and set to stain the coming eighties as these two cities, less than thirty miles apart, became each other's worst enemy. Similar in so many ways: politics, literature, music. But when it came to football, there was now a deep divide, neither side possessing the will to make peace. You could talk all day and night about the Manchester Ship Canal and the treble we'd ruined in '77, but once they had started singing songs and indulging themselves with flags and banners based on a plane crash that almost wiped out a football club and killed twenty-three people? 'Ten past nine, stabbin' time la...'

This time I couldn't go because of school the next day, but Dad and Uncle Al set off for Goodison Park, again in Dad's beloved Ford Cortina, with me longingly watching them through the window. The plan was to listen on the radio and then watch Sportsnight later on television, hopefully with Manchester United back at Wembley. I sat down on the couch in the living room, feeling like a balloon being inflated to popping point. I tuned into BBC Radio 2. I had my scarf round my neck and was breathing heavily with anticipation. I couldn't bear to speak to anyone. I tried desperately to imagine walking towards Goodison amongst the United fans, stopping for fish and chips with my dad and Uncle Al and chanting all our songs, shoulder to shoulder with so many familiar faces.

I closed my eyes. Mum came in to check I hadn't already fainted or broken anything. 'Don't go mad if we score, Nicky, Jane's having an early night as she has an exam tomorrow,' she said with a smile. I stared back and kind of nodded in agreement. I was far too nervous and wound up to argue over such a ridiculous comment that only a mum could come out with. Not go mad, as if!

The noise level on the radio told me that the teams were coming out as the commentator described how our supporters were down at the Park End of the ground. He spoke of a fantastic atmosphere that you could cut with a knife. This was coming through on my small transistor.

'United, United!' I jumped up on my feet clapping along, before there was a knock on the wall from Mum. The first stirring of 'You'll never walk alone' could be heard from the Liverpool fans. 'Oh, piss off,' I whispered under my breath.

As if determined to finish the game early, United flew out of the traps and only a heroic trio of saves from Ray Clemence denied Lou Macari, Sammy McIlroy and Stevie Coppell. We were running them ragged. On eighteen minutes Gordon McQueen shot over from just five yards; then, shortly after, a Joe Jordan header smashed against the bar. It was all United: Macari and McIlroy prompted, pushed and probed as Liverpool's much-vaunted midfield were left chasing shadows. However, their experience in European football of being able to soak up pressure then lash back showed itself on thirty-five minutes, when a Phil Neal cross found Ray Kennedy, whose header rattled our bar with Bailey well beaten, flailing. A timely reminder of just who we were up against. Nil-nil at half time. So tense. My nails were gone and I was weak with anxiety.

The second half was a far more equal affair as nerves took hold on both sides. The thought of losing was abhorrent. I was starting to panic and couldn't even look at the radio. God knows how I'd have been in the ground! Passes were going astray, thunderous challenges in midfield, no prisoners or mercy taken or given. It was ferocious with neither side giving an inch. The tension on the terraces rose relentlessly. I'm sure if I'd been much older I'd have had a heart attack. Twelve minutes remained when United broke forward and a wonderfully precise Mickey Thomas cross was headed low by Jimmy Greenhoff, past Clemence, into the net, igniting scenes of wild joy amongst the United sections of Goodison Park! Me ... well, I went mad and Mum came in to join me! And, that was it, we'd only gone and knocked them out in their own backyard! A lad I know, Sam Smart, was in the Park End and described the scenes.

'I thought the Park End top tier was going to crumble that night. A proper stand, bouncing like mad. It was shaking. The last twelve minutes from the half-way line, top and bottom was a picture of pure red swaying euphoria. Somehow you just knew they weren't coming back. Later, outside the ground, it was utter carnage. Only this time there were thousands of us, not a few hundred. A proper red-blooded battle ensued. Then, on arriving home in Manchester, the celebrations continued. Piccadilly Gardens at midnight was full of pissed-up Reds dancing and singing, while Kloisters, Placemate and the Cyprus Tavern to name a few, to quote Lionel, bounced all night long. There's nothing like being a Red and nothing better than beating that lot...'

The astonishing scenes of violence and chaos outside Goodison Park following the match are now widely regarded as amongst the worst ever witnessed between the two sets of English supporters. Ask any United fan who was there and they'll tell you the same. Meanwhile, round at ours, as Mum sat down with me to watch Jimmy's goal for the first time on Sportsnight, we both went mad again! Manchester United were back at Wembley and Arsenal awaited. This time I'd be there like in '77 to watch the lads. Listening on the radio to the events that night is something I'll never forget. But, there's nothing like watching the Reds with your own eyes.

Nothing at all.

Postscript

Unbeknown to most, that unforgettable night at Goodison Park was where the now-legendary Manchester United song, 'Scarlet Ribbon' received its first mass public performance. One now stitched into the rich tapestry of United's terrace classics, and a wonderful addition to the Red Army songbook. The writer was a guy called Mick Farrell, who perfected the words and music that same afternoon in the Nags Head pub on Lloyd Street back in Manchester, before setting off for the match. Maybe Goodison wasn't Naples or the Sydney Opera House, but as 'Scarlet Ribbon' roared out from the United supporters in the Park End on that Merseyside evening, there really couldn't have been a more fitting venue for its first throaty airing...

'She wore, she wore, she wore a scarlet ribbon,
She wore a scarlet ribbon in the merry month of May.
And when I asked why she wore that ribbon,
She said it's for United and we're going to Wemberley,
Wemberley, Wemberley, We're the famous Man Utd and we're goin' to Wemberley, Wemberley, Wemberley...'

GOING UNDERGROUND
CHAPTER THIRTEEN

In 1979, the USSR began sending troops into Afghanistan. In California, nineteen-year-old Brenda Spencer shot and killed two people in her school. When questioned by police as to why, she replied 'I don't like Mondays'. Sid Vicious of the Sex Pistols overdosed on heroin in New York City and died. Roots premiered on American ABC television. The US embassy in Tehran was taken over by Iranian students and a hostage crisis began. The Deerhunter won the Oscar for best film. Idi Amin was deposed as President of Uganda. Talking of despots, Margaret Thatcher became Britain's first female Prime Minister, the Clash released 'London Calling', and Alan soddin' Sunderland broke this young boy's heart.

With just five minutes remaining of what had proved a thoroughly depressing afternoon, Arsenal led 2-0 in the FA Cup Final and all I could think about was getting home. Across the Wembley terraces, the gathered massed ranks of the Red Army were resigned to inevitable defeat. Goals from Gunners midfielder Brian Talbot and then, right on half-time, centre-forward Frank Stapleton, heading home past Gary Bailey, after a wonderful dribble and cross from the beguiling Irishman Liam Brady, seemed to suck the life out of United, both on the pitch and on the terraces. Brady's poise, movement and silky skills placed him on another level to anyone else playing that day. A world class talent shortly to sign for Juventus, but sadly not before he'd finished with us.

Rarely did Dave Sexton's team not turn up in the FA Cup, but this had definitely been one of those times, and how typical to pick the final to do it. There was certainly no lack of effort – but the spark was just missing. The vibrancy and passion so evident against Liverpool in the semi-final had vanished. Terry Neill's Arsenal were a decent side and had clearly outplayed us, but what stuck in the throat was they'd hardly needed to move out of second gear to do so. I watched their supporters starting to ramp up their songs as victory inched ever closer. The banners and flags being waved now more in celebratory manner than probability. Only a miracle was going to prevent them seeing their team running around Wembley with the cup.

Only a miracle.

As in '77, I was in a different part of the ground to Dad and Uncle Al, and I could only imagine their faces as the clock ran down. On the pitch, United were still pressing forward without ever really testing Pat Jennings. For Arsenal, there was no last gasp, backs to the wall, giant effort needed to fend off the Reds; it'd turned into more of a canter. A victory parade. Four minutes remained when United won a free kick close to the touchline, ten yards outside the Arsenal box. Stevie Coppell swung it across and Joe Jordan played the ball back into a crowd of players, and Gordon McQueen, with socks around his ankles, clearly exhausted, stroked the ball low past Jennings. 2-1! The roar from our end, though deafening, became tinged with consolatory tones. Surely, it'd come too late? Around me, already empty seats from people who'd gone home and given up. A shred of hope remained, but was there really anything worse? From the kick-off, we immediately won the ball back, only for Jimmy Nicholl to lose it. The outcoming groans stuck in our throats as Coppell flew in and retrieved before passing forward to number four, Sammy McIlroy. Gliding into the Arsenal penalty area, McIlroy skipped past one defender, then two, we held our breaths, before Sammy rolled his shot agonisingly low past Jennings and into the net. 2-2! Yes!

What happened in the following thirty seconds is a blur. All I know is that for a short time I'd gone to Red heaven. There'd been an eruption of sound in the United end. Beer was flying everywhere, total strangers hugging and falling about on the floor. We'd somehow saved it at the last! Total madness. The only words able to escape my lips were 'Yes, yes, yes!' I was crying and laughing, but so was everybody else. 'Ya fuckin' beauties Reds,' a fan shouted behind, and as I turned around, he grabbed me in a friendly headlock! 'This is why we love em lad,' he said, with tears in his eyes, though smiling wide. 'This is why we fuckin' love em.' I noticed our substitute Brian Greenhoff stripped and ready to come on. It'd been a miracle, nothing more than a fully blown Manchester United miracle! God bless you super Sammy McIlroy! Those beautiful, dancing, Irish feet tip-toeing through the Arsenal defence. It was over, done. I'd resigned myself to defeat: the long miserable journey back home, we'd just not played, but now!

'Come on you Reds!' bellowed out around me. I joined in.

'How long to go mate?' Someone shouted nearby. 'It's over any second,' came the reply. 'Gonna be extra time.'

My eyes back on the pitch, Arsenal had re-started and Liam Brady had the ball with Lou Macari and Mickey Thomas in hot pursuit. 'Get him lads, bring him down!' The Irishman kept going, he spread it wide to Graham Rix. His cross whizzed over… out came Bailey, where the hell you going Gary?… Gary nooo! The roar from the Arsenal fans more in disbelief than joy: 3-2. How much more can we take? From joy to immediate despair. The super-seventies, perm-haired, moustachioed figure of Alan Sunderland arriving at the far post to win the cup, again, for the gunners. Oh no United. Why didn't you just break my heart once? To do it again, that's just cruel, it's just not right. I'm only a kid for God's sake.

Around me there's utter jaw-dropping disbelief and desolation. Many hadn't even seen Sunderland's goal as they were still celebrating our equaliser. I felt empty – how are you supposed to react after that? The final whistle blew and the entire Manchester United end burst into song. 'We'll support you ever more.' I tried to sing along but the words wouldn't form. United were my team. They were Dad's and Uncle Al's team. But, my God, it was a bittersweet love, laced with heartache.

You realise how much you love your football club when it hurts this much!

The following weeks were a haze. A miserable blur. I remember going to north Wales on holiday, staying at Butlins in Pwllheli. Every single night, in the cabaret hall, Man City fans would sing about Alan Sunderland's winner. The 'I am a music man' song was a tradition at the camp and performed nightly. Everyone got involved. The entire family. Your mum, dad, auntie, uncle, nan and grandad, the bloody lot. Normally it was fun, but not this year. To my indignation the Blue noses had changed the 'I can play the ukulele' line to 'I can play the Gary Bailey!' They did something similar to the chorus, which became, 'Where, where, where's the ball – where's the ball'. Here they'd all start waving their arms wildly about. This was rubbing rock salt into my raw open wounds. Many a time Mum glared as if able to read what I was planning. 'Behave Nicky, we're on holiday.' Oh, Lou, Mickey, why didn't you just chop Brady in half eh? The City boys were right though, what the bleedin 'ell were you doing Gary? I just felt like digging a deep, dark hole and wriggling underground and staying there. At least till August, when it would start again! Forty years on now and am I over it?

You must be joking…

WILKIE
CHAPTER FOURTEEN

Birmingham City at home. Let me tell you about Wilkie. A lunatic like no other and one of the original seventies United hooligans. Up there with the legendary Johnny one-eye off the Stretford End, but this guy was truly real.

Sad to admit it, but me and my mates loved a bit of aggro at the match. Watching and urging on the older lads squaring off to opposing fans. Trying to get at them, the sirens, the roar of a charging crowd! We'd attempt our own type of mischief, rascal-like, but it was always just an adrenaline rush. The police with their dogs on leashes or crashing around on horseback would strike down fast and nothing ever seriously kicked off. The few times I did get a crack, my face would be numb for days, but I daren't say anything at home in case I got another off Mum and Dad. Wilkie, however, was the real deal. He'd moved from Pendleton precinct to the end of our road, right on the corner house of Trent Drive, and had a vicious little bull terrier. The old adage of the dog being like its owner – well true in this case. Wilkie was an amateur boxer with a born gift of intimidating people – he was scared of nobody and nothing. Fearless, frightening and I'm also convinced now, utterly mad.

Come the late seventies at Old Trafford, it became far more common for away fans to make the official trip in larger numbers, as along with their nationwide counterparts, the Greater Manchester police force had seriously upped their game when it came to handling the much-talked about and maligned problems of hooliganism. Surveillance was hugely increased and police spotters knew all the faces in the Red Army. There were no secrets anymore. It evolved into a game, albeit an extremely violent one at times. Cat and mouse between the two sides. In the stadium, metal fences had also been erected around the pitch to prevent invasions, meaning, sadly, no more turf for our back garden, courtesy of Manchester

United. I'd truly convinced myself that the grass I had laid on returning home from that memorable evening after the Blackpool match had spread to now fully cover all our back lawn, and as I practiced and played mini-games of Wembley with my mates, I really believed it was the treasured pitch itself. Our privet hedges also worked nicely as fans, which I'd often dive in to celebrate with upon scoring a winner in an imaginary Cup Final.

By the 1977–78 season at Old Trafford, the away support had been allocated sections of the standing scoreboard end, next to the United Road paddock, and depending on how many fans were visiting, they were handed a certain number of pens. Around 800–1000 supporters. Most teams easily filled a pen, maybe two at most, and here would be where the Red Army could target their enemy, no-one more than our mad mate Wilkie. In the week leading up to the Birmingham game, Wilkie had been telling us all how he was going to enter the Brummie end and 'kick off'. We stood in awe listening to this living legend. In the presence of greatness.

'How many of you Wilkie?' I found the nerve to ask.

'Two of us,' he replied. Smashing a fist into his other hand. 'That's all we fuckin' need innit. Cos we're fuckin' United, aren't we?' His eyes bearing down on ours as we all nodded swiftly in agreement. Wilkie told us he would go down near the front just before the start and exactly ten minutes into the game it was going to go off! He was serious and I couldn't wait! Because of the atmosphere in the scoreboard paddock, I'd started to stand there with my mates. It was incredibly hostile and I loved when it simply exploded into life as all the older lads stamped down on the wooden steps, creating a right racket, before roaring 'Aarrrrgh!' at the often terrified away fans!

Beforehand, I'd already spotted Wilkie and his equally mad sidekick walk out of the away-end tunnel in the midst of the crowd, and I hadn't taken my eyes off since. There they stood amongst all the blue/white scarves. Cool, calm as anything. I swear I even saw Wilkie check his watch! Then, as promised, at exactly ten past three, they began throwing crazy, windmill punches at whoever was around them, causing mayhem before being absolutely pummelled back and dragged out by furious members of the Greater Manchester constabulary. There, in clear sight of the home crowd, Wilkie and fellow lunatic stood proud, looking totally bedraggled. As the away supporters screamed abuse, the two raised hands, taking the acclaim and receiving a heroes' welcome before being thrown into an all-embracing United Road by the police. Faces bloodied, battered, bruised and absolutely mad as hatters and lovin' it...

They claimed to the police that they didn't realise it was the away end, and managed not to get into any trouble from the coppers!

Crazy days.

Back then, Saturdays were just football, not only for our United-mad crowd but also for lads who didn't really follow it. Simply because there was hardly anything else to do, except hang around in town, bored, trying your hand at shoplifting, or annoying the shoppers. There was also the wrestling at the Pembroke Hall. You might remember it on ITV's World of Sport, just before the results, with Dickie Davies and his Mallen streak hairdo introducing huge characters like Mick McManus, Big Daddy, Giant Haystacks, Jackie Pallo, Johnny Kwango and the likes. I'd go with my mate Timmy Blair, whose grandma never missed a bout. It was fascinating to watch for me, more like a circus freak show, in and out of the ring!

Fixed?

What do you think?

Postscript

A sad parting tale on Wilkie. He went off me a bit when one summer I wouldn't jump over the wall of a farm at the bottom of Hilton Lane, catch one of the chickens and then snap its neck in front of him. Wilkie called me a shithouse and our relationship never really recovered after that...

PASTURES NEW
CHAPTER FIFTEEN

On the home front, Mum and Dad finally made the decision that it was time to leave Little Hulton and make home elsewhere. Various reasons. One was that the 'Comprehensive' school system had come in and whilst I was hardly academic, Jane was completely the opposite. Bright as a button. She went to Adelphi High on the Crescent, whilst I was packed off to Saint George's comprehensive in Walkden. I'd also found myself some dodgy company and pastimes such as thieving copper pipes and robbing from shops. Sports gear, sweets and such. It was nothing that others around me weren't doing and it simply felt normal. Not for Mum though. She got word and, with Dad grafting all hours on the business, she was more switched on regarding my 'out of school activities'. She dug her heels in. We were off.

Initially, they found a place in Chorley and fell in love with it, only to be gazumped at the last minute. Both were devastated. As for me and our kid it never felt like the world's end, but for them it was. Shortly afterwards, Dad noticed in the Manchester Evening News that same Thursday evening an old farmhouse in Hale Barns had come up for auction. It was basically nothing more than a shell of a building with a large garden but he saw potential, and when Dad set his mind on something, that was it. When I say it was in Hale Barns, Wythenshawe was only a stone's throw away across a field. In years to come, Mum, being Mum, always let it be known that we were on the right side of this particular field! In the end we paid twenty grand for it and the Welsh clan bade goodbye to Little Hulton and moved across to the posher climes of South Manchester. That the largest council estate in Europe was a mere stone's throw away never mattered, at least to Mum!

Now, it came to choosing schools! Whilst our Jane settled in comfortably at Loreto Grammar (11 O Levels our kid!), my educational adventures were about to enter a whole new phase. I found myself with a place at St Ambrose college, where to say I was like a fish out of water hardly does the saying justice. From the start I hated it. Now, the fact that rugby was played there and not football was bad enough, but with my background, it was a culture shock to find myself surrounded by these strange-talking kids who may as well have been Martians.

I did a little preparation for that opening morning. I decided I was no longer Nicky but Nick, and that I came from Worsley, not Little Hulton. During my first class the teacher brought me up to the front of the class and I was told to introduce myself to these posh Cheshire gits. The sniggers that greeted my Manc/Salford accent made me more angry than upset and I made my mind up that I would keep as strong a Manc accent as I could. Fuck 'em! Later that morning, at break time, still fuming, a lad pushed me through the door in front of everyone and I did what I'd seen in Little Hulton – nothing more than to turn around and smack him in the face. For me it wasn't really common. I was hardly a fighter, but with my pride sorely hurt, someone in that school was getting it! Off I was sent to meet the headmaster Brother Rynne – on my first day! A great start! He took one look up at me across his desk and I was sent home, not so much for the punch but more for wearing trainers and not the compulsory black school shoes. He was one of the many Christian brothers that ran St Ambrose and was a stickler for appearance, more than against violence, it appeared. It was a long walk back down the country lanes to our new gaff whilst I figured out how to explain this to Mum when she got back in from work. It didn't bode well. Ultimately, I made the tactical decision of not mentioning my act of wanton pugilism against the snobby little posh git and instead I told her it was only because of the trainers. Now, my parents, though never poor, had stretched themselves to the hilt for me and Jane. 'I can't afford to pay for new shoes Nicky, you'll just have to go back and tell them.'

The next day I discovered that, amongst my new classmates, I was now regarded as something of a 'rough'n' from the other side, and I have to admit I did play on it! It was a different world, but I did start to make some really good new friends. Pete Docherty, Barry Kilroe, Shay Ennis and Jim McGoff. Pete was the son of former United manager Tommy Docherty from his first marriage. Then, there was footy in the playground with Nick Roberts and Gez 'the lightbulb cruncher' Ford, amongst others. They soon realised that the kid from the other side who wasn't to be messed with could also play a bit. Not that it mattered in this place, because in PE and games they played with a different kind of ball. Rugby!

Come the end of term I was handed an envelope with my mum's name on to take home. A kid in the know shouted over 'Ha! You're getting paid for Welsh!' I'd no idea what he was blabbering on about, but when I got home, I asked Mum and she explained in full. Because I never passed my thirteen plus exam, they had to pay for me to go to Ambrose. When I say my parents were stretched, this is what I meant. Maybe I never appreciated it at the time, but I do now.

I've been blessed.

THE RIGHT SHAPED BALL
CHAPTER SIXTEEN

It was after a game for Parkside Athletic, who by this time had moved to Eccles, onto Brookhouse pitches, that I was told Manchester United had been watching me, and would I like to go training at the Cliff for a trial?

I couldn't believe it! I was thirteen years old and this meant everything to me and more. All I'd ever dreamt about was finally happening. The train to Old Trafford, the bus across to Broughton, then the walk up to the Cliff gates. The pearly gates – well they were made of sturdy wood painted in United red, but all the same! The entrance to paradise. The shale pitch, the huge gym. I'd been there many times before for autographs since being a nipper, but this was special. Nicky Welsh of Manchester United had a ring to it, and I was determined to make this real.

I was shown around the changing rooms, including the first-team room where players such as Georgie Best, Bobby Charlton, 'Pancho' Pearson and Gordon Hill had once sat.

'Get changed, Nicky. We'll see you outside.'

Then there was the kit. If I shut my eyes, I can still see it now. A yellow shirt with a badge on that was hardly ever washed. But did I care? What do you think? The burgundy sweaters, the baggy shorts, black socks with the United red and white trim. All handed down from the first team. You could smell the history – amongst other things – but did I care? You must be joking! I met all the trainers, physio and staff. The top man Eric Harrison, ferocious, hard but fair. Al Jones, Jimmy Curran, Harry McShane (Father of actor Ian). All great footballing men, steeped in United tradition and great characters to boot.

What I noticed immediately in the training session was the tempo. Eric Harrison called it the 'United way'. It isn't a myth – it really does exist. The ball on the floor, pass and move, two touch, make angles, all performed at a frightening pace. Knocking a ball against a wall until you could make it talk and dance. Both feet. Simplicity in its genius. There's nothing complicated about football, just sometimes the managers and coaches who make it so.

I'd go every Monday, Thursday and then most days during the school holidays. Living the dream.

Most of the time when I wasn't training, I'd walk around starry-eyed, just staring at the first team players. Bryan Robson, Martin Buchan, Gordon McQueen.

One time, I suffered a knock on the leg and they took me up to the treatment room. As I sat on a bench nursing a large icepack on my knee, I looked around at players such as Kevin Moran and Frank Stapleton being treated. 'How you doing Nicky?' I heard this Scottish voice say and I turned around. It's only Lou Macari! I can't talk. 'Which leg is it?' he asks, and I quickly point to towards the ice pack! Much to the laughter of all present! There were no airs and graces. I was just one of the crowd. A little Red Devil amongst giants in a footballing heaven.

Meanwhile, back in Cheshire Hogwarts, I was by now playing rugby for the school. I didn't mind it to be honest. No great love, but I was good. My speed saw them play me in any number of positions. On the wing, in the centre and I also took the conversions. Whilst holding my own out on the rugby field, back in the classroom, I was hopelessly out of my depth and always bottom. I should never have been at a grammar school. My parents' intentions were nothing but totally well-meaning in enrolling me there, but sadly, the reality was that I was a non-league player competing in the champions league with this lot. I do sometimes wonder if really it was just because my head was completely in the United clouds. All day every day my brain was at the Cliff. I didn't give a stuff about lessons and homework – I wouldn't need any qualifications because I would be a United player! Everything I thought about revolved around my football and United. As an example, I was set a subject to write about in English. The countryside. I presented an essay about football fields! Reasonable was the mark. But not the subject set!

In 1982, Manchester United were looking for the next year apprentices and wanted me to play in the B team the coming season. This was a year before the YTS schemes came into being, and of course I was flying amongst the stars with this news. It felt like it was all coming together. My United Road was continuing.

Thinking everyone would be equally ecstatic as I was, I asked the St Ambrose sports teacher, a Mr Hallis, if I could concentrate on my football instead of rugby. 'Not a chance,' he said. 'You're playing the proper game, Welsh.' Now, Hallis was a tough bastard, a brute of a man with a bent nose who'd once played for Salford rugby club. A legend in his own scrum. Hallis hated football so much that he would even confiscate the round balls from our playground. 'You're not playing that rubbish,' he'd mumble in disgust before walking off with them under his arm. Hallis couldn't stand me either. I'm sure it was because I so loved the real game. Also, while other pupils were always wary around him, because he stopped me playing footy, I couldn't help myself. We were fire and water. When the rugby season finished and I asked again if I could do football instead of athletics, and he once more said no, I lost it. I was close to fifteen by now. A cocky teenager, fuming with this man because I believed he was purposely trying to derail my dream. One day I told him that no way was I doing athletics and he started jabbing me in the chest. Now, these were different times. St Ambrose was run by Christian brothers. Some were OK, but others were inherently cruel. The cane, strap, slipper or just the back of their hands – all were used to painful and almost lethal effect. Hallis's action wasn't anything strange. However, me telling him to 'Get your fuckin' hands off me,' wasn't something heard often off St Ambrose pupils. Neither was 'I'm bringing in my old fella tomorrow to sort you out!'

'Bring him in, Welsh!' he yelled back in my face.

'Oh, I am doing,' I replied. 'You just wait!'

Anyway, I'd love to write that next day my dad went into St Ambrose and wiped the floor with Hallis and that I had achieved a moral victory. Unfortunately, however, that same night when Dad got home, I explained to him how I'd gone nose to nose with my bullying sports teacher, but it didn't quite go to plan.

'I told Hallis you're coming in tomorrow Dad to sort him out, once and for all.'

'You're joking!' exclaimed Baza to my surprise. 'He's a bleedin' nutcase, thanks a lot!'

So it was that next morning Dad came to the school under a flag of truce and, after a meeting with the headmaster, where it was explained that if I didn't play rugby, I'd be suspended, I admitted defeat. At least for the moment. Deep down, however, I'd no intention at all of going along with their peace plan. There was only one game that mattered and one club. One love, Manchester United and my dream to pull on that red shirt. St Ambrose, Hallis, the headmaster and everyone else trying to stop me could take the world's longest running jump. That'd be the only athletics I'd be doing. My masterplan was simple, but brilliant. I'd claim to be injured whilst at the same time turn out for United's B team. Unfortunately, this all went horribly wrong when somebody informed the school after they spotted my name in the programme line-up. This caused me no amount of trouble on the home front, but ultimately I was still propelling myself forever onwards towards my true goal. A career with the right shaped ball.

CHANGES
CHAPTER SEVENTEEN

Early 1980s: Corbieres, Bowie, the underground market, Stolen From Ivor, Sergio Tachini, Ellesse, Oasis, Placemates, Pips 'behind the Cathedral', Roxy Music, Peter Werth, Perrys, Rotters, Arran jumpers, fringe flickers, The Jam, Adidas Kagools, Austin Reed, Lacoste, Penguin, Pringle, Cellar Vie, Justin's and MUFC!

I was a teenager. I was United through and through. I was in the youth set up – on my United Road. I had the attitude. I had the fringe flicker, the Lois jeans, the Fred Perry shirt, the Peter Werth or Slazenger jumper and I was looking out from the inside. I really thought I was the dog's bollocks. Walking down Market Street with your mates, you had the gear, the strut, the looks. Halfway down you'd swing onto Brown Street and down the steps to the underground market, or into Justin's or Stolen From Ivor, for here was where you'd get most of your stuff.

After 1979, there'd been a huge change, fashion wise, that obviously resulted in what you wore going to the game. Perry Boys was the term. The Manc alternative to the Scousers' Scallys. In Manchester and Salford, it started with lads wearing jumbo cords, Arran jumpers and the unmistakable Perry cut, or wedge. To really pull this off, you needed a fringe flicker!

A compulsory match-going top for 1980 was a slightly striped burgundy Peter Werth sweater with a polo collar, often with a navy pack away Adidas Kagool and Stan Smith trainers. The need to be kitted out then was no different than the three-star jumpers with Oxford bags that everyone had on back in the 1974 second-division days. Times and fashions had moved on (some might say thank God!). The Perry Boy was a much cooler look, and very quickly became the most popular.

Back then, nobody had heard of the phrase 'Casuals', but it was certainly born in the North West of England, before ultimately the rest of the country latched on. No arguments though. It began jointly with our mortal enemies down the A580, East Lancs Road – 'the best thing to come out of Liverpool after the Beatles,' as good old Tony Wilson once memorably said. As the early 80s stepped up, Liverpool supporters, it hurts me to say, were in front of us with regards to trainers and tracksuit tops. They were the first I knew to wear the rarefied brands of Adidas footwear and especially Lacoste tops. This was down to their many European away jaunts. Spotting what was going on across the channel and helping themselves – without paying – to the best foreign gear that was limited back in the UK at the time. Classy stuff that simply blew you away.

I remember Austin Reed, on the corner of St Anne's Square. A posh shop, we thought, for middle-aged business men. Well suddenly, it became the go-to place, for they were one of the very few stores who sold the Lacoste brand. Also-Penguin and Pringle golf sweaters. Purely and simply a treasure chest for any wannabe, aspiring or match-going casual. You simply had to have it, by hook or by crook! Come weekends, gangs of lads would head in there trying to figure out how they could possibly get something through the door without being sussed. Meanwhile, the suited and booted 'Are you being served'-type, snobby shop assistants watched, utterly confused without an inkling of what was going on! Who were these well-dressed boys hanging around the shop for hours on end? For times were truly changing. Young Manc hooligans were no longer dressed like hooligans, but they were hooligans all the same! When the Mickeys came to Old Trafford we'd meet them near their coach for a proper scrap, but equally to see what they were wearing. It was just the way things were. Looks and fashion mattered just as much as getting the first punch in and chasing them away.

By now the atmosphere with Liverpool had turned beyond toxic. Looking back, it was probably not just them singing Munich songs and waving aircraft arms – it was jealousy too. It should have been us!

Boxing Day, 1980. For me, a defining moment in the rivalry. Earlier that month John Lennon had been shot dead in New York and, sick to the teeth of the Scouser's derisory Munich songs and flags, United supporters retaliated with a chant of, 'All we are sayin is Lennon is dead,' to the well-known tune of 'give peace a chance', inspired by the legend himself. Cue unadulterated violence both outside on the Old Trafford forecourt and in and around Manchester's city centre that night. Foremost around Piccadilly and Victoria stations. There were only so many times you could stomach 'Who's that dyin' on the runway' before hitting back. The rights and wrongs of the argument for attacking the Scousers may, nowadays, be debatable. 'You should've risen above it,' some may claim, but easier said than done, for back then all felt fair in loathing and war.

The following year, Bill Shankly passed away and his sad demise was added to our song list. So, it evolved. A hateful, venomous period where anything went. There was a slyness about them. The Stanley knives, the slashing, the swift cut and they were gone. Blood on your hands, pouring down the face. The Mancs never partook in this. That was their style, not ours. If a stag do from Merseyside turned up and went to Rotters, or elsewhere, the word would go around town and it'd be mayhem. Same in their city. Anyone with the wrong accent in Liverpool faced the distinct possibility of – not putting it too finely – getting your 'ugly Manc face' kicked in. Things turned so rough that eventually Manchester-based coaches stopped travelling to Liverpool. Journeys were only possible by car, van or train. After every game between the two clubs there was chaos and that continued throughout the eighties, nineties – and to this day, to some extent. It won't ever go away.

A northern thing.

This was the period in my teenage years when I'd starting going regularly to away games such as Derby, Stoke and Villa, before graduating onto proper, moody big days out to London, with the infamous Man United Red Army. Football specials were laid on from Piccadilly, but (if selected) I'd even go on the normal British Rail services, meaning you were travelling to step off at the destination without the normal police escort. To say I'd become besotted with the craic and violence was an understatement, but something happened that shocked me back to normality. Made me realise I was acting like an absolute idiot.

At this time I was fifteen years old. I was suffering the nail-biting wait to see if United would take me on as a first-year apprentice, and here I was pretending to be Johnny one eye, but better dressed. We were at home in a midweek league cup tie against Everton. As ever, I'd got involved in a ruck outside the ground, and a police dog had almost taken a piece of my arse off. I could live with that; the fact that it'd ripped my Lois Jeans was far more distressing.

Following the match, which we'd lost, I was hanging around in the K Stand with some mates, sniffing for more trouble as there had been loads of Everton fans in the seats as well as those standing in the terraces below, in the normal away team supporters' pens. Suddenly, from over the seats, a hand taps me on the shoulder. I turned around and it was United's chief scout Joe Brown. 'What are you still doing here Nicky?' he asked. Now, Joe was a lovely man and he'd no idea what was going on – thank God! It was an innocent question, but at that instant a lightbulb flashed in my head. My moment from Damascus as my religion teacher at St Ambrose would have described it! 'I'm just waiting for my dad Mr Brown,' I lied, before skulking away quickly. It was like an alarm clock going off in my head. 'What are you doing ?' I thought to myself. If I were to get caught scrapping or nicked even, my permanent dream would be over. United would toss me away like garbage, and rightly so. I had to cut it out.

I just had to change… Not a moment too soon, as it turned out.

NICK OF TIME
CHAPTER EIGHTEEN

'I should've trained with a United scarf wrapped around a wrist. Maybe even tucked my autograph book down a sock as well and used it as a shinpad.'

Back in the seventies/early eighties, if you wanted the real thing there were only two places to buy your football boots in Manchester. Cookes on John Dalton Street or Tyldesley and Holbrook on Deansgate opposite Kendals. They were the best! Cookes had the most rickety old stairs down into the boot room – and a smell like no other. Looking around in wonder at all the glass-fronted wooden cabinets – what lay behind them? For some reading this they will remember that unmistakable library smell – but for me it's got to be that exciting smell of a proper old sports shop. I wish it could be an after shave! This was serious stuff – getting the right Mitres that Pancho wore. I never liked Gola but Gerry Daly did. Mind you Liverpool's Emlyn Hughes started wearing Gola too, so bollocks to that!

If you were serious about your footy then you simply had to have the best, for these were the tools of your trade. Puma Lima with that great white curved line and Adidas Chile with their three white stripes. I still smile when I close my eyes and imagine stroking these things of beauty. Black and white works of art. No fluorescent green or blue – or even non-matching – ankle guard boots that footballers all seem to wear nowadays. Class!

It was the Easter break, and as happened every school holiday, myself and all the other United schoolboys aged 13–15 years, were required to – well, lucky enough to – turn up to train at the Cliff, in preparation for what we all hoped for on finally leaving school – a full-time apprenticeship at the club. The path to our dreams coming true. Our yellow brick road – our United Road. On Wednesdays we'd do fitness/stamina training, but in these holiday sessions, it was much more about technical skills. Keep-ball, attack against defence, one, two touch, before releasing it, and of course there were always the practice matches. During one of these games I was asked to play centre-half rather than my usual up-front role. This positional switching was done deliberately by the coaches, playing us in different positions to educate and give us a more succinct insight into the game. We had to understand the challenges of every role to make sure we knew the weaknesses in every position. It was all an essential part of your footballing development/apprenticeship – to learn different skills across the pitch, and most importantly, you played and thought about the game the Manchester United way.

We kicked off and I was put up against this big, burly centre-forward who was two years older than me. A fearsome sight. Frightening to be honest, but what a footballer. A hard-looking skinhead from Northern Ireland called Norman Whiteside. My god, it was a masterclass, and it felt like one of the longest games of my life as he virtually tore me apart, both physically and technically. Norman was brutal, but in terms of touch and vision he was on a different planet to any of us. Like a top snooker player thinking a shot or two ahead. Similar to Paul Scholes in later years. That was our Norman. An amazing talent. And, god was he tough, a handful like no other! Elbows in your throat, arms all over you. This was a boy in a man's body, but a kid on a mission and in a rush. For one challenge Norman came charging in and it felt like he'd snapped me in half. This was playing to win with a vengeance and a little bit more. Hit first! I always remember Eric Harrison shouting to him on a different occasion in a training-match, as he was busy carrying out GBH on some other unsuspecting player.

'Norman, go easy now, these are your teammates and friends!'

'I don't have any friends on a football pitch,' he shouted back over in that broad Northern Irish brogue of his.

After training, we'd all head back into the changing room and there'd be two huge tin jugs of weak orange cordial. You'd be so thirsty so everyone would grab and fill a plastic cup and drink it as quickly as possible. Being young lads, we'd often lark about and sometimes start throwing what was left of the drink at each other just for a bit of amusement. This one time, a youth teammate, foolishly launched his cup over Norman who'd just walked in. Fuming, he picked one of the jugs up and smashed it over his head, knocking him senseless. The poor lad was left a crumpled mess in the corner. Imagine a cartoon character with stars twirling around his head. 'That's all folks!' As everyone stared on in horror, a still seething Norman turned and declared, 'I don't play stupid games like that!' He simply didn't want to get involved messing around with us young lads, for Norman Whiteside had bigger plans that involved making the first team as early as he possibly could.

Born and raised on the Shankhill Road, Belfast (he used to hear gun shots next door on a terraced row where people would be getting knee-capped), Norman is one of the hardest lads I've ever met and, over the years, like Billy Garton, has become a true friend for life. A great lad with a heart of gold. I'd like to place on record that if it wasn't for appalling injuries and an operation on his knee at just sixteen years of age, Norman Whiteside would've without question have achieved more in the game than nearly everyone else. Though, when it came to FA Cups and World Cups, I don't suppose he did too badly as a Manchester United and Northern Irish legend! If I shut my eyes now, I can still see Norman curling that low beauty past Southall in the final back in 1985. Funny how whenever I shut my eyes I think of football memories!

Some years later, after his playing days had finished, I remember him being in The Griffin pub in Bowdon, when Roy Keane was still enjoying a drink. Typically, Norman was having a laugh by jokingly winding up Keano. Especially with his taunt one time of, 'Keane, take one step back from the bar for every World Cup you've played in,' then proceeding to do so for Spain '82 and Mexico '86. Not surprisingly his hot-headed fellow Irishman took the bait. Luckily, Ned Kelly, the ex-SAS United security guard was there to keep them apart. A box office showdown between two men who could, let's just say, look after themselves! Imagine the final fight scene in the Quiet Man between John Wayne and Victor McLaglen, but much more brutal!

My time at school was almost over. The trouble with Ambrose College after my suspension lingered like a bad smell and they were by this time refusing to even let me turn out for United's junior teams. They even threatened expulsion if I did so. It was war. This lot were standing in the way of my dream. I'd been asked by Cheshire, with another lad, to go for rugby trials, but I didn't bother to turn up. This really irked my arch enemy, Mr Dave (the bully) Hallis, the sports teacher. He couldn't think of anything worse than turning down a chance to represent your county and, of course, St Ambrose College, for it meant a little ray of sunshine and self-esteem bouncing off his daft head. Well, looking back now, you reaped what you sowed Davy boy. You can stick your egg-chasing game up your arse! Or as the Jam put it so brilliantly in their call to arms song, Eton Rifles:

"All that rugby puts hairs on your chest.

What chance have you got against a tie and crest?"

There was a Blackpool FC scout who lived over in Atherton, who'd watched me throughout my Parkside career. He'd already approached my dad and said they were interested in offering me an apprenticeship. Burnley were also a possibility, although I never actually received an official offer. It felt great to have these two clubs after my services, but there was never a chance in hell I'd play in their colours. There was only one offer I wanted on the table. United were the team for me. It was them or nobody else, yet Blackpool wouldn't go away. I kept the faith in my head. Red or dead. Make it happen Nicky. Besides, I hated their tangerine kit anyway. To prepare for the worst, I'd even started looking into courses to become an apprentice joiner, for as I said, it was United or nothing...

Then it happened. By fate, I'd a free weekend with no rugby match coming up. Jimmy Curran had asked me on the Thursday night after training at the Cliff whether I'd be available to play the coming Saturday against an Irish select X1 under 16 team, over from Dublin. 'Can't wait Jimmy,' I said. 'What time do you want me here?' Instead of my normal position up front, I played in centre-midfield that morning which I also loved, and I had one of those special games. After ten minutes I smashed a thunderous effort against the bar and sometimes you just know when everything is ticking. I couldn't put a foot, pass or a tackle wrong all afternoon if I tried. I'm sure it's the same in all sports when everything just clicks. We won 4-0 and without ever wanting to sound big headed, I'd run the show. The rest of the United team were mostly made up of lads definitely starting full-time at the club that summer, and without wanting to sound cocky, I'd been the man of the match by some distance.

After a few pats on the back and a chorus of 'Well played, Welshy,' and 'Good job today mate,' from the lads in the dressing room, I was flying! I was on top of the world. We'd got changed in the first team dressing room and I swear when pulling that red shirt over my head, I could've burst with pride. Just as Eric Harrison was walking out the room, he turned around and looked over towards me. 'Nicky, bob up to my office would you, when you've had your bath.'

'Yeah, no problem,' I replied, still on a high from the game and not really giving it a second thought. Once I was changed, I set off up the wooden stairs to the offices on the first floor, my hair still wet and legs feeling the ninety minutes against the Irish lads. I walked past the manager, Ron Atkinson's office towards the coaches' and knocked on the door.

Eric and Jimmy Curran were sat there having a cuppa. Both smiled on seeing me. 'Come in, take a seat' said Jimmy. I did so facing them. 'Some game that today you played, Nicky lad. A great performance.'

What's going on here I thought? The world slowed down, my head went quiet...

Then Eric spoke those magical words.

'Nicky, how do you fancy signing for us as an apprentice for next season?'

Boom.

It was surreal. A dream. One of the best feelings ever in my life, and for a moment I couldn't breathe. Is this real? 'Well,' I replied, stuttering. Still dumbstruck. For some reason it must have been nerves or shock, but what came next out of my mouth was probably the most stupid thing I've ever said. Another of my Tourette moments! 'I don't know. I've already told Blackpool I'd sign for them.' Did I really just say that?

Eric stared at me with a puzzled look as if to say, 'Have you lost your mind son?' Whilst Jimmy, though appearing equally shocked, couldn't help but smile. 'Blackpool?' Eric said. 'Don't they make rock?' That was all it took. We all started laughing and I swiftly told them that of course I'd love to sign. My head was just all over the place. 'Thank you, thank you,' I said to them many times over! 'Of course I'd love to sign! Of course!'

It was like all my birthdays and Christmases had arrived at once. At that moment it was impossible for me to be any happier. Ecstasy. I could have levitated to the ceiling and floated onto Bury Old Road and all the way to home. I'd never done hard drugs so I can't say how that feeling compares to a trip on some mix of chemicals, but I'm sure nothing could ever give anyone as high a high as I was on at that moment. Nothing can ever fully take me back to the place I was in when Eric said those words. I wanted to cry, but thought best not to in front of Eric and Jimmy. They'd hammer me!

I'll wait till I get home, I thought!

'We'll put it all in writing,' replied a smiling Eric. Seemingly glad now that I hadn't gone nuts. I shook hands with both and I swear I glided out of that office and down the stairs like Billy Elliott, without touching the floor, and out onto the car park where my dad was waiting for me.

He knew by my face I'd had good news.

Dad, you're not gonna believe this!'

On the way home it began to sink in. I was now more sure than ever that I'd be wearing a real number 9 shirt someday soon.

I wondered who I'd see next... Nowadays there would be an instant tweet or post on something or other, or at the very least a call on your mobile. But in those days it would be an hour or two before I'd be able to tell my mum and my mates – and of course Mr Hallis (couldn't wait to knock the smirk off that face), and meanwhile I'd be bursting with pride, passion and joy.

For the next few days I was first to the letter box. No emails or texts or WhatsApps in those days! Finally, a few days later, the official Manchester United confirmation was delivered. Heaven sent. Never has a postman been more welcome! I ripped open the letter and unfolded it. It was typed out on United's official letterhead, showing the cantilever stand at the top of the page. I was told when to report to the Cliff Training Ground in Broughton at 9.30am with all the other new year apprentice players, where we'd be given a run through of all our expected duties and the weekly format. You won't be surprised that I still have the letter... One of my most precious possessions.

Over the past three years I'd tried and ultimately succeeded in finding the fastest way possible to make it across to Lower Broughton, every Monday and Thursday night. I'd head over the field at the back of our house into Wythenshawe, onto Newall Green, then take a 101 bus straight into town, followed by a walk to the arches by the Irwell and another bus down to the Cliff.

Jimmy Curran used to live in Sale, so after evening training sessions which ended around eight o'clock, he'd always give me a lift back across town in the club's famous little red minibus. I got to know him really well over time. A lovely man. We'd jump in and he'd immediately light up a cigar and more often than not put on a Frank Sinatra, Shirley Bassey or Johnny Mathis tape. Jimmy was a great coach. The good cop to Eric's tougher persona. An understatement if ever there was one! Originally a goalkeeper, although not particularly tall, when he joined in training he was always difficult to beat. I once remember him turning out in a B team game after our normal keeper was ill with the flu. A little over the age limit, but no one bothered!

Jimmy said that the young players, living in digs in Stretford or Chorlton, always got to Old Trafford at 8:45am, for a lift over to the Cliff, and I should do the same from now on. So, it was back on a beautiful June morning in 1983, that I stepped off the train from Altrincham at Warwick Road station, by the cricket ground, and headed to the ground with my favourite Patrick moulded boots under an arm, two stripes on the heel. I felt I could run like the wind with them on! The number of times I've walked that route both before and since!

The Manchester United laundry room was based under the K stand and Jimmy had said for me to get there early and help him load the kits onto the bus. I all but skipped across the forecourt, feeling ten feet high, swinging my boots, and down to the red wooden gates under the Munich clock. I knocked on the door and Jimmy answered. 'C'mon on Nicky lad.' I followed Jimmy under what was the centre of the Scoreboard stand into one of the most breath-taking places I've ever experienced. On the surface it was a simple laundry room, packed full of washing machines, baskets and tubs. There'd be kits, shirts, shorts and socks folded neatly in piles which you'd expect, but it was what adorned the walls that left me stunned. Every inch was covered in photographs of past and present United players. Many were inscribed with personal messages. One particularly caught my eye. A black and white photograph of a handsome young man. On it was written 'With best wishes and thanks, Duncan Edwards.'

The whole place was nothing less than a Manchester United Bayeux tapestry. Living and breathing history. Buried deep in Old Trafford, an everyday hubbub of normal life. Well, here, away from the razzamatazz, this was the club's true heartbeat. I stood open-mouthed, as if hypnotised. There was Matt Busby, Jimmy Murphy, Georgie Best, legends all. More recent ones also for me personally, such as Gordon Hill and six foot two, eyes of blue, big Jim Holton. I could've just stood there all morning, but a gentle slap on the back of my head off Jimmy brought me back to earth. 'Your first day Nicky, you don't want to be late for work. Grab a tub!' I did as asked, but remember having a last glance and thinking, one day I'll be on these walls. One day, I dared to dream.

FEELS LIKE HEAVEN
CHAPTER NINETEEN

In the summer of 1983, I was sixteen years of age and joining the club of my boyhood dreams, Manchester United. I signed shortly after we'd won the FA Cup against Brighton and Hove Albion, and was released two years later, following another cup victory at Wembley, courtesy of Norman's epic strike against Everton. The two years in between those finals were the best and worst of times for me. I didn't so much as fulfil my dream as have a gloriously short nap before waking up with the hangover from hell. Though, for a while it really did feel like heaven…

The First Day: I couldn't believe it was finally happening. Sat in the back of Jimmy Curran's red minibus after stepping on at Old Trafford and now heading for the Cliff training ground. Along the way we picked up other lads, Billy Garton amongst them down on the dock way. 'Baby give it up' by KC and the Sunshine Band was playing on the radio. I'll never forget that – will probably have it played at my funeral!

Once at the Cliff, we were each allocated our kit and a squad number. Being polite and a bit laid-back, I just wanted to soak everything up, so I waited near the back. Suddenly, I noticed that the numbers were getting higher and higher and by now we were up to forty-six. I clocked on the notice board that they stopped at fifty and started thinking, they're set to run out of numbers here, and I'm not going to get one! So it was that polite Mr nice guy, Nicky suddenly disappeared out of the window and I thought bollocks to this! By now only three remained and discreetly as possible, it was elbows out, edging in front of David Platt. Panic over. The kit man Billy Watts passed over my neatly folded, clean white Manchester United towel, navy sweatshirt, shirt, shorts and socks and he noted down on his clipboard: Nicky Welsh: no. 50. Any joy I felt momentarily disappeared when the kit man then handed Platty no. 29. 'Oh, we'll have to go down the numbers. Now, there you go David.'

It turned out the better the player, usually the lower the number. Any disappointment swiftly vanished though, for I was just happy, more relieved in fact, to have a kit! Embarrassing to admit now, but for a split second I'd honestly thought what if they've messed up on numbers, didn't realise, decided to change their minds and I got sent home? Innocence of youth eh? Just holding all the kit in my arms felt like Christmas as a ten-year-old. Since I was a kid, I'd always loved the Manchester United FC white towel with red lettering. Even back to when Best, Law and Charlton had been photographed with them after winning trophies, and seeing the towels draped around their shoulders or waists in the dressing room. Now it was my turn, and even that felt like such a privilege.

The opening day also saw the fuss, with the press and television people turning up for interviews. Myself, David Platt from Chadderton and Alan McLoughlin, another local lad from Burnage (same class at school as Noel Gallagher). A lot of us were local in those days – and we were the first footballers to be taken on at Manchester United under the government's new YTS (Youth Training Scheme). This, as with everything to do with the club, was big news, both locally and nationally. We found ourselves front and centre. Swiftly finding out, if only a tiny crumb's worth, just what it felt like to be part of the greatest club in the world. The Manchester Evening News plastered us all over their front page 'Red babes on the ball'. In the photo I was positioned between Gary Bailey and Gordon McQueen, whilst the other two were on the first teamer's backs!

'I've supported United all of my life, and my favourite player is Bryan Robson,' I told the reporter Simon Spinks. 'I'm hoping to pick up some great playing tips.' We also featured on both News at Ten and Granada Reports, where I got to have a short kickabout with Stevie Coppell for the cameras. Among the many memories etched into my mind from that very special day was the moment when club Captain Bryan Robson and senior pro Roy Wilkins came into our apprentice changing area, situated next to the boot room for obvious reasons, to wish us all the best of luck. Robbo had with him a large sack of New Balance boots he'd brought back from Boston – USA, not Lincolnshire – after signing an advertising deal worth £30,000. Thirty-grand! It seemed a fortune at the time. We were earning £25 per week on the YTS. Robbo tipped the boots out onto the floor. 'Help yourselves lads.' A class act was Captain Marvel, both on and off the pitch. Wilkins said that if we ever needed advice just come and see him. He also reminded us, 'Remember, you've not made it as a footballer until you've played 300 league games.' A line Wilkins repeated a few times when he felt it needed drumming home to help stop us becoming prima donnas. Again, just class, a lovely fella. God rest his soul. All in all, I floated through that first day, and to celebrate in the evening Dad took me for something to eat at a Bernie Inn, as Mum was working. There's no doubting where my work ethic and grounded personality came from. Baza and Eileen.

Any full-time professional player will tell you that pre-season training is a strange and arduous time of year. It's usually in June, heading into the height of the British summer. The start of the playing season still feels a lifetime away. Most of the emphasis, particularly in the first couple of weeks, is about getting fit, and you don't often see much of an actual football. To achieve the standard required we ran and ran! Just a couple of miles down the road from the Cliff was Heaton Park, Europe's largest municipal park. Simply perfect to build up stamina and experience the joy of running endlessly up and down the hilly heights. I knew the park so well as it had been my childhood playground. Just a stone's throw from The George pub my Grandad H had in Cheetham Village. Running around it again, trying to keep up with the front runners, Bryan Robson and Frank Stapleton, was such a strange but wonderful feeling for me. Paradise? If such a thing existed then I was in it. You know the feeling when it's Christmas morning, maybe you're off on holiday, or a birthday? The sight of your own babies when they are born. Well, that was me, day after day, week after week. Getting paid to play football and rubbing shoulders with my heroes...

We had to clean the boots. No problem. Our heroes' boots after all! Sweep the dressing room. Why not? I loved it – bring it on. I especially loved all the banter between the first team players – no headphones worn by players with more languages than the Tower of Babel in those days. The humour could be ferocious, but it was also such great fun. I was pretty sharp – well, sharp enough not to get wound up too much by the big names, because if they saw a weakness, by god they went for it! All part of learning the game that you just had to ride and become stronger in doing so.

One of the stipulations on the new government-funded YTS apprenticeships was that all first-year players attended a day release at Stretford college on the Monday morning. It was a specific course aimed at young footballers and, if I'm honest, we all felt it was a waste of time and viewed it as more of a laugh and a chance to let off a bit of steam. Also present in the classes were Manchester City and Oldham Athletic lads, which was a little off-putting because we played them at A- and B-team levels at least twice a season. The City game in particular was pretty serious stuff. Eric would wind us up to the point that it'd be war out on the pitch. I always got on well with their defender Earl Barrett, but the other Blue in the class was Steve Redmond. A Scouser playing for City. Could there possibly be anything worse? We simply never gelled. He'd turn up on a Monday morning wearing a red, white and yellow Liverpool beanie hat. You can imagine how that went down? The bare-arsed cheek of it. Myself and Aidan Murphy, another mad Red from Blackley in North Manchester, used to look at each other in disbelief. Wearing that in our backyard. How bleedin' dare he? Redmond knew the script. He was a real wind-up merchant and I don't think we spoke a word the whole year.

While waiting at the bus stop one early afternoon on Broughton Road after training, United's first team defender, Arthur Albiston pulled up in his car and wound down the window, permed hair flowing. He'd recognised me from the Cliff. 'You heading over to Old Trafford?' he asked with that Edinburgh drawl. I nodded. 'Jump in then, I'll give you a lift.' Arthur asked me what digs I was in, and I explained I lived over in Altrincham. 'So, do I. I'll drop you home then, no problem,' he said. And that was it. I got on famously with Arthur, but who wouldn't? Such a warm and unassuming guy despite playing 379 – yes 379 – games for Manchester United and over 500 professional games in total. A great. 'I'll pick you up in the morning,' he added. 'Save you getting the train.' Amazing, here I was being paid for living the dream, and now chauffeured into work! Is this for real, Welshy? I very swiftly became great friends with Arthur, and eventually even better drinking buddies! His ability to memorise games was and remains extraordinary, a man who possesses a wealth of footballing knowledge and a true gent to boot.

Finally, after the ordeal of stamina training for the first ten days or so, it was time to get the ball out! At last. Now I could show what I could do, I thought to myself. The Adidas Tango balls – still leather and prone to get heavy on wet days – were ready and primed. All pumped to perfection, and I should know, for I blew up most of them in the corridors at the Cliff! The first practice match was a concoction of first teamers, reserves and youth players.

My dad and my good mate Gez (the infamous lightbulb eater), plus his old man Tony Ford, used to call Ray Wilkins the crab, because in their opinion, he always passed sideways across the park. 'Too negative,' they said. I wasn't having that and remember arguing long and hard in a London pub on the Saturday night after the first Brighton final. To be fair, a lot of United fans I knew were pretty mixed on their opinion as to whether Wilkins was, as we like to say, a 'United' player, despite his 160 games for the club and despite our fans voting him player of the year that season.

Well, let me tell you something.

After the first fifteen minutes of my first full Manchester United practice game, playing on the same side as our 'Razor' Wilkins, I was left in total awe. I'd always prided myself on having decent vision and for being able to pick a pass. That day, however, I'd had the ball on several occasions in midfield and couldn't for the life of me see anything on. Here was Wilkins though. One touch and bang, it was gone in the blink of an eye. Finding teammates through gaps that simply didn't appear to be there. Hitting inch-perfect, forty/fifty yarders to feet with total ease. It was incredible to watch and experience. A totally different level to anyone I'd played alongside previous. Total class. I remember thinking if only Dad, Gez and Tony were stood here watching this first hand. Some bleedin' crab! I also realised that I seriously needed to up my game if I was going to hack it around these parts. An understatement if there ever was one, for this was an early reality check that I have to admit shocked the living daylights out of me. The same scenarios also were occurring in the sprints and shuttle runs. All my life, over ten or twelve yards, I'd always been way ahead. Billy Whizz. In sharp contrast, here at the Cliff there were seven or eight players of similar, if not greater pace. The challenge was set: any lowering of standards and, even early doors, you'd be handed your arse on a plate by Eric Harrison and his staff. It was full mettle, no hiding, but I was up for it. This was my dream and even if there was a chance that it might not turn into reality, I was determined that there would be no chance that it could ever be said that I hadn't given it my all. As I had always made clear to all around me, it was going to be United or nothing, and nothing wasn't an option.

I began well for the youth team despite playing in the unusual position of centre-midfield, instead of up front. I impressed against Bolton and Leeds at the Cliff and then came a hat trick at Halifax, when everything just seemed to click into place.

Life was good. In training I was working like a trojan, listening and taking everything on board. For some reason, after my game against the Irish select XI the previous season, the United coaches had seen a different part of my game and so came the centre-midfield switch. That's fine by me, I thought. I'm obviously being groomed to play alongside Bryan Robson. Wonder if I'll captain England as well as United? Always the dreamer. Still in wonder and needing to pinch myself that this all was really happening. Surreal, but still hard work. Especially now I was in a new role. I'd always loved playing up front and had done so throughout my junior footballing career. One of my strongest assets had been a tremendous turn of speed off the mark. My old fella always taught me from being a kid that you could gain two yards mentally on a player by being like a coiled spring, or an Olympic sprinter when the gun goes off at the start of a race. 'No one can mark that,' he'd say. 'They simply can't stop you Nicky son!' On your toes and bang! You're off with a two-yard start. We'd practice it time and again. But that was then, and this was Manchester United.

Another special memory of the early days for me was going into town one Tuesday afternoon that Autumn, to an olde-worlde tailor's shop, directly under the CIS building – the tallest in Manchester at the time, and once the tallest in Britain. You were sent on different days to be measured up for your club blazer. I always wondered if the other lads felt just like I did. Proud as punch. Buzzing every single day back then, I really was living out my childhood dream. On entering and handing over my form, out came the tape measure and the old fella went to work.

'How long before it's done?' I asked him.

'Around ten days,' he replied giving me a sideways look as if to say 'Don't you even dare try to rush me young man!' That's a long time, I thought. I was so impatient.

'Can I see the crest? Do you have any here?' By now I'm clearly getting on his nerves. He looks at me with disdain, shakes his head, then walks back behind the shop counter searching a set of old wooden drawers. I leaned over to watch to make sure he looked for it properly! Eventually, the old man brings one over, and lying flat in the palm of his hand was a thick piece of cloth pocket with the crest on. Wow! For me this was everything. The crown jewels, and soon my crown jewel. All my life I'd seen the photograph of the Busby Babes taken before the fateful flight to Belgrade. All wore the crest this old man held before me. They'd wear it for one last time. These were the treasured footsteps I was following in. Tread carefully Nicky lad. Tread carefully.

Around this time, Aidan Murphy, Alan McLoughlin and I were approached by Frank Stapleton about the possibility of representing the Republic of Ireland at youth level. Aidan said no and went on to play for England schoolboys and England youth. I turned the offer down too – but Alan did go on to represent Ireland, including playing at the World Cup! Thinking back now, that's one of the very few decisions in my life I actually regret. I should've played for the Irish. My mum's side were from Ireland, and we'd go over to the family cottage in Ballyhaunis, Mayo virtually every summer. I loved the people there; the place; the craic. Deep down though, I also knew that England was my birth country and my home and I think I'd have been kidding myself, although I remain deeply proud of the Irish roots. A Soldier's Song always brings me a warmth within and touches my soul. A little piece of Mayo, like United, will always be a part of me.

Because of the rugby background at Ambrose, I'd never had an opportunity to play football at county level, let alone England, although I don't necessarily think I'd have got that far because of what the FA looked for in young players back then. Two United lads, Simon Radcliffe and keeper Fraser Digby from our year were the only ones that represented England schoolboys. Simon actually captained the team. Our mentor Eric Harrison, God bless his soul, was brought to United by Ron Atkinson and outstayed him. He had been a player in the lower ranks but his skill was as a coach, recently having become recognised as one of the best there has ever been. Coach to the Class of '92. Now Eric had a real downer on the English youth set-up. Both Simon and Fraser would go off to Lilleshall during the international breaks, when it was run by the FA's director of coaching Charles Hughes. On returning to the Cliff, they'd report back on the training methods with tales that sent Eric mad. 'Football should be played on the ground, not in the air!' Hughes had bought into (and preached like a religious zealot) the long ball philosophy that claimed most goals in football were scored by three passes or less. A player had to aim to get in the 'POMO' position (position of maximum opportunity). Wimbledon and Watford, more than any other clubs, adopted this style and they did have some success, albeit relative, with it. To Eric, however, this was 'Ale house' football and went against everything he and Manchester United stood for. Also, it saw very talented lads discarded just for not being of sufficient size and build, in place of bigger, stronger, tall ones, often with far less ability. If you ever wanted to rile Eric Harrison, and believe me, few ever dared, all you had to do was just mention the name Charlie Hughes and stand back.

Every few weeks at the Cliff, Eric and Jimmy Curran called the youth players in for a one-on-one chat to check on their progress, though each moment of every day was already like an ongoing appraisal. You'd constantly be asked how things were. How do you think you're doing? During the actual meetings, it was a case of sitting down and taking on board what they told you. Good and bad. Neither missed anything in training and each could spot a hangover at a hundred yards. They'd mention if you were being too slow for the second ball in open play. Anathema for those two wise old crows. Basically, that was about not being fast enough either on your toes or in your thought process – or both – each of which was unacceptable. You had to be ready if the ball ricocheted back into your area of play. The basic stuff, but if you were going to have a chance at United, you had to be better and faster than your opponent in body and mind on the pitch at all times. The chats were not used as opportunities for rollickings. My god, as if they needed an excuse, for rollickings were handed out with both barrels there and then on the training pitch, within a game, at half or full time. I never had the experience of a Sir Alex Ferguson hairdryer within my short footballing career, but I'd imagine it was very much like an Eric Harrison blast. Peas in a pod.

He'd go nose to nose screaming vitriol in your face, calling you names, offending you personally if he felt it necessary, for Eric was building character and you either took it and learned, or fell by the wayside. Sometimes, you were picked out just to see how'd you react: hit back or shrink? I remember Eric almost scrapping with a youth player, Lawrence Pearson, but that's football. That's United. It's a passionate place to play a brilliant game, and you have to care. You really do. Ask any Manchester United youth team player from back in the day, even the class of '92. We would all agree that, when playing a competitive game at the Cliff, the worst sound you could ever possibly hear was Eric's dreaded bang on the window! No one else did it. You knew it could only be him. Somebody could produce a wonderful pass, score an unbelievable team goal or make a last-ditch saving tackle. Nothing. You'd never hear that bang. But woe betide if he witnessed something that irked him. Slack marking, not running back, lack of awareness… then would come the clatter on the window and without a shadow of a doubt, he'd appear raging, and ready to give out a no-holds-barred rocket in your face, in front of whoever was present. Good on you Eric Harrison. All of it was only ever done in the best interests of Manchester United, and even today, Eric's words, harsh at times, have left me in good stead. It was more than just a football education; his were lessons on life. I can see that now. At the time, though, he could fill me with dread and inspiration in equal measure.

It was during one of the appraisal chats that I somehow plucked up the courage to say, 'You know, I wouldn't mind having a go up front. I think I could do the business, Eric.' He looked at me for a moment and I thought, oh no, he's gonna lose it here! Instead, Eric simply smiled and nodded his head. 'OK,' he said. 'You can have a go at centre-forward next game.'

'Cheers Eric,' I replied, grinning widely, still not quite able to believe he hadn't thrown me through a window. The game was to be against Burnley at the Cliff and I performed really well. Feeling pleased with myself, I remember heading up the stairs to the canteen after the game and seeing him in there. He looked over, smiled, and that gave me the confidence to say rather cockily, 'I told you I could play up there didn't I, Eric?' Thinking back, I'm cringing right now. 'Yes,' he replied, the smile now gone. 'But it's OK doing it against the likes of Burnley. Can you do it against the Liverpools and the Manchester Citys of this world?' I was sent packing with a flea in my ear, but the opportunity approached to show Eric that I could produce similar form against those two, because coming up in two weeks were the Scousers.

Sadly for me, I didn't actually get the chance to find out, for the following Tuesday in training I went to sprint for a ball and then I felt it… My right groin had gone again. I first had issues with this when I was around thirteen and it went in a hundred metre sprint race at school. As I made my way off the pitch, I knew it was the same issue recurring, but I buried this because nothing was going to stop me. The physio Jim McGregor had been monitoring the problem for the last three years and he would sort it, I told myself, for this was United. The biggest and the best. Nothing to worry about. Nothing.

Nothing.

I came back after a large chunk of the season had been lost, and then it went again. I remember being sat up on the treatment table, legs stretched out with Jim McGregor assessing the damage. Also present, watching on was the manager Ron Atkinson, who just so happened to be in the room. Just my luck. McGregor looked up at me and shook his head. 'Welshy, I have to say, you have legs like Trevor Francis, you run like Trevor Francis.' He paused and before he had the opportunity to carry on, Big Ron piped up, 'Yeah, but he plays like bleeding Claire Francis!' We all started laughing, because if you don't laugh, you know, you really could cry. Right?

The Boss, the Gaffer, the Manager. Whatever anyone called him, one thing was for sure: Big Ron was a football man. Following Dave Sexton, Manchester United had shifted gear back to a front man. Outgoing. Brash, and to quote Billy Joel: 'Quick with a joke or to light up your smoke.' Sexton came quietly and left Old Trafford quietly – a fleeting shadow. Missed by nobody. Whereas Ron? His unofficial CV had arrived on our chairman, Mr Edward's, desk on that frosty, snow-filled Christmas afternoon back in 1978, when his West Brom team tore us apart, playing football the United way. Whatever anyone ever claimed about his teams, like spectators in the Colosseum watching gladiators, fans were always entertained. Big Ron was larger than life around the place; a joker and he always had time for everybody. From the laundry ladies and the apprentices to the first team players. He had a warm character. He wasn't a bully. He was approachable to all and – quite simply and most importantly – a true student of the beautiful game. Wingers were like fresh air to him – essential. Ron Atkinson, despite the public persona of the sunbed in the office (which was true) and a quip for every occasion, was a proper footballing man. He also loved to join in the practice games if the first team had played the night before, or were given a day off. Ron always played left wing. 'Who should I be today lads?' he'd ask us. 'Platini, Zico, Puskas!?' Ron always reminded me of the PE teacher from the Ken Loach film classic, Kes. A footballing romantic with the pitch as his stage and one he simply could never leave. Never bothering to get changed into training gear, Ron preferred to stay in his pristine, Adidas tracksuit. He simply had to look the part, even to a bunch of lads, despite the fact that if he said jump, we'd ask, 'How high gaffer?'

There was this hallmark trick of his that he'd pull off time and again. The legendary lollipop. Big Ron would shout for the ball, often close to the left-hand touch line. 'Here, knock it into me,' he'd shout, if the play swayed to his side of the pitch – and if the gaffer says knock it into me, you don't mess about, you knock it into him! In fairness, he had a decent first touch for a big fella. Then it'd come – we all knew it was coming! The lollipop. His left foot sweeping over the ball and in the same movement stroking it softly over with the outside of the right one, whilst dropping a shoulder. This was a skill in itself, but try and pull this off whilst flipping your long, combover strands of hair back into position in the same motion – believe me, it took some doing. Absolute genius. This became my party piece in the dressing room and I could pull it off to a tee along with other impersonations of the gaffer, one in particular as he spoke, always touching and squeezing the bridge of his nose.

One winter's morning at the Cliff, Big Ron had got involved in another of our practice games being played on a rain-lashed, mud-splattered surface. Typically full of enthusiasm and armed with that one great trick. 'El Lollipopio,' he had the ball at his dancing feet trying to go past someone, when suddenly the gaffer slipped and went over. This was no ordinary fall to earth, for Big Ron, dressed immaculately in a brand new light blue tracksuit, never did anything bland. With the greatest respect, it was like watching a baby elephant fly through the air and splat! Face first into the mud, landing on top of the ball itself. Almost impossible to pull off, but the gaffer had done it.

No one laughed – we daren't. Though so wanting to, we knew it wasn't the done thing. It'd been like a sniper on the Cliff building roof had picked him off in the way he hit the floor. Almost apologetically the ball sat under Big Ron's armpit. He never moved, all was silent. Everyone was looking at each other. Is he dead? Alan Mcloughlin was standing nearest and, after about ten seconds, he slowly tip-toed his way towards him and gently started to roll the ball away. 'Ahem, you OK boss?' said Alan. 'Sorry Boss, but there was no foul.' That said, we played on, although all of us watched from the corner of our eyes to see him finally stand back up, arms out, mud dripping off everywhere and slowly walking off up the banking to the dressing room. Soon as Big Ron vanished over the hill, play stopped and everyone just fell about laughing. Even Eric Harrison couldn't help himself, and that was a rarity.

Big Ron – a legend!

Let me tell you, he never left that touchline again.

After breaking down the second time, it was decided by Jim McGregor and his medical staff that I needed to go in for an operation on my right groin. A manipulation op, which in basic terms means that, whilst under anaesthetic, they stretch the leg further than you naturally allow if you're actually conscious. I hoped and prayed it'd solve the issue and allow me to play a few games and impress, but deep down, although I hardly allowed myself to think it, I knew almost inevitably that it would happen again. Being out injured is, for a footballer – well, for any sports person – the worst feeling in the world. I'd gaze out of the window at the Cliff and see the lads getting on and progressing. You just so wanted to be out there amongst them. It was eating me up inside. I had to face facts. Things weren't looking promising. The first year of my contract was almost up and decision time was dawning. Finally, the day arrived for me to find out my future. I was waiting at the bottom of the stairs at the Cliff before being invited in to see the Gaffer. I knocked on and heard his voice. 'Come on in, Welshy.'

Big Ron was sitting behind the desk in his trademark Adidas tracksuit. The sunbed was across by the window. I remember a couple of occasions when in the height of winter, as we were flogging ourselves training in all conditions, running endlessly around the pitch with the wind and rain hitting us in the face, we would suddenly see the flickering blue reflection of the sunbed! I recall my good mate Martin Russell, from Ireland, as he ran next to me one time saying in his strong Dublin accent, 'Not being funny Welshy, but shouldn't he be watching us, by the way?'

I can still see the big red phone on the desk. I was nervous as hell. Once again breathless with anticipation. Dreading anything negative. Big Ron looked across at me. I just wanted him to get it over with. No slow kill, just tell me straight out.

'Nicky,' he said. 'We've decided to give you a one-year professional contract.' My heart leapt to a new high! 'And we've booked you in for a full operation at BUPA to sort out your leg. We've seen enough to know that, when fully fit, you have something to offer.' Relieved was probably the understatement of the century. 'Thanks so much, gaffer,' I replied, whilst firmly shaking his hand. 'You won't regret it, I'm telling ya!' I walked back down those stairs with the certain belief that next season would see me rise through the ranks of my beloved Manchester United. Bring it on... M.U.F.C OK...

THE BITTEREST PILL
CHAPTER TWENTY

To my eternal surprise, from our group only myself and David Platt were to be handed professional contracts, and so we switched dressing room from the apprentices to the reserves. Billy Watts took us through the footballing rites of passage, where we'd both be given a dressing peg with our number and name. Mine was next to a young Irish centre-half from Dublin, who could play a little. A kid called Paul McGrath, who we all know would go on to be one of the greatest ever Irish players.

Although I'd hardly set the world alight on the pitch the previous year, it had to be said that I'd been getting one hell of a different kind of apprenticeship – in Manchester, Salford and Trafford's watering holes. It all became so normal. Getting a lift home and to training with my friend Arthur and, at times, Captain Marvel himself, Bryan Robson, I was often invited to join them on their infamous midweek boozing sessions. Here was where I got to know Big Norman Whiteside really well and, therefore, his mate and fellow Irishman, Big Paul. What an outstanding, outstanding defender. Whenever pitched up against Paul in training, I hardly ever got a kick or a header, or even made it past him. He was remarkable and those size 13 ½ feet of his got everywhere. After one particular practice match, first team against reserves, when Paul had all but made a fool out of me, I remember going home on the bus thinking, I'm kidding myself here about making it at this club if Paul McGrath was the standard, for he was beyond the stars. A different class. Watching him some years later putting Italy's Roberto Baggio (considered to be the best striker in the world at the time) in his back pocket at USA '94, made me feel a little better. Great player and a lovely lad – those nights out around Altrincham, Hale and Bowdon were legendary!

There was a lot of emphasis on the offside trap at the time, and we'd do attack against defence drills for weeks on end. Frank Stapleton pulled me to one side one day and said, 'I've been watching your runs, Nicky. If you set off making a run down the channels, arch your run back, so if the centre-half steps up you don't go offside. In reality you should never be caught offside again, as you've got enough pace to get away with it.' It was great listening to a wise old pro and so obvious what he was saying. Stapleton had taken the time out to advise me and I've never forgotten that. I tried taking it on board and always used it to good effect. (Unless up against Paul McGrath, who was that fast I'd need a five-yard start, and he'd probably still clear up.) I always thought Frank would go on to become a great manager because of the way that he thought about the game. A first-class professional, as was the Dutchman Arnold Muhren, whose left foot could open a tin of peas. I don't think they enjoyed the drinking culture that existed at United, but with Robbo at the front of the training runs and Norman and big Paul nearly always our best players every Saturday, there wasn't really much to hang their hats on.

Back then it was a different ball game with all the socialising. After the game, the players would drift away to the local pubs and clubs. Crossford's in Sale was a popular haunt. By then, I'd become really good friends with Norman and his then wife Julie, a lovely local girl from near Gorse Hill, Stretford. We'd go out as a foursome with my then girlfriend Sally, end up in Friday's nightclub in Didsbury, and then carry on for a curry. Proper athletes! I remember one particular night in the club. We were at the bar chatting when this brute in a suit went right into Norman's face, virtually nose to nose, calling him a 'Munich bastard.' He just looked away and turned his back on this idiot whilst the bouncers arrived to sort him out. I couldn't believe it and said, 'I don't know how you keep your cool big man?'

'Quite straight forward Nicky,' he replied. 'If I rose to it every time I went out in Manchester I'd be fighting every weekend!'

In more recent times I experienced a similar situation at Haydock Races with Sir Alex Ferguson. He'd generously helped me out with a charitable cause and I'd thanked him with a couple of bottles of wine. We'd walked across to put them in his car and a couple of lads with Scouse accents shouted over to him 'Eh Munich!' For me, to say this to a footballing legend was despicable. I was livid but he just said quietly to me, 'Arh just ignore them Nick'. Not all Scousers are as bad, I must add. The older generation show more respect. The boss though, like Norman, just rose above it. Situations like these have shown me just what Manchester United legends have to contend with whenever they are out and about in public .

Without saying it, everyone knew the script. I'm sure the same has always applied at all the large football clubs. The best way to progress as a young player is to have a good run in the FA Youth Cup. For us it was the big time. The closest we'd get by that time in our careers to the real thing. You'd play in the main stadiums, travel on the official club coach, have pre-match meals – no different from what the first team did. Plus, the entire management, first team players and even senior directors would often be there to watch. All a little different to stepping on Jimmy Curran's little red minibus and heading off to Marine or Formby for an A team game. In 1984 we'd drawn Leeds United – and we were playing them at Elland Road in the second round. I knew this was my chance to shine. I was totally focused. It was Thursday 6th December 1984, three days before my 18th birthday. I began the game on fire. After just 3 minutes, I went past a defender and put a nice dinked cross in for Martin Russell to head home from a couple of yards. Well done Welshy, keep it going. With their fanatical crowd behind them, Leeds hit back and come the second half, they'd taken charge to race into a 3-1 lead. Undeterred, we kept going at them. I had a header saved on the goal line by a defender's hand and Tony Gill smashed home the resulting penalty. 3-2, and now it was all set up for a grandstand finish.

Five minutes remained, and I'd managed to nutmeg the Leeds left-back Terry Phelan, just inside the edge of their penalty box. It'd opened up and as I set myself up to shoot, I suddenly felt that familiar pain in the leg. Oh, God, not again, please no. Instead of letting fly, I took the easy option and tried to cross to fellow striker Gary Worthington, but it got blocked. The game ended 3-2. Not good enough, I remember thinking, This isn't in my script. I felt it in the depths of my guts. A second-round exit in the FA Youth Cup, by Manchester United's high standards, could not be tolerated. My uncle, Steve Toal, had travelled over the Pennines to watch me. Afterwards, we met up. 'Why didn't you shoot near the end Nicky?' I never even responded or mentioned the leg to him. I was sick of it. I still often wonder though what might have been if I'd crashed in the equaliser to take them back to Old Trafford for a replay. But, such is life…

Although events were starting to turn a worrying shade of pale on the pitch, off it I was starting to look international class at holding a pint pot. The laughs and craic were aplenty. Big Ron would openly say to his players, 'So long as you do the business on the pitch, I don't care if you have a drink.' He was one of the old school who considered boozy nights out to be team bonding. There was a standard two-night club curfew before a match, which was always adhered to, but if we had no midweek games, it'd be all out on a Wednesday session that could be anything from ten to twenty pints. Not only that, but at the Cliff there was a lovely Irish lady chef called Theresa. Her speciality was fish, chips and peas on a Friday, and jam roly-poly with custard for afters. This was the afternoon before a game, after we'd attempted to drink Manchester dry only two days previous!

Three weeks previously, I'd broken down on the Astro Turf in the big indoor gym, and Eric Harrison had gone absolutely berserk. 'Get off the fuckin' pitch Welshy,' he screamed at me. 'You're like a pane of glass.' I tried to walk a little faster, but simply couldn't. Eric was obviously frustrated, but not half as much as me. I can honestly tell you that. We were set to take on Manchester City in the Lancashire Youth Cup semi-final at Old Trafford. If I didn't play it would be game over, pure and simple. The City match was going to be my very last chance and it was on the hallowed turf that I'd never performed on competitively. I'd trained there, had team photos taken there, but never actually put on a red shirt in anger. Somehow, I just had to play. I had to. Jim McGregor knew this. He suggested I have a cortisone injection which just totally numbs any pain. The fact that it could be damaging the injured area even more didn't matter to me at the time. It was now all or nothing. Last chance saloon. In the end, I was picked for the sub's bench, because I hadn't trained. Alongside me was a lad from Hyde called Lee Martin. My dream was still alive. Just.

With twenty-five minutes remaining, we were losing and Eric turned to me, 'Go on, get on there Nick, and turn it around.' My moment of truth. This was it.

On I ran, the world stopped turning and I looked around at the stands in awe. This had been my dream since that first game with Uncle Al. Now here I was, actually playing footy on this magical turf. My destiny.

With the clock running down and us chasing the game, I won us a corner at the Stretford End. The ball had gone behind the advertising hoardings and I rushed quickly to retrieve it. As I rolled the ball up the wooden board, I suddenly looked through the bars and noticed that this was where I first used to stand back in 1975. I saw myself as an eight-year-old staring back. It was a surreal moment for me. The game was literally over. We were 3-1 down, but I kept on going, running myself ragged. The referee was checking his watch as I chased City winger David White down the wing by the United Road, with the cantilever stand again towering over me. Exactly in the same spot where many years previously I'd ran down the wing in my Oxford bags and six-hole cherry red Doc Martens, to help myself to that piece of turf for our own Derwent Close back garden. It felt like a lifetime ago. The final whistle blew and somehow, I knew...

I just knew.

Once more I'm walking up those Cliff steps to the Manager's office. I knock on, and this time Big Ron is smartly attired in his suit. Not a good sign. The red telephone and sunbed remained in place. 'Sit down son.' I felt sick. 'Nick, we can't wait forever for you,' he began with. 'So, we're going to have to let you go.' I knew it was coming, but for some reason couldn't accept it. 'No, you can't.' This was sheer desperation talking. 'No boss, you know there's more to come. Much more.' Big Ron stood up and went to open the door. He turned facing me. 'Sorry son.'

I panicked. 'Boss don't do this. I tell you what, just give me six or seven weeks pre-season. You don't even have to pay me. I'll wash the cars, whatever, just one more chance to prove myself. Please?' I was pleading.

He simply shook his bronzed head. 'Please don't make this harder than it is Nicky, we've made our decision.' That was it. I upped and left. My head was buzzing and already what felt like a cloud had gathered in my mind. Although I knew this was going to happen, upon hearing it out loud from the gaffer it really did feel like a dagger in my heart. This time around there was no Billy Elliott moment. Heading back down those stairs, I just felt numb. My United, how can they do this to me. Me? I was beyond upset, my world had come to an end. Turned out I was no different after all. United's youth set-up was simply a conveyor belt, and they'd just ran out of patience with me. There had been thousands before me and would be thousands after me and only a special and lucky few would ever get to step off it and into the first team.

My head was all over the place. What happens next? The club had been my entire life. This wasn't in the script. I headed over in a daze towards The Priory pub, directly across the road from the Cliff, with a couple of Irish lads who had been given the same news and also been released. David Platt had been let go too, but I don't remember seeing Platty. You simply had to deal with it in your own way. The three of us stood at the bar, no one really spoke. Some senior players were in, and offered condolences, but we weren't really good to be around. Alan Brazil (Bazil as we fondly nicknamed him during his time in Manchester) sent £20 over to buy us a drink – fair play to him. I just thought he was being nice at the time, but looking back now it's obvious he was just relieved that a fellow striker had been let go and his place was safe for another season! The next few days were a blur. I went home and never said much. Everybody knew and left me alone. I simply sat in my room, absolutely gutted. I cried, got mad, and the same thought kept racing around my head.

What on God's earth am I supposed to do now. Since I'd been knee high to a corner flag I'd lived and breathed this football club, and now they'd tossed me out like garbage. Unrequited love. Is there anything worse? My dream had just ended and slowly it was starting to sink in and break my heart.

ROAD TO NOWHERE (NOBBY)
CHAPTER TWENTY ONE

Life goes on they claim.

Well, I was entering the Twilight Zone. After being given the big heave-ho off Manchester United, I could've gone two ways. Walked away, picked myself up, dusted myself down and started all over again. Or, hit the beer, sulk and see what more damage the angels could do to derail my life. I went down the latter path. I'd received the inevitable news that I was out from the Gaffer before the 1985 FA Cup Final, but, like any other job, I needed to work my notice, which meant I remained officially employed up until the end of June. Ten days before the final, Big Ron called all the reserve players and apprentices into the little gym at the Cliff to announce that everyone was going to be measured and fitted up with a Cup Final suit, the same as the first team squad, and Phil Black, a local boutique clothes shop owner would be in tomorrow to do the measuring up. Great, I thought, at least I'll get a decent suit out of it. I was already in my head trying to get around the fact that I was no longer going to be a United player. Once again, I'd be the fan, but this time without the dream. It wasn't the end of the world, I'd tell myself. United would remain in my life, just as they'd always been. I cheered myself up with the thought that I could travel to away games now with all my mates – every cloud and all that. Who was I trying to kid?

Come that glorious Cup Final, May morning, we all met up on the main Piccadilly Station concourse. Kitted out of course in our super-cool, grey Van Gils suits and scarlet red ties. Courtesy of Big Ron and Blacky. You were allowed to bring a guest and I brought along Shay Ennis. A huge United fan who was my best mate and partner-in-crime in the pubs and nightclubs of Manchester throughout our teenage years. I recall David

Platt who was released the same week as me brought along his brother. Platty had already been given the opportunity of playing for Crewe Alexandra the following season and had already packed his boots immediately on being given notice by United to start training there for the final few weeks of the season. He'd go on to have a fabulous career, whereas I and the other rejects? We thought sod it, let's enjoy the day out to London, courtesy of the club who had broken my heart.

As soon as the train pulled out of Piccadilly the beers appeared, and by Birmingham, the Reds were in full on party mode. Come London, we were absolutely flying! Not only our group, but virtually the whole two/three carriages of players, including the younger apprentices, who were the worst of all and close to being out of control. An age thing! We'd all been there. A local lad from Wythenshawe, Denis Cronin, jumped on the train's intercom to jokingly ask if anyone wanted to buy his Cup Final ticket for 'One and a half?' Not good, for there'd been a flurry of press leaks about tickets turning up on the black market. Also travelling and listening into Denis on our train were club staff and officials. There were many annoyed faces and it has to be said a few worried ones amongst them. Cup Final tickets back then were viewed by certain people involved at United, and every club, like a plumber or an electrician treated a foreigner. Money on the side, a perk of the job even.

When we were just a few miles from Wembley Central station, word reached our carriage that one of the younger lads was 'broken biscuits', as we say. He was sat on the toilet, singing and talking utter rubbish, clearly in no state to be seen in public. A conversation swiftly took place and it was agreed that we couldn't leave him on the train, for inevitably someone would find him and he'd be in for the high jump. So, the lad in question was coming with us, even though this future United first team player had lost the use of his legs. The time was touching one o'clock – two hours until kick off. We'd have to move fast and spread the load: it was decided that two at a time, one either side under his armpits, we would carry him upwards towards Wembley Stadium. Everyone else would crowd closely around and hopefully no one would notice our mate, rat-arsed in the middle. Astonishingly, despite many curious looks, it worked! We managed to get him through the turn stiles, scarecrow (Wizard of Oz style) and placed him under the concrete stairs, sat against the wall like a Guy on Bonnie Night. I remember taking his red tie off as if to protect him, in my mind anyway, from being identified as a United player. A rota was organised between twenty of us so that every five minutes or so, someone would check on him. All this worked a treat until early in the second half when one of the lads came back with the shocking news that our man had thrown up all down his club suit. Now, he was truly done for. Luckily, there's a happy ending for this same kid, sleeping off the beer and covered in vom, but with a half-smile on his face. He would later achieve greatness wearing a red shirt in an FA Cup Final replay, six years later.

Good on ya, Lee lad!

Back to events on the pitch, and what a goal to win the FA Cup in extra time by that skinhead kid from Belfast. We were right behind it as Norman Whiteside took aim and placed a shot of unerring accuracy past Neville Southall into the bottom corner to ignite Wembley's United end! It was a truly incredible strike and one I'd watched him do on so many occasions during training. Norman would use a defender, this time Pat Van Den Hauwe, as a shield to totally block the goalkeeper's view and then let fly. He'd hit the target every time.

'We've won the cup, we've won the cup. E, eye adio, we've won the cup!' All achieved with ten men after Kevin Moran had, unfairly in my opinion, been sent off in the first half after tripping Peter Reid, becoming the first to be sent off in a Cup Final. It'd been some performance by the remaining lads, brimming with huge heart, determination, and no little skill. Not a classic – but who cared? We'd won! We'd also denied a brilliant Everton team of a domestic double, which made the victory even sweeter. Following the match, we partied on throughout the weekend and then, still groggy from all the celebrations, I played a final game for the United A Team the following Monday night.

With my very last kick of a ball officially in a red shirt, I scored a penalty. Luckily, it went in off the post. Just imagine if it hadn't? That would've topped it all off eh? I was never a penalty taker, but the other lads, who I was about to say goodbye to, were just being kind. For despite me trying to act all Billy big bollocks, I'm pretty sure they knew inside just how much I was really hurting. They'd have been right doing so, for as the final whistle blew on that early May evening, a massive wave of sadness washed over me. Over the next few weeks I decided in my foggy, depressed head that it was all over. What chance did I really have? You're nothing but a dreamer Welshy. You've come to the end of your United Road and did so by falling down a huge manhole. Stay down it, time to find a proper job and get in the real world. I definitely knew one thing for sure.

I was finished with football.

To try and help me think straight, I went with my girlfriend at the time, Sally, on holiday to Marbella.

We were sat outside Sinatra's bar in Puerto Banus, drinking with Paddy and Noreen Crerand and their son Patrick and his then girlfriend. A lovely family who I knew really well. I was enjoying the company and for the first time since arriving I was starting to feel a little like my old self. Paddy could make a tree smile. He mentioned in conversation that Nobby Stiles, who was working at West Brom, was asking about me, and if I'd found a new club?

'I'm not interested Paddy,' I replied. 'Let's have another round eh, my shout!' I just didn't want to hear about football, never mind play again. I called the waiter over. 'Same again mate.' Guess who then appears walking towards us? Big Ron and his good lady, plus Phil Black and his. I couldn't believe it. Talk about dancing on my grave? Childishly, I pretended not to notice him, but he'd obviously clocked me, or perhaps Paddy more like. Next minute a tap on my shoulder and it's Big Ron. 'Welshy, how you doing? Can I buy you a drink?'

Suddenly, it all came back, the fog returned. I so wanted to say to him, 'Just another month, please Boss, I've been on two runs this week and feel great. My leg is sorted, and...' Instead, I kept my head down and muttered, 'No thanks, I'm sorted.' I finished my drink soon after and said to Sally, 'C'mon, let's go.' She knew and understood. It'd been five weeks since being handed the P45 from my dream job and it was still a massive open wound.

We met up with the Crerands again later that week, and Paddy was like a dog with a bone. He wouldn't leave it alone, bless him. 'Why don't you speak to Nobby, Nicky son? They really wouldn't mind taking a look at you. Johnny Giles is getting things together down there and it might not be a bad move for you.' I'm still not certain if it was the San Miguel or the sun, but I suddenly had another road to Damascus moment. Or in my case, motorway to the Hawthorns. Now, Big Ron had come from there and he's not going to last forever at United. What if he does get the chop and they decide to look at Giles and Nobby? I could be the next Remi Moses, or, dare I say it, Bryan Robson, with a transfer to follow. It all made so much sense in my messed up state of mind back then. God does work in mysterious ways and it's a common fact that he's also a Red! I wondered if they'd sign me on the pitch. I really did.

Back at home the phone rang not long after the holiday. I recognised the raw, but in some ways slick, North Manchester accent as soon as I answered the phone. 'Is that Nicky? It's Nobby Stiles here.'

'Hello Nobby.'

'Paddy has passed on your number and I wondered if you fancy having a run out for a few games while we take a good look at you? I can sort out expenses, and also I live in Sale, just off Brooklands Road, and travel there daily, so I'm happy to pick you up and give you a lift if you like?' How could I say no to that? To Nobby Stiles? As a kid, I'd sometimes attended Mass twice on a Sunday morning at St Patrick's in Collyhurst, when staying at Nana and Pop's. No, I didn't have plans to go into the priesthood, it was to try and catch sight of the great Nobby Stiles in the flesh. If he wasn't at the early 8 am mass, Nobby never missed the 9:30am. He was a living legend. Similar to Brian Kidd, who was also occasionally present in the Saint Pat's pews and who I hear still goes to mass most days. Another son of Collyhurst with no airs or graces who helped us to win the elusive trophy that Sir Matt Busby had strived so hard for after the Munich air disaster. The European Cup.

Nobby arranged to pick me up the following Monday morning from St Margaret's church in Bowdon, and we'd travel down the M6 to the Midlands. I was a little in awe when he first pulled up. Nobby gave a friendly wave, but didn't get out and I walked over. He smiled and signalled for me to jump in the front. Blimey, I thought, after all these years and a thousand Hail Marys, I'm finally going to meet Nobby Stiles. Bloody 'ell, he looked small behind the wheel. 'Nicky, lovely to meet you. Let's get going because the traffic's always heavy down there on a Monday.' By the time we'd reached the Midlands, it was like I'd known him all my life. Why wouldn't it be. He was a proper Manc. Arriving in good time at the Hawthorns, Nobby reliably informed me this was officially the highest ground above sea level in England. A fountain of footballing knowledge was my new mate!

The training started well and I enjoyed it. As expected, it was mostly running, but also, we saw more of the ball. Something that never occurred so early in pre-season at United. The lads were friendly, down to earth, and I got on particularly well with a lad called Carlton Palmer. A second-year apprentice, a good sort and also a little mad in a nice way. Another was full-back Nigel Burrows, who went on to to play for Liverpool. A Midland lad. 'Tell us a joke Nicky,' he would always say to me in his thick Brummie accent. There was also a shy centre-forward with longish hair called Steve Bull, who wouldn't say boo to a goose, but was also good as gold. Everything felt so much more relaxed than at Manchester United, friendlier even somehow. No Eric Harrison! I sometimes thought it was because the pressure wasn't quite so intense. At least for me.

I kept telling myself that I was almost over my United experience. It was like being dumped by a beautiful girl which hurt really deeply, but time is a good healer, and my legendary, personal chauffeur from Chester Road, Altrincham to the West Midlands helped this healing process in a way that few others ever could have done. In so many ways Nobby was priceless, and no more so than as a storyteller. Without bad traffic it took seventy minutes travelling to the West Brom training ground at Field Road, whilst a few miles further along the M5 was the Hawthorns. To this day I cherish those memories. I loved those times, absorbing those wonderful tales from the past that Norbert Peter Stiles reminisced about. I'd even think the night before in bed before nodding off, who or what should I ask him about tomorrow? It was a daily personal Q&A from the legend himself, and you can only imagine the questions that I, the ultimate 'Rent-a-fan Welsh', would have lined up for him. The only problem was that, God bless him, Nobby was as blind as a bloody bat! He'd sit low in his seat with his head just about above the top of the steering wheel and drive in a not particularly relaxing manner, taking one hand off the wheel every fifteen seconds or so to push the thick black spectacles back over the bridge of his nose.

One of the first tales Nobby shared with me was about Georgie Best in training. 'Nobody could ever get the ball off him in a small sided game Nicky, so we'd make it two touch, but again he'd still be running the show. Then it'd go to one bloody touch! The trouble being though Bestie was that good he'd knock the ball back off the opposing player's shin like a one-two. Still, the little bugger would run it until finally, we'd just have a normal game and try to kick him!' Nobby also spoke about the toughness of the truly great players. He said Pelé was absolutely 'Hard as nails.' 'They all were. If it came down to mixing and putting your foot in, Nicky lad, all the greats were capable of doing it. Eusebio, Cruyff, the lot of 'em.'

One time going down we'd reached around Walsall, still on the M6. It'd been raining hard and the inside of the car windscreen had steamed up. I'd decided the topic that day was the momentous events of the 1968 European Cup Final. Something I still never tire of hearing about. Anyway, a passionate Nobby was explaining in great detail how United winger Johnny Aston played such a pivotal part in beating Benfica that night. He spoke about Aston tracking back, preventing the Portuguese wing-half getting forward, and how it released Bestie. Nobby became so engrossed. It was enthralling to just sit back, watch him and listen. He started drawing a dot on the window condensation. 'That's Johnny Aston,' he said, then a curve with the left index finger. 'Here's Bestie out this side.' Another dot. As Nobby is speaking, I catch sight through the passenger window of a huge juggernaut's wheel coming to within inches of the car. 'Bloody 'ell, Nobby!' I shout. 'Never mind Bestie's goal!' I swiftly grabbed the wheel with my right hand, steering the car back across into its correct lane that we were supposed to be travelling in! 'Let's just get to training in one piece, eh!' Good old Nobby was so engrossed in the story he forgot about the driving. I loved him.

The many stories were simply fantastic, and I remember them to this day almost word for word. I chose to ask one afternoon coming home about the Munich disaster, and where he was when he heard the news? Nobby had been at Old Trafford doing his apprentice duties, sweeping the main terraces in the old B Stand, amongst other stuff. It was such a sad tale told with tears in his eyes. Like so many Reds of that era, Munich scarred their souls and would do forever. He went on to talk of Duncan Edwards. 'The best player ever, Nicky lad,' he said. 'Duncan was the greatest. Before all the United first team away matches, the referee would ring the bell or blow his whistle for the lads to start making their way onto the pitch. As they prepared to leave the changing room, Duncan would either stand in the face of a teammate, or grab the front of their shirts with both hands, before declaring, 'C'mon now chief, we've not come here for nothing!' Nobby would say all this in Edwards' strong Dudley accent. The emotion in his voice was uncontrollable at times. He continued on, 'These other players, Nicky, they were older, established international players in their mid-twenties, and Duncan—' His voice once more choking. 'Duncan was only seventeen.'

Apart from the unforgettable stories I'd continue to hear and absorb like a sponge from Nobby, the one thing he truly amazed me with was how good a player he remained when joining in games at training. I always had Nobby down as a stopper, a nuisance on the pitch with orders from Sir Matt to unsettle the opposition, but he had so much more. Nobby could ping a ball, Ray Wilkins style, and hit a beautiful 35–40 yard pass with ease. You never saw many clips of him doing this, but I suppose when you're playing alongside the likes of Best, Law and Charlton, you probably just leave it to the experts. Right?

West Bromwich Albion, the 'Baggies', were a lovely, friendly club. I recall meeting on a few occasions arguably their finest player, or at least goal scorer, Jeff Astle, who seemed to work helping out behind the scenes at the Hawthorns. I'm a little embarrassed to say, but at the time I'd never heard of him. What a nice gentleman. When he passed away in 2002, he was the first British professional footballer confirmed to have died from chronic traumatic encephalopathy (CTE), a progressive, degenerative brain disease found in individuals (usually athletes) with a history of head injury, often as a result of multiple concussions. In Jeff Astle's case, it was the repeated low-level brain trauma believed to have been caused by heading the ball.

In an attempt to avoid the leg problem, I played right midfield for West Brom reserves, thus not having to tempt the devil by too much sprinting and turning as I'd have to do up front. In my mind I was doing the right thing. Able to read the game, I felt all was going OK, until one particular, pre-season reserve team friendly at Field Road, against Arsenal. I came up against the type of quality I'd only previously experienced in Norman Whiteside and Paul McGrath. That old sinking feeling returned tenfold as I received the type of football lesson that made me once more question whether I was out of my depth. I ended up having to try and kick this kid because I couldn't get anywhere near him. He was like a flashing red shadow, dazzling touch, then gone. Finally, Nobby subbed me before being sent off. He knew the signs. Afterwards, I checked their team sheet to find out my tormentor's name. It was a kid called David Rocastle. What a player! Rocky had everything and went on to have a wonderful career with Arsenal, before his tragic, untimely death at just thirty-three years old.

My cunning West Bromwich Albion scheme to use them as a stepping stone back to M16, and home to Old Trafford, wasn't quite going to plan. First team manager Johnny Giles experienced a horrendous start to the 1985/86 season, drawing the first match and losing the next nine consecutive matches which resulted in him offering his resignation. My mate Nobby was drafted in as temporary caretaker. My Manchester United, however, were the opposite. They'd gone off in the opposite direction like a steam train, winning their opening ten games and playing in exhilarating style. Big Ron had them on the right track and the media were actually talking of this being the season that United could actually win that league title again.

My initial surge of renewed enthusiasm had waned dramatically. Perhaps more importantly, when I pulled on that famous navy/white top with the embroidered WBA logo, it meant absolutely nothing. For me, West Brom were nothing more than the girl you jumped into bed with after that one true love left you heartbroken. An illusion that was never going to last. Thanks a million, though Nobby. Thank you for the memories.

MALAYSIA: MONEY FOR NOTHING
CHAPTER TWENTY TWO

Thursday 22nd August 1985. After playing for West Brom reserves against Everton the night before at the Hawthorns, I was having a leisurely lie-in after returning home late from the Midlands. We'd won and I'd had my usual half-arsed, average game on the right wing on this occasion. I knew I needed to step up, but...

I was woken up by the sound of dozens of ambulances racing at full speed up and down our lane. It was surreal. What the hell was going on? It turned out that a blaze had broken out on a Boeing 737 aeroplane bound for Corfu on the runway, at nearby Manchester Airport. Tragically, fifty-three passengers and two crew were killed, but as the sirens raged outside ferrying the victims to the closest hospital at Wythenshawe, I'd no idea. For this was before the internet, Sky and mobiles. There wasn't any such thing as breaking news. Still half asleep, our telephone rang, and as I was the only one home I was forced out of my pit to answer it.

'Hello, is that Nick?' this foreign-sounding voice asked.

'Yes' I replied, puzzled.

'Hello Nick, my name is Steven Sya. I am ringing from Kuala Lumpur, Malaysia. I have football club, Cheq Point FC. We want to sign you. You've played for Manchester United, yes? You must be very good player, yes? I want to sign you. I come to London.'

No way, a wind up, I remember thinking. This had my best mate Shay Ennis written all over it. The king of practical jokers.

'Fuck off Shay, it's too early!'

'What!? Who is this Shay?' Suddenly, alarm bells go off in my head. Maybe, just maybe, this wasn't Shay and the guy was serious. 'No, my name is Stephen Sya. I get your number from PFA. I want Manchester United player – future superstar to come play for me in Malaysia at

Medeka stadium.'

I glanced through the window and the ambulances seemed to be getting faster and the sirens even louder. 'What is that noise, is that a police car, Nick? Are they chasing you?'

'No, Mr Sya. You were saying?'

'Nick, you know where Malaysia is?'

Even though I'd got a Geography O level, I didn't actually have a clue. My guess was the Middle East, but I thought best to just hang up. What with the sirens and the caller's strange accent, it all felt like I was in some kind of nightmare. As I was about to put the receiver down, he continued on. 'Please take my number and I will see you in London next week in Park Lane.' I did as this guy asked and then ended the call. Outside, the scenes continued with ambulances and police cars roaring past with red lights flashing, horns blaring and sirens deafening filling the air. Something terrible had obviously occurred, but it wasn't until much later that day, when we were all at home watching the six o'clock news, that it became clear just how horrific the fire on the plane had been. So very sad, those poor people excited about going on their holidays and then, gone. I suddenly remembered the strange phone call and decided to mention it to try and cheer everyone up a little. 'Hey Dad, I got a phone call about half nine this morning from a Malaysian guy in Kuala Lumpur. Can you believe that?' I went on to tell him what he'd said.

'That sounds interesting,' replied Baza. This shocked me because I thought he'd laugh it off. I should have known better. 'Where's his number? I'll ring up and suss him out for you.'

Off he trundled to the phone. Impulsive never did my old man justice. Simply full of enthusiasm and adrenaline in everything he did. 'Dad, no,' I shouted after him. 'Don't ring him now, it's bleedin' two o'clock at night over there.'

Thankfully, he didn't contact Mr Sya that evening, but did so the very next morning! Typical! Up and flying around at the crack of dawn, that was him.

'Up you get, rise and shine!' Baza would shout when knocking on the bedroom door to wake you up! 'The early bird gets the worm.' He had such a fantastic work ethic. Dad's favourite saying, or at least one of them, was 'If you can wake up in the morning, get out of bed, tie your shoe laces, go out your front door and walk left or right, you're a lucky bastard.' I'm sure I used to wind him up, for I was so much more laid back. He'd often claim, 'If I'd had your talent, I'd have cleaned up. Always back to football with Dad, an excellent centre-forward, whose best assets were being brilliant in the air, and a desire to win that at times was frightening. So, it was hardly surprising that after speaking with Mr Sya, Baza informed me that we were off to London the following Thursday to meet him in person...

I didn't want to go, but Dad was insistent. He even drew me up a contract at work. You can only imagine my face on reading what Dad put in for the wage.

£1000 a week tax free.

Free medical care.

A sports car.

An air-conditioned luxury apartment.

Free flights for my family and my girlfriend Sally.

Plus, eight others to be taken into account...

I thought he'd lost the plot! No way would this Sya character agree to all these. I mean, I was Nicky Welsh, not Kevin bleedin' Keegan!

After being finished at United, I had decided to cheer myself up by splashing out £300 on a gorgeous khaki green leather jacket, with flaps that came down over the shoulders. The eighties... Flush with two months of paid-up money, I thought 'Why not?' and sauntered into Flannels in Manchester, like Billy big time and came out with that beauty. Come the following Thursday, I wore the jacket travelling down to London. Baza insisted, however, that I try to be smart. 'At least stick a bloody shirt and tie underneath and show him some respect.' Incidentally, my mum went berserk over the cost of the jacket, still a sore point today!

We met Steven Sya in an apartment just off Park Lane. Parked outside was his red Ferrari. Sya was doing interviews with various other players and, whilst waiting for my turn, I noticed Glenn Hoddle stood with a taller lad, around 6 foot 4 – his younger brother Carl. He would prove to be my partner in crime during our adventures in Malaysia. Sya's PA appeared and she was absolutely stunning. I later learned that he'd married his previous PA, so this one obviously knew what was coming. Out with the old, as they say.

The PA ushered myself and Dad into a large, lavish suite where Mr Sya was waiting. He came across and shook both our hands. I noticed that behind him, amongst his entourage, were two serious, hard-looking guys who simply stood staring at us, arms folded. It later turned out they were bodyguards and Sya was connected to the Triads. At the time though, I knew nothing of this. Immediately, Dad went into his sales spiel and I have to admit, he was brilliant! It would have been obvious to a blind man that Sya was impressed. He replied by telling us all about the vision for his club, Cheq Point FC, and how he intended to up the attendances five-thousand-fold by bringing in foreign stars. At this, I nodded my head knowingly.

'Nick is interested, Mr Sya' said Baza. 'And this is what we are looking for.' He passed over the contract. Here we go, I thought. This is where we get frog marched out of the building. Sya read it through, his face giving nothing away. Then, to my disbelief he pulled a pen from his jacket, smiled and said, 'This is good. Where do you want me to sign?'

What? No way, you can't be serious?

As we left the apartment, I was still arguing with Baza. 'Give over Nicky,' he replied. 'This is bloody brilliant. That sort of money for a nobody like you!' Put like that, it was hard to argue with. There remained one problem to resolve before I set off to rescue Malaysian football. I'd told Sya I was earning £350 a week at United, not the £110 that I was on, and he'd expressed a wish to see my contract. More out of interest than checking on whether I was telling him the truth. Whilst I thought this would definitely scupper the deal, Dad never saw the problem. He set about dealing with this like he did everything else in his life. Not making a fuss, just getting the job done. 'This is what we'll do Nicky.' So the next day, he got his secretary at work to tippex out the £110 and type over it with £350, then they photocopied the contract. Crumpled it a little and put it in the first-class post. Job done. On receiving it, Sya expressed his delight and could not thank us enough.

Now that it was all sorted, I was off to more exotic climes...

The evening before I was due to fly off on my great adventure in almost another hemisphere, I gathered all the lads from United and mates from elsewhere together for a farewell drink. After a long, drunken sojourn through the usual haunts we finally ended up at the Amblehurst Hotel in Sale. A normal late spot to carry on boozing, long after the pubs had rung their bells and stopped serving at eleven. The hotel was owned and run by a guy called Mike Prophet, and on joining the club many United players would reside there whilst they searched for a house. Ironically, Mike was a fanatical City fan, but he was also huge friends with Bryan Robson and other first team players. He always ensured the Hotel was a safe environment and that they felt comfortable and able to relax properly following a game, or as a final call after a night out on the tiles. Similar to Paddy Crerand's pub, The Park in Altrincham. In both places there was no such thing as last orders. Trust and respect were the main words and they summed up Mike and Paddy perfectly.

As ever, in the Amblehurst, we were having a great time and the thought of a twenty-hour flight to Kuala Lumpur via Brussels early the next morning was as far away as possible from my thoughts. Ten or more pints does that to you. However, events took a rather sour turn well past the witching hour when my mate, a very drunken Gez 'the light bulb cruncher' called Manchester United full-back John Gidman a 'Scouse bastard.' Now, Giddy loved to play the guitar and had been doing so when the argument had broken out. A few silly words, drink taken and the next moment our defender tried hard to bury his guitar into the light bulb eater's head. Luckily, we managed to jump on him and things were swiftly sorted out.

As for my top mate Gez – unfortunately not long after this he ended up a heroin addict in Wythenshawe and tried to take his own life. Luckily, Gez's attempt failed and he saw the light before ending up in a monastery somewhere in the Scottish islands. These days, good old Gezbo lives in New Jersey, working with addicts. He's got himself clean and sorted, thank God, and is still a huge United fan who never misses a match on the box. Happily, the lightbulbs and the drugs are now a thing of the past. The incident with Gez and Giddy did kind of help to sober me up a little, and as I stood waiting for a taxi home, I looked up to the skies thinking, Christ, this time tomorrow even the stars are going to be foreign. What are you doing, Welshy?

It was yet to sink in that I was travelling to the other side of the world to work. My old journeys from Little Hulton to Manchester, then onto Collyhurst to Nana and Pop's, the endless bus and car rides to the Cliff: all this now looked like a trip to the bathroom. What was waiting for me, I'd no idea. Probably something along the lines of Altrincham FC or Mossley? When I questioned Baza, he just said, 'For the money they're paying you, does it really matter?' True! 'Just get out there, Nicky!' Cheers Baza!

All those years working every hour sent were finally paying off for Dad. He'd built his company, TBS (named after the three brothers), to the point that they now employed more than a hundred staff, and even had an executive box at Old Trafford, which he was so very proud of. We were actually the first to have one – even before Salford Van Hire. They were our neighbours! This was all something my Uncle Al had a great hand in sorting. The Crumpsall chameleon with his many connections and sparkling charm! Baza would sometimes say how he'd have loved his dad, my Grandad Harry to have lived to see it all. H's lads, through nothing but brains and hard graft, now had their own family business – and one that was prospering, going from strength to strength. Also a box at United that even had a telly in it! Baza often used to entertain clients in there and Big Norman, Robbo, Arthur and the lads would sometimes come up after the match to say hello and have a drink with them. It worked a treat.

As for me, it was 'Tara our kid'.

Weary-eyed and hungover, I decided to wear my tracksuit for comfort when travelling over. I said my goodbyes. Even Mum had a tear in her eye, and she never cried. Ever. Baza dropped me, my two suitcases and sports bag off at the airport, which was only ten minutes from our house. We said our goodbyes.

'Go on mush, sock it to em.' Then, not wanting to hang around, he was gone and I was left alone. Look after yourself, Baza!

I made my way inside and the long haul unfolded. A swift transfer at Brussels, followed by the 9.45am Sabena Airlines flight A5730, to Kuala Lumpur. It had to be said I felt rotten, with the previous night's shenanigans striking back. Once on the plane, before I knew it, we were in the air and the smiling air hostess with the drinks trolley was by my seat. I daren't, I just daren't! I told myself I wasn't off on holiday, this was work, so I politely turned her down.

You're growing up Welshy!

I'd informed Steven Sya's PA over the phone of my flight details, and she'd confirmed someone would be there to greet me when I landed at Subang airport, Kuala Lumpur. I was more than a little pensive, because I literally had no idea of what lay ahead. I'd done no research and was basically clueless! Once on the ground I waited for my luggage off the carousel, which seemed to take forever before finally arriving. I looked around, hunted down a trolley, took a deep breath and pushed my stuff through a set of green 'Nothing to Declare' double doors, and into the main international arrivals hall. I was suddenly bombarded by a blinding sea of flashing lights. I covered my eyes. What the... Stood before me was a huge mob of photographers and cameramen, easily over thirty strong. They'd obviously had me mixed up with somebody else? I felt a tap on the shoulder and appearing from nowhere was a smiling Steven Sya. He hugged me tight.

'Welcome to Malaysia, Nicky' said Sya. 'Leave your bags here, they shall be taken care of. We have a press conference waiting upstairs.' What? The most I expected was a taxi to pick me up, but a press conference? How happy was I that I had turned down the beer on the plane, can you imagine if I had turned up five sheets to the wind? It didn't bear thinking about!

Walking up the stairs, I noticed a slim figure, a young man waiting at the top. Sya does the introduction. 'Nicky, this is club Captain, Lim.' We shook hands. 'It is good to meet you Nicky,' said Lim. 'We have heard so much.' That doesn't sound good. Sya watched on like a proud father. 'Come,' he announced grandly. 'Let us go and introduce all Malaysia to the great United player Nicky Welsh!'

Oh no...

We entered this large, elegant, wooden-panelled room, crammed packed with rows of loud Malaysian journalists and even more photographers and cameramen. In front, facing them, was a long table set-up with microphones. Sya settled down in the middle chair with myself and Lim alongside him. I was utterly confused, but smiling nonetheless. He began, 'I would like to introduce you to a future Manchester United and England star, Nicky Welsh!' Huge applause and chaos breaks out! The cameras click, flash and the questions come at me like bullets.

'Nicky, what you going to do to improve Malaysian football?'

'How many goals are you going to score?'

'What does Ron Atkinson think about your move, and will he have you back?'

What on God's earth has Sya been telling these people, I thought to myself?

'Nicky, how do you think this move will affect your England under-21 chances?'

Playing along with the charade, I tried to answer them all as honestly as possible. It's by now obvious to me that Sya has built me up to be a cross between Bryan Robson and Bobby Charlton, and I was going to be expected to score a hat trick every other game. Well, were they in for a bleedin' shock. I smiled and nodded loads, hoping my bravado would hide the fact that inside I was having kittens. The press conference went relatively quickly and once I'd stopped shaking I was actually starting to thrive and believe the stuff being said about me. Afterwards, I shook hands, signed autographs and had my photo taken with a couple of fans. This is the life Welshy, I thought. Why not milk it until everything goes pear-shaped?

After the press conference had finished, Steven Sya pulled me aside to say we'd be flying on directly to Penang, a small and beautiful island off Malaysia's West coast, much favoured by Australians. This would be where, just three days later, I'd play my first game and start producing miracles for Cheq Point FC. This appeared to be the plan – and Steven Sya had no doubt that with me in his team we would win every game.

Sya had also dipped into his pocket to sign another English reject, like myself, but this one was from Tottenham Hotspur. The guy from the corridor back in London, Carl Hoddle. Strange, I thought, I half expected Sya to announce he had Johan Cruyff's long-lost cousin, Diego Maradona's second nephew and Zico's twin sister also on the payroll.

It was evening and already dark by the time we eventually reached the Golden Sands hotel resort in Penang. Waiting for us at the airport was one of Sya's white Mercedes limousines. On top of the boot was what can only be described as a huge white boomerang. This was the aerial for the television in the car – unheard of back in 1985. He'd obviously seen Back to the Future. With the jet lag and nervous excitement of the day catching up with me, I headed straight to my room. In no time I fell on the bed and went out like a light.

A day an 'arf Baza. A day an 'arf.

I awoke to the shrill ring of the telephone – the 9am wake-up call I'd asked for – and I was still more than a little disorientated. I rubbed my eyes before climbing out of bed and opening the large, floor to ceiling, thick blackout curtains. I looked out and couldn't believe my eyes. Maybe not Little Hulton, but close. Paradise on this earth. I was gazing out at the most beautiful, pristine white beach I'd ever seen in my life. I've still never seen a better beach. Real Robinson Crusoe desert island stuff. I turned around and took a deep breath. The sheer size and class of the suite I'd been given by Sya hadn't really sunk in till that moment. I noticed a bundle of newspapers had been pushed under the door. I walked across to pick them up and who's on the front page? Oh my god…

I saw myself smiling back – in print. 'WELSH – I'LL DO MY BEST' was one of the many headlines reporting on the previous day's press conference. I'd been set up like the second coming. Fuckin' 'ell Welshy, you're in it now mate.

I made my way downstairs to the restaurant for breakfast and to meet my new teammates. All Malaysians and remarkably friendly, they couldn't do enough to make me feel at home – despite me probably being paid as much as the rest of them put together. A clause in the contract I'd signed with Cheq Point FC back in London was that I'd help out with coaching. To pass on my expertise and know-how, with me being a future Manchester United and England star, of course. We set off for training and all piled into a small van that bore more than a passing resemblance to the Scooby Bus from Scooby Doo. I sat up front with the driver, where I had plenty of room. It made Jimmy Curran's van appear executive-like. I looked back over my shoulder, and wondered how on earth everyone had managed to squeeze in there. We drove a couple of miles and despite it being only 10 am, I was already sweating through my shirt. No air conditioning either – a little different than being in the Chairman's limo yesterday evening.

We eventually turned down an old dirt track, lush green walls of jungle-like foliage on both sides, filled with pot holes and with mangey dogs chasing after the van. We rocked and bumped our way along for a few hundred yards before the landscape opened out into a large field surrounded by more trees. Our training pitch. The grass, well more weeds than grass, grew half-way up your shin, and we had only one set of clapped-out goal posts. No changing rooms. No office for the gaffer. No physio, team doctor – just us, as we piled out of the van. Roy Keane would've loved this. Not sure where it came from, but a bag of balls appeared. Right, I thought, start earning your money. Come on Nicky. What would Big Ron do? Or the Doc? The magnitude of what I was up against was dawning on me. I was Georgie Best and Sir Matt combined – the football Messiah. If the pitch had been water the lads would have expected me to skip over it and score a hat trick!

All the lads were staring at me as I tried to present a calm and organised front. I was taller than most of them, and bigger and stronger – despite still being only 19 years old!!!! If I was managing to look kind of calm, inside I was panicking. I could feel the blistering sun on my face: no sunblock applied, no injections, no insect repellant, no power drinks – I'd never needed any of that on the Red Rec or at the Cliff! I was sweating buckets and could hardly breathe with the humidity. It was like the Bridge Over The River Kwai!

My eyes scanned around my surroundings – here I was, half the world away from home and I was clueless. What am I supposed to do here? So I just did whatever I was used to. I treated it just like any other day at the start of a new season.

'Right lads, get in twos,' I decided. 'We'll have a warm-up,' (warm-up!) and I proceeded to lead them off in a run around the wobbly, uneven perimeter of the field. Very soon, in fact after no more than ten minutes, I started to melt. The rest of my new teammates, however, looked as though they were on a leisurely Sunday morning run. Me... I was frying! I put it down to the strong German beer I'd been putting away in the Amblehurst, now the other side of the globe. Oh to be back there with the lads, sinking a few after training!

After cutting the run short before I collapsed, I asked the keeper to go in goal and picked two seven-a-side teams, coming up with the genius idea of shirts v skins, defence versus attack, with me joining the latter. No revolutionary ideas from my young head! I removed my soaked Nike t-shirt and it was back to Little Hulton on the fields as an eight-year-old. It really doesn't matter where you are in the world, so long as you have a ball and a net. 'Let's play footy lads!' It was a decent work-out session and although I swiftly noticed the standard didn't appear great, the lads were enthusiastic and super fit. As for me, despite the blazing heat, I was happy enough to enjoy myself just kicking a ball around again. Some things would never change.

We finished off and it was a case of all back on the Scooby Bus to the hotel. As I stepped into the shower in my palatial apartment, I suddenly felt the water hit my shoulders and back and learnt a first painful lesson in Far-East Asia. They could've heard me scream back at the Cliff. Don't ever play on the skin's side without applying sun screen. My back had been burnt to a crisp, and in the mirror I looked like Captain bleedin' Scarlet!

Match day arrived and I woke up excited. This was it. Cheq Point were due to play the home side Penang later that evening. My first match and my first opportunity to impress.

We were told after breakfast to meet at 2pm in a private room just off the hotel foyer for a 'team bonding' session. Really? Anyway, I was there on time, more than a little quizzical as to what to expect next. Steven Sya was already there with my teammates, who were all sitting quietly in front of him. One chair remained – mine. I took my place and noticed that Sya had a guitar and was busy tuning the strings. Is he really going to sing? Surely not.

'Good afternoon team,' he said in English, whilst beginning to strum the guitar. Even Big Ron had never pulled this stunt. All the lads began to clap along before bursting into song. They obviously knew this one.

'Cheq Point, Cheq Point FC, the kings of the whole Far East.'

This repeated again and then a verse about kicking the ball into the goal.

What the fuck?!?! Am I dreaming this? It felt more like some kind of weird religious cult, but, not wanting to offend anyone, I clapped along with them. It was quite an easy one to learn in fairness and I also began to sing. The stuff you do for a grand a week! Finally, Sya stopped and we all applauded. Loudly. He smiled, but it was like the smile of a James Bond villain. He just needed a Siamese cat on his lap to stroke! 'Excellent,' he said, clearly enjoying himself. 'Now, let us take time to think about tonight's game. All close your eyes.' I knew I daren't laugh, but just for a moment I tried to imagine doing all this with Eric Harrison...

We arrived early at Penang's stadium, which was surprisingly decent. A large crowd had gathered, with hundreds of people milling about on the concourse. A frenzied mixture of polite clapping and loud boos greeted us as we stepped off the bus. Then, I heard it for the first time. 'Welsh, honky man!' What did he just call me? I thought I must have been hearing things, but ignored it and off we strode to the dressing room. Once we'd got in there, Steven Sya pulled me aside. 'Nick, I want you to go out on the pitch ten minutes before kick-off and wave to the crowd. It would be good if you smiled a lot, and did some keepie-uppies when you get out there. Can you do any?'

The cheeky Bas....

'You do this good,' he continued. 'Many locals have come just to see the

Manchester United star.' Blimey, I thought. The big time. I didn't really fancy this, but it was 'in for a penny' now, as they say, or in my case more 'in for a grand'. If the boss says do it, it's simply a case of throw me the ball! The time came for me to make my first guest appearance in front of the adoring Malaysian audience. I walked out into a half-full ground over a red running track and I think it's fair to say that I didn't actually receive a hero's welcome.

The crowd basically ignored me. Then I noticed a large chunk of something white hit the ground nearby. Then, I heard it again. 'Ha, honky man!' This time around I knew I wasn't imagining it. 'Fuck you honky man!' So here I was, far from home, being abused by fans before my first game, when suddenly, another block landed at my feet!

These blocks were being aimed at me!

Charmin'! I did as the boss asked. A few keepie-uppies. A last wave to a totally unappreciative audience. Then the team headed down the tunnel – and suddenly one of their missiles walloped me on the shoulder.

Once in the safety of the dressing room I asked the lads what was being thrown at me? 'It is ice, Nicky!' laughed our Captain, Lim. 'They are big ice cubes. Some supporters bring in buckets to the stands to keep their drinks cold, and to try and knock out opposing players with. Try not to get hit my young English friend, for they hurt like hell!'

That pumped me up – twats! The game went well. It was played at a fast pace and I really enjoyed it. Technically the teams were hardly brilliant – maybe that's why I fitted in so well! But, as I had clocked the previous day in training, these Malaysian lads – on both teams – could run forever and they gave it everything. We won 3-1 and I'd managed to set up a couple of our goals. Everyone, even the Penang fans, seemed happy with me. There'd been no more ice boulders thrown and I was even stopped and asked to sign loads of autographs before boarding the coach. Being treated like a superstar was something I could easily become used to. I had to admit it – I loved the attention and, in my head, this was how it was always going to be here in Malaysia. We drove directly back to our hotel and a couple of the lads talked about going downtown to one of the local nightclubs. After my schooling by the very best in Mancunian post-match night outs, I thought why not? Check out my newly found stardom. 'Win, lose, have a booze!' Not sure how that translates into Malaysian, but I was about to receive one of my life's hardest lessons.

Nothing is ever what you think it is.

We hit the town with Sya's blessing because he was delighted with our victory. His rousing performance on the guitar had obviously worked a treat. After half an hour in the nightclub, I remember thinking that I should ring home when I got back to the hotel and give Baza the good news that we'd won. I'd worked out that it would be mid-afternoon back in Manchester so I could catch him at work. This settled in my mind and I went to the bar to buy myself another cold beer. Standing at the bar, in my favourite leather jacket again, waiting to be served, I felt this leg next to me rub against mine. It happened again a few seconds later, and I realised this was no accident. Hello, I thought, turning around to set my eyes on one of the prettiest girls I'd ever seen in my life. Tall, very tall actually, with a fine pair of headlamps. Long dark hair, deep brown eyes and a statuesque physique. OMG! Uncle Al would definitely approve. She smiled back at me in the most seductive way. Bloody hell, welcome to Malaysia Welshy!

'Hi,' I said. 'You OK?'

'Yes', she replied. So far, so good.

'Can I buy you a drink?'

'A gin and tonic please.' So she was sophisticated too! By now I was starting to get excited.

I ordered her drink and got myself another beer. Next I gave her what I thought was my best, but was in fact probably my goofiest smile. This is the life. She obviously knows who I am? Nicky Welsh. The English superstar. Future Manchester United and England Captain. Why not eh? Robbo can't go on forever. The drinks arrived, and as I paid for them, she continued rubbing her leg against mine. All we ever got off Eric after a good win was a slice of orange. Looking absolutely drop-dead gorgeous in a black sequin dress, I couldn't believe my luck.

'Where you staying?' she asked seductively, fluttering her eyelashes at me and drawing her hand across those headlamps.

'The Golden Sands.'

'How do you fancy we go back there?' She teased me. She slowly inserted an ice cube into her mouth and started sucking it, smiling intensely towards me. Ice again, but this was more like it! Normally, I'm quite a fast drinker – but this one was easily my all-time personal best. I downed the beer in one then grabbed her hand. 'Come on, we're off!'

I abandoned my teammates – after all, there would be many more nights to bond with them – and we set off for my hotel, where my amazing suite awaited. I began to imagine where it would all unfold and what I'd be doing with her. Feeling like the king of the world – and pure George Best – we began to climb the luxurious carpet stairs leading out of the club and back through the foyer, into the road. I was smiling like a grinning chimp when I suddenly saw our Captain, Lim, coming towards us from the top of the stairs. He didn't look too happy and, to my surprise, he grabbed my dream lady by the throat and started going crazy at her in Malaysian. Oh no, I thought. It dawned on me. This is obviously Lim's girlfriend. I held both my hands up. 'Lim, I had no idea she was with you.'

He let go of her and she grabbed her sparkly handbag and quickly scurried off up the rest of the stairs and raced off into the darkness when she reached the top. Her high heels rattled at speed and I was taken aback at the suddenness of it all. My blood was still stirred and I was unsure how to react in such an alien place. My new Captain turned towards me with a look of real concern etched upon his face. 'No Nick,' he said. 'You don't understand. That a boy, not girl.'

I couldn't believe my ears. Is he really trying to tell me that...?

'No way mate,' I replied. 'She was lovely and what a pair of...' I motioned and Lim simply shook his head.

'No, no, no Nick' he said, this time wagging his finger towards me. 'You gonna have to be very careful here. Katoey, many katoey in Malaysia. I show you.' We walk back into the busy, beating heart of the club. Lim points at a group of four beautiful girls 'There's one, there's one. Another one. And there!' We were surrounded. I was seriously shell-shocked.

'How do you know then?' I asked.

Lim shrugs his shoulders. 'Very, very hard sometimes. Maybe Adam's apple, and hips. If they not have wide hips, not girl!'

Fuckin' 'ell – ladyboys. It scared the living daylights out of me if I'm honest. This was the era that AIDS arrived on the scene. There'd been television adverts back home in the UK for ages warning against the potential dangers of unprotected sex. Not that I was interested in that of course with 'Miss no name.' Not much!

Talk about the Great Escape! I could have been confronted by meat and two veg!

The Captain and I had a few more drinks. He had plainly been told to keep an eye on me and was taking his orders very seriously. We had a few – quite a few – more drinks and played spot the ladyboy.

'What about her?' I'd ask Kim.

'No, OK normal girl,' he'd reply. Or if not, 'Katoey, Nick, definite katoey!'

I wasn't getting much better at spotting them! This was worrying.

We stayed in the club until closing time and, with me feeling deflated, especially after my opening first hour in the club, Lim decided we should go and find somewhere to eat. Outside the club, the late-night streets were quiet and only dimly lit by weak street lamps. Suddenly, a large cat-like creature shot across our path and disappeared into the darkness. 'What the hell is that?' I screamed. Lim's head went back on his neck and he looked at me again quizzically, as if he was staring at a young lad who needed seriously educating in the ways of his country. 'That was a rat,' he smiled. 'Lots of rats in Malaysia. We have open drains. Some rats nearly bigger than you Nicky!' At the time I honestly thought he was being serious!

We ended up in what can only be described as a pigeon shed. The food on offer was nothing less than fish heads in some kind of watery stew. I was desperate for a Holland's steak and kidney pudding with chips, peas and gravy, or a donner kebab! From nowhere, I felt a small wave of home sickness. It wouldn't be the last. I looked at my watch and I'd not been there seventy-two hours.

All had been going perfectly well until I'd bumped into Foo Foo Lamarr's eastern nephews!

In all, I went on to play sixteen games for Cheq FC and, despite the arrival of Carl Hoddle, who I gelled with instantly, events both on and off the pitch began to sour pretty quickly. We were culturally just too different. Our own fans turned on us quickly, because they'd expected Pelé, not a United 'reject'.

After five or six games, Mr Sya called me into his office for a chat. Here we go again, I thought!

At first I thought I'd got it wrong. I thought he was just going to sing me another morale-boosting tune, but there was no guitar in the room. Oh no! Oh no! He looked up from his papers and paused before starting with 'Nicky, I think you're trying too hard – running around too much.' I didn't have the heart to tell him I was just trying to get the bleedin' ball. There's a limit to how well you can play if your team aren't great and won't pass to you. 'You need to slow down. Let the others play the ball to you and then you do your stuff. Also, I must say, I thought your shoulders were much bigger when we met in London?'

What was he talking about? Then it dawned on me. I'd been wearing my trusted new leather jacket – with the massive shoulder pads! My Joan Collins Dynasty jacket had probably got me the job!

Despite us being hopeless in the league, our one saving grace was that we won the cup with Cheq Point FC – their only ever win – and the winning goal in the final against our great rivals and top team, Selangor, was a free kick orchestrated by myself and Carl. That cup win apart, we struggled. It was a hard slog and our opponents were always prepared to get stuck into the nearly famous Englishmen. We were their targets. They were small, fast and at times like Triad hitmen. During one game I was smashed in the face and, I must admit, I saw red. The wrong kind of red! I chased after my assailant and when I caught him, in true Cantonesque fashion, I nailed him. It was an away game (not that it mattered much by then) and their crowd went wild, howling and screaming God knows what at me. There was one insult I did recognise – because I'd become relatively used to it. 'Honky man!' I was lucky not to get a three-month ban for that retaliation but, being Mr Manchester United, I got away with it. The truth be known, we did put good numbers on the gates for a while, but results-wise, it never really worked out. After playing against one team managed by the Czech Dr Josef Venglos (who later went on to manage Aston Villa), he approached myself and Carl and said, 'I recognised you as English players by the way you passed the ball into channels.' To this day I'm not sure if this was meant as a compliment or an insult.

The more homesick I became, the more important the arrival of the Manchester Evening News Football Pink newspaper became – always a week late, sent by Baza. It helped me stay sane. A dash of normality once a week. I missed watching United and reading all the results. When I think back, I can't believe how the Evening News managed to get that paper out so quickly on Saturday afternoons – ready for us when we got home from the game with all that day's results for every big team in the country and every smaller team in the area, and all the write ups!

The 1985–86 season began while I was half-way around the world. The season's start saw Big Ron and the boys win their opening ten games, and it finally looked like the title was heading back to Old Trafford – and I wasn't there to enjoy it. It made me even more miserable. Bless her, my mum tried to give me a taste of home. I used to love the chocolate rice krispie cakes from Marks and Spencers. So, in her infinite wisdom, Mum wrapped a couple in bubble wrap and parcelled them up, and with Dad's Pink, my version of a Red Cross food parcel was dispatched – Malaysia bound. Needless to say, on arrival, I received the parcel and was intrigued by the rattling coming from inside. I opened it and low and behold, the crumbs of the broken rice cakes fell out all over the floor and party time began for the cockroaches. It was the thought that counted though. Cheers Mum!

Winning the cup with Cheq Point FC gave myself and Carl more or less superstar status amongst our fans for a while. It even gave me the opportunity to open a nightclub with Miss Malaysia. What a darling she was. The real thing – and you can be sure, remembering Lim's advice, I checked her out. I did quite enjoy this small shot at fame if I'm honest. Being stopped for autographs in the street, I even had my own newspaper column. Events then took a strange turn when Steven Sya called me in to tell me that I was being leased out to a side called Negri. Negri were a regional club and were due to play in a four-month tournament beginning in the new year. Carl was going to join me. We had no say in the matter. Sya would continue to pay our wages and that was that... We were gone.

Negri was around twenty-five miles south of Kuala Lumpur. Carl and I commuted daily.

One time I crashed our car, but luckily we avoided trouble with the local police, who said that if we gave them tickets for the next match it was the end of problem! Imagine trying that in Salford! Malaysia was interesting like that. Gambling was off the scale and everything, and I mean everything, had a price. As I'd soon discover. The club was run by another colourful character, a Malaysian military officer called Captain Ahmed Hadi. Full of enthusiasm, a really nice guy who loved his football. Our first match for Negri was against the Malaysian national team. Myself and Carl began on the bench, but we came on to help earn our new team a draw. We were feted afterwards. It looked hopeful, for if we could play like that against the best players around, all boded well for the future. We were getting ahead of ourselves!

The next match we got hammered 4-0, and from then on we fell off a cliff. The only highlight for me was Sally coming out over the Christmas period. I loved having her around and, for a while, life was good. However, when it was time for her to return home, I'm not ashamed to admit it, I got really upset as she boarded the plane. A sign of my new-found fame, a Malaysian man sidled up to me and said 'Don't be sad, Nick Welsh. Come back to my home, meet my family and have something to eat.' When not hurling ice at my head and calling me 'honky man', the Malaysians really were the most lovely people.

Before Sally left, we made up a foursome on New Year's Eve with Carl and his girlfriend, who'd been with him from the start. Problems had arisen when Negri demanded we attended a training camp over the New Year. I'd insisted to them that the New Year celebration was a very important English tradition and must be celebrated. We'd be turning up late. My ego had by then outgrown my talent. Anyway, it was a lovely evening and the four of us had a wonderful time. Far too wonderful – for a photograph was taken of myself and Carl with manic grins on our faces. He had a daft plastic party hat on. I was giving it full blast on a party blower and both of us were clearly merry. The following day it appeared in a local newspaper and, when in the next game we were battered 4-0 in Singapore, myself and Carl were obvious scapegoats. One headline was particularly memorable.

'WASH OUT WALSH AS HODDLE HOBBLES!'

They'd even misspelt my name.

After that, everything started to go downhill on the pitch – and there was an awful lot of other stuff going wrong! Apparently it was all down to the English lads! We were the whipping boys and it became hard to stomach. The end started to approach when one evening we were out for a drink with our coach, a friendly Malaysian guy called Tony, who informed us that the word was that seven of the team were on the take, including the goalkeeper. I did say that everything had a price, and it seemed that they all thought we'd taken our price! Suddenly, it all started to make sense. One game shone out like a lighthouse. We'd played on some island in the outback, east of Malaysia. We had flown there in a small plane. It was a hostile place. The previous year the team coach had been torched! We were beaten 3-1. We missed two penalties and our keeper dived over the ball like he was jumping away from a grenade. I looked at Carl and for him it was the last straw. He went home straight afterwards. Now I was alone. I was going nowhere. Who else would be mad enough to pay me a grand a week?

I missed Carl. Sadly he passed away at the tragically young age of forty. He was a lovely, funny man, and we shared some good and strange times! Carl had echoes of his famous brother's talent. He played in the same laid-back manner. We kept in touch for a while, but such is life. Ultimately we drifted apart. RIP big man.

With my heart no longer in it, my form deteriorated further and Negri tried to get rid of me. However, I was determined to see my contract out. I went to see Steven Sya, digging my heels in. Captain and my now good mate Lim had another quiet word in my ear. He told me not to push it because Sya had strong connections to the Triads and I was a long way from home. This worried me a little, although I never let on. I used to always sing to Lim the Billy Ocean song that was out around this time, 'When the going gets tough, the tough get going'.

I did confide in Baza though and, shortly afterwards, he wrote a letter to Sya. An extract read – 'If you're a man of honour, get this sorted out. Malaysia is only an eighteen-hour flight away and you'll know my face when you see me again.' That was Baza for you.

Before one away game I remember lying despondently on my bed in a hotel room watching dozens of cockroaches going up the wall and across the ceiling like an invading army. Another time, whilst rooming with a Negri player after Carl had gone home, I pointed to a red arrow on the ceiling and made some throwaway remark. Next minute he'd stormed out and, later, I was accused by the club of mocking the Muslim faith. Turned out the arrow was showing which way to pray towards Mecca, which I didn't have a clue about in honesty. After that they all refused to room with me. When it rains Welshy?

It continued: I had this huge rat in my apartment running wild, so I rang the security guard. He turned up, armed himself with a broomstick and beat the rodent to death. Holding it up by the tail he turned to me smiling and said, 'Ah Nicky Welsh, you should have just kicked it, but you would have probably missed!' The dream was definitely turning sour...

Finally, lonely and missing home badly – and not forgetting the warning from Lim not to antagonise the Chinese owners too much – I decided to go home. I signed a confidential agreement to say I wouldn't speak to the newspapers on the understanding they paid my money up in full to the end of the season. It was time to say goodbye. There was an old Malaysian saying that's rather apt to end with. 'Bersatu teguh, bercerai roboh.'

United we stand, divided we fall.

A   B

C

A   First day at work under Eric Harrison's watchful eye

B   The best uncapped boot cleaner at the club on the right! With Platty and
       Alan McGloughlin in the Cliff boot room

C   Pre season pic Old Trafford 1984 - Sitting too close to Big Ron's tackle

D   The Gaffer - Big Ron

E   On my way up the ladder - or so I thought

F   With my team mates me bottom left with ball, Paul McGuinness right.
       Lee Martin top left

G   Proving one of his favourite sayings to be right - "nothing moves faster than the ball".
       Big Norm's magical winner in 1985

D

E

F

G

Cheq Point on Nick's mind now

By DAN GUEN CHIN

Nick Welsh ... 'I'll give my best'

Welsh eager to meet the challenge

MANCHESTER United reserve midfielder Nick Welsh is eagerly looking forward to his new role as player cum coach for Cheqpoint soccer team.

Welsh, 19 this December, is well aware of the high expectations in Malaysia, after signing up with Cheqpoint for a $100,000 contract for one season, and is ready to meet the challenge.

He is due to arrive in Kuala Lumpur tomorrow, with the experience of having played as a striker and a centreback, besides being at home in midfield.

"I know it's a tough job for me especially coming from a club like Manchester United. But if I can do something good for the Malaysian football, and I think I can do it, that will be wonder

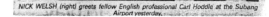

NICK WELSH (right) greets fellow English professional Carl Hoddle at the Subang Airport yesterday.

THE STAR
WEDNESDAY, December 4, 1985

Cheq-Point's Nick Welsh attempts a header against Taisco at Merdeka Stadium last night. Behind him is teammate Carl Hoddle. Talasco won 2-1.

F

G

H

A   I'll give my best?! Back tracking on arrival
B   What a challenge it was!
C   Meeting Hod with Chairman Steven Sya looking on
D   Playing for Negeri Sembilan
E   The only star is above the date
F   Cup Winners - me bottom far right, Hod back centre
G   Homesick and on the bench
H   "We don't want them" - you couldn't write it but they actually did!

MOET MASON
CHAPTER TWENTY THREE

I flew home to Manchester in the spring of 1986, just delighted and so relieved to be back. I'd missed my family, my girlfriend and my mates. Smoky pubs, Coronation Street, Boddingtons, Guinness and Carlsberg, fish, chips and peas, the nine o'clock News, and last, but not least, Manchester United! I knew I'd hardly set the footballing world alight in Malaysia, and they'd never be building a statue of me over there, but overall it'd been an unforgettable experience.

Did I enjoy it? Well, I'll never forget it... You always remember when things go wrong – and plenty did over there – and I did have a load of laughs.

The night after I returned I went out with the lads into town and we ended up at a club called Brubaker's. It'd been a really harsh winter in England and there was me, tanned like Des O'Connor and, to be honest, looking and acting like a bit of a poser. Come throwing out time at 2am, a few of the lads I was with were having serious words with a gang of other lads outside on the pavement. I'd walked over, happily drunk, when one of them shouted, 'Who the fuck are you looking at smiler?' I just couldn't stop smiling, because I was just so pleased to be home! Saying that, I also knew the script and, this being no friendly encounter, belted him to get things started. Cue mayhem. Before I knew it, the police had arrived and we were soon outside Collyhurst Station. One of my mates was actually on parole, so they'd brought him in and he was getting a grilling. Whilst waiting, I'd taken myself outside and I remember standing there looking over Rochdale Road, at St Patrick's Church, and further down towards the junction, where I'd first learned about headlamps from Uncle Al. It really was great to be home. Once he had been released, we all headed off to Chinatown and Manchester's original Chinese restaurant,

Charlie Chans, to continue our evening. Believe it or not, these were the kind of nights I'd so missed. Manchester may not have had a beach or a wonderful climate, but at least I didn't have to worry about the ladyboys.

The 1986/87 football season was about to begin. I'd still no inclination to play again. Malaysia had put a few quid in my pocket but to actually wear someone else's shirt over here – and not United's? No thanks. I did actually go down to Altrincham FC's Moss Lane for a couple of pre-season training sessions. However, this was more about staying fit rather than looking for a team. During the second week back, we got the ball out and had a practice game. I tried a low cross-field pass, drilled it a fraction too hard, and it went out of play. It wasn't the worst I'd ever done, believe me, but the first team manager went mad. 'There's 30,000 feet up there,' he shouted pointing towards the sky. Smartarse. 'And you can't even keep the ball in play?' It was probably the worst piece of advice I'd ever received. Charlie Hughes at Lilleshall may have said he had a point, but that's not my type of game. I knew at that moment that this wasn't for me. If footy was meant to be played in the air, God would've given us wings, not wingers. I was gone. Surprisingly, they didn't seem that bothered!

I did need to shift gears and make a living though, because there wasn't a chance in hell Dad would've put up with me lazing around the house and not grafting. I wasn't in Baza's good books anyway. He made no attempt to hide his disappointment of me losing interest in finding a new club. 'A waste of bloody talent,' he'd often mutter under his breath, so I could just about hear. 'More interested in going out with your bloody mates on the piss.' Baza hated it if people were good at something and weren't using it to their maximum. I had to sort myself out. I came up with an idea, more of a gut feeling really. I'd been told of a business called Star Sportswear over in Wakefield, South Yorkshire who made football kits. Not branded types like your famous Umbro, Adidas or Bukta, but they'd design and make, to order, any colour combination of shirt, shorts and socks you wanted in quantities of twelve or more. All this was done at a decent price for great quality. With this in mind I started to go to Hough End and all the main pitches around Greater Manchester and Salford. Mersey Bank, Brookhouse, Rabbit Hills. Wherever I'd played as a kid got a visit. I'd go on a Saturday, Sunday and even on the Wednesday for the midweek leagues. I always made a point, on the touchlines, of finding out who the manager or team secretary was. I'd even visit the dressing rooms to track them down and hand whoever I thought would act on it a small A4 flier that I'd had made. I struck up a special start of the season offer until 1st August. £225 all in plus VAT, which their sponsors could always claim back anyway as a business expense. For this they got a full new team strip, any colour combination and 1–12 numbered shirts. This also included a padded elbow keeper shirt (the keepers loved those!) and a full-colour sponsor's logo and lettering on the chest. I'd hit the jackpot, and the kits were huge sellers. The mere fact that a pub, brewery, the local butcher, pet shop, baker, or even candlestick maker could sponsor the team and have their name plastered all over the front of it went down a treat. Strange to say, but until then such a thing had never existed. Many a time the sponsors paid for the strip and the lads got a spanking new kit to start the season with. Everyone won with this deal, for some of the rags these teams were forced to play in were pitiable. You look good, feel good, play better. I was off and running!

My rates were so much cheaper than a high street sports shop, as I had very few overheads. If you were to go there and order from the likes of, say, Umbro, it'd cost £350, with no sponsorship logos or extras like the padded elbow keeper shirt. I couldn't get them printed fast enough. After just two weeks I already had thirty teams signed up who, as part of the deal, paid half the money up front. The actual kits cost me just under a £100 per set and I passed on the cost of the logos, which were done at a screen printers on Dale Street in Manchester. All in all, I made a hundred per cent mark up on the kit itself. Not bad for a beginner and I'd no idea what I was doing! Everything was trial and error and a whole load of Hail Marys!

I was on a roll.

I also got in with huge local firm ICI Colours and Fine Chemicals, based in Blackley, through a good mate Lawrence Gee, who worked there. They wanted to order their team's new kits. The lad I had the meetings with asked what else in terms of personalised sporting goods I did? Being a Welsh salesman, with Baza's DNA, I quickly replied, 'Everything! Why, what are you interested in?'

'Well Nick,' said the lad, 'we order ICI golf umbrellas, golf balls, T-shirts and sweaters for handouts. I'll tell you what I pay for them and if you can match the price, you can have the business.' We shook hands, and although I didn't have a clue where I'd get the stuff from, I refused to let such a minor problem deter me. Isn't that what the Yellow Pages are for? I was up to my eyeballs working all hours God sent, but I was happy and loving it. More so, Baza had stopped scowling at me and was smiling again.

He had his lad back.

On the home front, Dad's TBS toilet cubicle business was flourishing and he'd bought a townhouse villa with his brothers in between Marbella and Fuengirola, which all the family took turns to use in the summer. Once the football season had finished, I'd booked in my two-weeks' vacation there for myself and Sally. Also staying in different locations along the coast were my mates: Jim McGoff and Shay, and their girlfriends. Prior to setting off (no mobiles back then), we'd arranged to meet up on Cabopino Beach by the marina and make an afternoon of it. Come the day, we all got together as agreed and, just as we were set to go and get settled on the sunbeds, Jim said, 'Let's just hang on five more minutes. I met this lad on Saturday night outside St Vincent's in Knutsford, after 5.30 mass. His Dad's just moved in on the Mere. Anyway, he's due out here this week and I said we were meeting up and for him to come along.'

'Bloody 'ell mate,' I moaned at him. 'What you doing that for, I thought it was just us?' I didn't want our afternoon to be ruined having to put up with some stuck-up Cheshire git.

If you owned a house on the Mere everyone knew you were rich. Properly minted. Known fact. If I'd learnt one thing in my short life it was that the vast majority of that lot were so far up their own backsides they could see double. A couple of minutes later we heard a whistle, and there's a lad sauntering down the beach carrying this heavy looking orange cool box. He gave us a quick wave. He'd a couple of girls, real lookers, with him. Coming ever closer, I remember thinking, he doesn't look like your typical Cheshire git? This one had streaked hair, boating pumps with mad patterns on them. Christ, I thought. You could only snap those things up off places like Eccles market. In time, I found out that's where he'd actually bought them. Jim made the introductions and whilst we sat on a wall we began chatting. 'Where you from mate?' I asked.

'Eccles originally, but I live in Monton now.'

Without being dramatic, it was a life-changing moment, because that day I'd met a friend who's been the closest thing to a brother I've had ever since. In so many ways we were similar. Our dads had their own businesses that they'd both started from nothing. His mum grew up on the next street to mine, by Strangeways prison, although they didn't know each other. He also knew Nobby and Bernard White, the Welsh lifesaver in United's ticket office. This guy drank at the Albion in Little Hulton on a Sunday night, and was friendly with some of the same lads I'd gone to school and played footy with. Oh, and guess what? He was a Red!

'Do you fancy a drink everyone?' he asked, pointing to his cool box. I noticed him looking across to the girls first. Old fashioned manners my new mate had! He opened up the box and lay there, packed in with San Miguel cans, surrounded by crushed ice, were three bottles of Moet & Chandon Champagne.

Meet 'Moet Mason!' What other nickname could I possibly give him?

After meeting my new, not so posh after all mate, he'd asked what I did for a living and I explained, chapter and verse, how I'd been destined to be a United legend, but had experienced a rude awakening, so now I had to focus on making a real living in promotional sportswear. 'Can you do printed baseball caps?' he asked.

'Of course,' I replied. 'Welsport–' (class eh!) '–offer everything a reputable company could ever need. We really are cutting edge, Ged.' Actually, I didn't offer caps, but soon we would do! As for cutting edge? Where did I pluck that from? Baza would be proud.

'Come see me and my Dad Gerry, Nick, when we both get home. I think we can definitely give you some business, he'll love your promotional stuff for our Morson golf days. Do you know Clarendon Road, Eccles, where we're based?'

'I do yeah, my mate Billy Garton lives in the flats opposite there.'

'I know Billy as well,' he replied smiling. 'What a small world eh?'

Small world indeed. Moet Mason... A one off.

Myself and Ged were eventually christened 'Beavis and Butthead' by his dad Gerry and, to be fair, considering some of the scrapes we'd found ourselves in, it was hard to argue with this to be honest.

In 1991 myself and Moet travelled to France to watch United take on Montpelier. On boarding a train south from Paris, we noticed how quiet it was. The only other person on the train was a cleaner, and she got off on the first stop. Where was the vast Red Army? Looking out the window a train was approaching nearby on another line bedecked in United colours. Flags and fans hanging out of windows. Banners and scarves waving, the songs resonating out of the carriages. We'd only got on the wrong train...

Gerry was right, he'd summed us up to a tee!

As I write this more than thirty years later, Morson is now truly a worldwide concern, my friend financially richer than most, but he remains the same lad who walked down that beach with those boating pumps from Eccles market. Sadly, Gerry passed away in 2017 and, determined to keep his dad's name flying high, Ged has turned Morson into something quite extraordinary. Needless to say, Gerry will be watching on proud that his boy who took phone calls at five years of age – and more importantly, wrote down name, number and reason for calling – has not just continued, but enhanced the Morson mantle beyond the stars. Nothing is impossible if you work hard enough and never give up. World domination (almost!), a private plane, racehorses, a premiership rugby club (Sale Sharks), cars. Most importantly though, a loving family with Soraya, Georgie boy and Matt.

The only downside for our Moet Mason is that to this day he remains stuck with me!

UNCLE MATT – (PART ONE)
CHAPTER TWENTY FOUR

'Oh, flower of Scotland, when will we see, the likes again?'
6th November 1986

I'd been over the Pennines to pick up some finished football kits, and was taking them to my printers when suddenly I had the urge to divert to the Cliff training ground. Why? No idea, just a flashing thought. Since returning from Malaysia I'd been putting off going back. Nerves and embarrassment each played a part. Would anyone remember me, or want to? Plus, the pain. I'd kept it hidden deep, but it was still there. The nagging feeling remained that this club had broken my heart. I also had my pride. Why should I go back? Just get on with your life Welshy. You're a fan again now, not a player. Your boot-cleaning career there is truly over. That particular ship had sailed. Then, could someone please explain to me why I was suddenly back on Broughton Road with butterflies in my stomach and heading through the Cliff gates? I took a deep breath and parked up next to the large gym wall. It would be nice to see the lads again, I told myself. Not forgetting Teresa the cook. I'd still never tasted a better jam roly poly!

As I stepped out of the car it was a strange feeling. I looked around. I'd been going through these same gates with a Shoot magazine or a United programme under my arm to get signed ever since I was a kid. Nobody was around. I thought for a second of getting back in my car and reversing away and speeding off before being noticed. Then again, I realised this was still my life. A second home. The first person I bumped into was the kit man, Norman Davies. A lovely, genuine man who lived and breathed Manchester United. His stories were legendary, and all true! Norman got the job from Tommy Docherty after previously working for the Doc as a taxi driver, ferrying him round after he lost his licence. At the time, United were bringing so much kit from Old Trafford to the Cliff that Tommy suggested Norman come on board to organise the kits, and the rest is history. A classic tale of his from taxiing before joining United was a wonderful Tommy Cooper story.

Norman picked up Tommy from Piccadilly Train Station one evening. Tommy asked to be taken to the Midland Hotel, just a short distance away. He remembered being disappointed that the comedian was unusually quiet for the trip, content to just stare out of the window. Finally, on dropping Tommy outside the Midland front doors, he leaned over Norman's shoulder and slipped a note into his pocket, patted it and said in that familiar drawl, 'Have a drink on me son.' The big man then walked off up the steps and into the hotel foyer, leaving behind a smiling Norman, convinced inside the note was a more than decent tip from the world-famous funny man. It was only when Norman had driven off and checked his pocket that he realised that Tommy had actually treated him to an unused teabag! That was a favourite trick of Tommy's apparently – always worked!

Nothing had changed – Norman was really pleased to see me.

'All the lads are over at Littleton Road, Nicky, the first team have got the day off but the others will be back in the next half hour. Why don't you hang around?'

Music to my ears. 'OK if I go upstairs Norman and see Jimmy Mc in the treatment room?'

'What do you think? Part of the family son. You know that.'

I walked through the main door and a few of the press lads, including David Meek and Tom Tyrell, were milling around. Neither are with us any longer. True gentlemen, both. I nodded hoping they'd remember me, before jogging up the stairs, and just as I reached the top, who was coming out of his office but Big Ron. He smiled widely on seeing me. 'Welshy, the last I heard you'd gone to Siberia. I thought you'd never be seen or heard of again, especially if they got you in those bloody salt mines!' We both laughed and shared a genuinely warm and long handshake. I'd long got over any bitterness towards him about being released. Big Ron had always been more than fair towards me. I remember he appeared tired. Weary even. United hadn't been doing too well and I knew the press and fans were on his back. The stick was cruel but, looking at him, that familiar, wide grin and deep tan, you wouldn't think it, though the look around his eyes told a different story.

After saying goodbye to Big Ron, who was off to meet the press lads downstairs, I took a deep breath and entered the treatment room. As ever, it was a busy place. On spotting me, like Norman and the now ex-gaffer,

Jim McGregor and Jimmy Curran looked delighted as I walked in.

'Bloody 'ell, its Welshy!' stuttered Jim, as he continued with his ultrasound transducer working on Remi Moses' leg. We had a proper catch up and they loved hearing the Malaysia stories. No surprise, the ladyboy tale topped their list. They told me of a similar story with another United player in the Far East. This one reached the bedroom before the discovery was made and, in a fit of rage, he'd knocked out the poor sod! Still fuming, he waited for the ladyboy to come to – before sparking him senseless again! The lads also explained that events weren't great on the pitch and the pressure was truly on Big Ron. Somebody had even scaled the Cliff walls not so long ago and painted in massive letters 'ATKINSON OUT'. The following day United had been forced to shut the doors to the public whilst it was scrubbed off. After the previous season, when they had won their opening ten games in magnificent style and appeared almost certainties to finally win the title for the first time since 1967, United collapsed through injuries and loss of form, finally staggering to only a fourth place in what was felt at one stage to be a one-horse race. This had all added to the mounting pressure on the manager, and I felt that Big Ron was almost out of time. There was that feeling of impending doom in the air. A sense of foreboding. The hushed voices and faces of resignation. It wasn't healthy.

Suddenly, I heard a commotion outside the treatment room and downstairs the clack of studs on the floor that could only mean the reserve-team players had returned. I shook hands with Jim and Jimmy and went outside to meet my former teammates. Nothing had changed. The conversations are eternal. What are you wearing? Your shoes, haircut? You always had to be ready for a put down! Before you went out your thought was never about how you looked but about what you'd get the piss taken out of you for. The banter was fierce, funny and for me emotional, but I tried hard not show it. Fifteen months had passed and there was a lot of new gossip. We chatted for ages. The Remi Moses–Jesper Olsen altercation on the training pitch, when Remi had sparked out the Dane, was one story that I desperately wanted the inside track on.

'It isn't good Nicky,' one lad said to me. 'The gaffer is putting on a good act but they're murdering him in the press.'

We decided to head for a drink and it really was as if I'd never been away. The same faces cracking the jokes, the quiet ones keeping their heads down. 'Brill Cream' Billy Garton was only ever ready to roll twenty minutes later than everyone else due to doing his hair. I was truly, after a period of self-pity, back on my United Road.

A few weeks later I bumped into David Platt when transferring trains at

Crewe station. It was good to see Platty again, though with him it felt more like meeting someone that was in your class at school – a bit more formal.

'Who you playing for then?' he asked.

'The Chorlton Irish Club,' I replied.

'Seriously,' he frowned. 'I'd heard you had a spell in Malaysia. Surely you can get in at a lower league club?'

'I'm not interested mate,' I told him straight. 'I'd rather watch United on a Saturday.' He shook his head. Clearly thinking I'd gone mad. This same conversation happened a few times. Once at Manchester airport, a Belfast lad called Mark Todd who was a year younger than me and had moved to Sheffield United, obviously misheard me. 'Charlton Athletic?' said Mark. 'In London?'

'No mate, the Chorlton Irish Club. In Chorlton!' Being schooled at United almost certainly ensured you were guaranteed a career elsewhere but, if you didn't possess the necessary endeavour and passion to do so, as in my case, then what was the point?

November 1986 turned out to be a truly eventful month both for me and my United. After losing 4-1 at Southampton in the League Cup, Ron Atkinson was finally sacked as manager of Manchester United. In typical Big Ron style, he went out singing 'My Way' and throwing a party for all the first team players at his Rochdale home. No more would the blue reflection of that sunbed flicker through the dark Salfordian skies over the Cliff in winter time. So long gaffer.

The white smoke churned from the Old Trafford roof to signal a new man had been chosen for at the helm.

Born in Govan, not Glasgow! He'll tell you that!

A certain forty-five-year old Alexander Chapman Ferguson, who'd done a remarkable job with Aberdeen in not just ending, but blowing away the Old Firm dominance of Celtic and Rangers, arrived on a cold and chilly Mancunian November afternoon. November 6th 1986 – another date now stitched into the rich tapestry of Manchester United history. It was the very start of Fergie time! Like most fans, I didn't know so much about him except the obvious. I recalled watching Aberdeen playing some brilliant football to beat Real Madrid back in 1983 in the European Cup Winners' Cup Final, and a television interview Ferguson had given on the Hampden Park pitch, only moments after the Dons had beaten Rangers in the Scottish Cup Final. Even though they'd won, he was fuming at how his team had performed. This was no Big Ron and I sensed there'd be a few worried faces down at the Cliff amongst the first team. It would shortly be tin hat time.

Later that same month something happened to me personally concerning another certain Scotsman who, you might say, also had some bearing on the history of Manchester United. My sister Jane married a local lad called Terry O'Donnell who was, of course, a Red. Our Jane is a Welsh so she checked this out early doors. The wedding was in August at Mere golf club and Dad threw not just the sink at it, but the entire kitchen. This was his only daughter, remember. Only the Georgie Best for Baza's girl. He promised a knees up of epic proportions, and so it turned out to be. There were hundreds at the evening reception. Rich, poor, good, bad, mad, a beautiful big-hearted crowd all there to celebrate our Jane's big day. The night was pure perfection until it came to that moment when the DJ puts on the last record, and what did he choose? Gerry and the bleedin' Pacemakers, 'You'll never walk alone'! I ask you. I've never seen so many lads move as quickly over a dance floor, and I was surprised my leg didn't go again. In the end it was young Pat Crerand who was first to reach the DJ's console, and he all but ripped the offending vinyl disc off the revolving deck.

'What are you doing lad?' somebody yelled at him. 'That's a hanging offence putting that on round here.' Red faced, shameful and fully aware he'd come close to bringing the Smith's 'Hang the DJ' track to life, he couldn't apologise enough.

'Put Dirty Old Town on you numpty!'

During that evening, I'd asked a girl out who I'd often seen at mass. She happened to be the daughter of Mum and Dad's friends, Peter and Lynn Molloy. Kaaron was a few years younger than me and the old man was a strict, disciplinarian, old-fashioned Irishman, who wasn't too impressed with me seeing her. Peter had witnessed at first hand the United players in action around Altrincham and Hale and, fully aware that I was good friends with all of them, his thinking was probably that Kaaron could end up dating an out of control party animal. Now this was not entirely true. I did manage to take her out on a few dates without causing civil unrest, and a major breakthrough occurred when I was invited out for a Molloy Sunday lunch with the entire family at the Four Seasons hotel to celebrate Kaaron's birthday.

'Sounds nice' I said. 'Who's going then?'

'Well, obviously me, my sister Siobhan, Mum and Dad. Oh, and my Auntie Sheena and Uncle Matt.' Sounded a bit boring but hey ho. A nice meal at least.

I wanted to look fresh and present a good impression for my first meal out with Kaaron's family, and so I made sure I didn't have too much of a late night with my mates after watching United beat QPR 1-0 at Old

Trafford. The goal came from a free kick by full-back John Sivebaek, meaning our new manager, that Alex Ferguson fella, had finally got a first win under his belt. Come the following day, around three o'clock, I entered the Four Seasons in my Sunday best and headed for the bar. The first person I bumped into was a lovely old Irish lady called Kitty, who ran the bar. I knew her from down the road in Chorlton.

'Hiya Nick,' she said in a soft Irish brogue. 'They arrived early and have already gone through, just around there,' she explained, pointing. I thanked her and on turning the corner couldn't believe my eyes. I honestly thought I was seeing things. This came after a relatively early night and being good. Uncle Matt was no painter and decorator from Wythenshawe or Urmston. He was actually born a little further afield in a small mining village in north Lanarkshire, east of Glasgow. You would never believe it – Uncle Matt only turned out to be Sir Matt Busby!

For the first time in my life I was tongue tied and, apparently, I went a strange whiter shade of pale. I'd obviously seen Sir Matt at times around Old Trafford as he still had an office there, but I'd never dreamt of saying hello. I was simply too much in awe. It turned out the Molloy family were extremely close to the Busbys. Kaaron and her younger sister had grown up around them since they were babies. Although not blood related, they were so close that they referred to them as Aunt and Uncle.

Star struck and in an utter state of shock, I can't recall much about the meal if I'm honest. I just stared at the great man! I do remember when I got home later that evening ringing up my close mate Billy G who had by now elevated himself in to the United first team squad.

'How'd it go Welshy?' he asked. 'Hope you disgraced yourself?'

'Billo, you know I said her aunt and uncle were also going to the lunch?'

'Oh, you didn't, not the auntie?'

'No, no, no. Not that!'

Blimey Billo, give me some credit. I couldn't get my words out quickly enough. 'You're never in a million years going to believe who Uncle Matt is?'

'Go on?'

'Only Matt bleedin' Busby!'

For a moment Billy goes quiet and then I hear him start to laugh. 'Bleedin' 'ell Welshy! The lengths you'll go to try and get a game for United!'

SIT DOWN
CHAPTER TWENTY FIVE

Towards the end of November 1986, Manchester United embarked on a short tour of Bermuda and following a game, a number of the senior players took themselves off to a nightclub. No last orders with this mob, despite the new manager demanding higher professional standards. Time to end their Viking pillaging around the pubs and bars of Cheshire. The only shorts allowed would be those worn on the field and in the short back and sides haircuts he started to insist upon. Around 2am, Fergie had gotten word of their whereabouts and he turned up, seething, and frogmarched them back the not-inconsiderable distance to the hotel. These were seasoned professionals, mostly in their mid-twenties, internationals, some even Captains of their countries, and they didn't care for being treated in this manner. Like kids, or so it felt to them. Besides, although this fierce, strong-willed Scot had turned up from the back end of Scotland, some fishing town called Aberdeen with a decent CV, a potful of trophies, this was Manchester United. The big league. A drinking club like no other, although Liverpool ran them close. On his first day at the Cliff, Fergie promised clean slates, but demanded in return a curb of their lifestyles. In other words, the ale. Forget that – they'd done all right by Big Ron with a couple of FA Cups, and don't forget the night against Barcelona at Old Trafford. I was lucky to be on clean-up duty in the dressing room that evening and can still remember like yesterday Bryan Robson seething with Diego Maradona for keeping them waiting in the tunnel.

'Who the fuck does he think he is?' Robbo raged. A historic and stunning 3-0 victory to come back from a 2-0 deficit at the Nou Comp set the old place alight! Not bad, they had thought, for a bunch of piss heads. Time for a beer, and another, and… Cut down by injuries and a last-minute goal by Paolo Rossi in Turin, United lost out in the semi-final to a brilliant Juventus, but the quarter final against Barca rightly entered into Old Trafford folklore.

On returning to the hotel, Fergie was brutally honest. He'd get it right, but these were players, especially his captain, who would be desperately needed. He wanted to be reasonable but booze was something Fergie detested and the battle of wills between them began and would continue. He demanded loyalty and minimal drinking – if not total sobriety. It ultimately came down to either respecting the badge and shaping up – or he'd get rid.

'I'm Alex Ferguson, sorry lads – it's my way or the highway...'

Fergie openly admitted that he'd no chance of making them change the way they wanted to live their lives – but it was simply a case of him or them. The high road or United Road. He needed, as Jimmy Murphy so succinctly put it, 'his own apples.' Young lads he could rear, if not exactly in his own image, then kids who would give everything and live only for the club. Instill into them with varying degrees of kindness, cajoling, mind games and at times outright fear, an obsessive passion for Manchester United. One, all consuming, so much that it mattered more than booze, cars and girls. Live, breathe, eat, drink, sleep and dream about that red shirt, whilst on the training pitch they'd be educated and schooled every day in how to play in the true, traditional Manchester United way. One, two touch, keep the ball. Never lose your composure, wear teams down, nothing is over, the Reds are never beaten – they just sometimes run out of time. From small acorns, mostly Mancunian, the man from Govan set in place a footballing revolution that would shake not only the foundations of English, but also European, football.

From my time at Manchester United, only two of our youth side made it into the United first team that played in that semi-final game at Old T against City – Lee Martin and keeper Gary Walsh. For the Blues that day, however, ten lads had progressed into their first team. Drastic change was needed at United. These were the questions Fergie was asking. Why it was that City had such a superior youth system to the Old Trafford set-up? What on earth was going on? Ken Barnes, the head of City's academy had six scouts in Greater Manchester, whilst the Reds had only half that number? The Blues were cleaning up. It was no contest. A determined Fergie immediately went to work and, within a month, he'd brought past legends and local St Pat's lads Brian Kidd and Nobby Stiles into the fold, along with sixteen other scouts. Their mission: take it all back. Both he and assistant Archie Knox attended every Monday and Thursday night training session looking at the local 13–16-year-old schoolboys. That had been me, once upon a time. Nothing, no one was missed. Including a thin little will of the wisp winger from Salford, stolen from City by the name of Ryan Wilson. As Sir Matt and Jimmy had built their success on youth, so it was Alex Ferguson would do the same. He just needed that one thing, so precious and essential to any football manager with a dream to succeed... Time.

That first season was a period of consolidation for Fergie as Manchester United eventually finished eleventh. The following campaign of 1987–88 saw a vast improvement with a second place, albeit nine points behind – guess who? The highlight by far was a remarkable match against Liverpool at Anfield, over the Easter period. A time when the greatest comeback since Biblical times took place. For those of a United persuasion, what occurred in the Scouse bearpit on bank holiday Monday on 4th April 1988 even gave biblical events a run for their money.

Come 1988, the animosity between United and Liverpool had transcended even that of the late seventies and early eighties. Two years previous, tear gas had been fired at the visitors' coach on arrival at Anfield, injuring even their own supporters. What kind of mentality pulls a stunt like that? Inside it was beyond poisonous: open warfare. United fans with blow-up Bill Shankly dolls, Scousers roaring out Munich chants. 'Stanley' rearing its razor sharp, slicing ugly head, Mancs bravely – or foolishly – scattered around the ground.

We hadn't lost at Anfield for nearly ten years but that day looked as though it was going to change. On the pitch we were being taken apart, 3-1 with goals by Beardsley, Gillespie and McMahon – this after Bryan Robson had given his team an early lead. Liverpool then revved up like the all Red-killing machine they were back then and tore United apart.

Enter Norman Whiteside and Jesper Olsen. Big Norm wasn't in a good place. After endless frustrating injuries and spats with Fergie about events off-pitch, he was wound up and ready to snap. Many of the rows with Fergie had involved his huge mate and partner in pub crawls, Paul McGrath. Norman had handed in a transfer request. Fuming at hearing his name being booed by United fans, the Ulsterman's state of mind when he crossed that white line into this cauldron of passion was one of 'I'll show em.' What happened next has become enshrined in the rich, fascinating, if truly tempestuous history between these two northern tribes.

Colin Gibson's dismissal early in the second half reduced us to ten men – against the likely champions – and a savage, humiliating mauling looked certain to be on the cards. Norman looked like he could burst!

They hadn't banked on Big Norm! Whiteside's first act was to bring two of Liverpool's main architects of their lead to heel with his devastating strength pumped up with seething anger. After dealing first with a deliberate foul on Scouse hardman McMahon – retribution for getting Gibson sent off – he gave John Barnes a crack in the face. Game on!! The tide of the battle had well and truly turned and United ultimately fought back to gain a memorable 3-3 with a riveting end to the game. Goals from Robson and a Gordon Strachan equaliser ignited riotous scenes of revelry amongst the travelling Mancunians. Strachan's legendary celebration of smoking an invisible cigar in front of a comically irate Kop a lasting portrait, alongside Norman Whiteside's introduction, of an afternoon on Merseyside never to be forgotten. It could've been even more dramatic as United winger Jesper Olsen went so close in the dying moments. Sadly the result took Liverpool 11 points clear and they went on to secure their last top flight title for thirty years. Especially annoying was that we were banned from Europe despite finishing second – the Scousers' fault (in my opinion) due to all English clubs being banned from Europe after the Heysel disaster!

Following the match, Fergie clashed with Liverpool manager Kenny Dalglish and it was clear that the vitriol on the terraces was shared by both teams' coaching staff and players. On a much smaller note, whenever we played them even at lower youth and junior level the contests were equally no-holds-barred clashes. You daren't lose or not perform well. It was also known for both clubs to move players across or down a notch to strengthen their teams, for whenever the whistle blew to start against the Scousers with the liver bird on their shirt, all that mattered was to win.

Win… At any cost!

The following season, 1988–89 again proved hugely disappointing, with Fergie seemingly struggling to come to terms with the English game. He'd never get as long nowadays – thank God for me, my family and friends that he survived!!

We had started the season with massive excitement, especially as Sparky had returned from Barcelona. We missed out on signing Gazza – still the player that, I am told, Fergie most regrets getting away. Imagine how different he might have been if he'd been moulded and protected by Fergie! Sad.

Murmurs of disapproval were already beginning to sweep across the terraces. Manchester United finished eleventh between Millwall and Wimbledon. The results, like the football on show, were underwhelming, and it became clear that the manager had to start showing the Old Trafford fans much more. Come the end of the campaign, it felt a little like the end of an era for me as Norman Whiteside and Paul McGrath left the club and another member of that era, Remi Moses, was forced to retire due to injury.

My own personal memory of Remi stems back to when I first signed for United on my YTS apprenticehip. I was interviewed by the Daily Mail and happened to mention that I'd named my dog after Remi Moses. Thinking nothing of it, a couple of days later, I was getting changed at the Cliff when a furious Remi stormed in with the said paper and grabbed me. 'What the fuck are you doing naming your dog after me?!' Worried at what the hot-headed player might do to me I quickly explained in a stutter that it was a compliment to his battling abilities and being a hard bastard! He smiled widely and I realised that Remi had been winding me up – though for a moment, I honestly thought Welshy, you're dog meat here!

Reinforcements arrived in the summer when Forest's Neil Webb and Norwich City's Mike Phelan were signed; however, events were about to turn from disappointment to an extraordinarily surreal farce at Manchester United with a certain Michael Knighton coming onto the scene. You honestly couldn't make up what happened to us next!

Cue the circus…

In the summer of 1989, a former headmaster, Michael Knighton, claiming to be heading a fabulously wealthy syndicate, made a £20 million offer for Manchester United and for a while, every Red supporter across the land thought our boat had sailed down the Irwell. Sadly he was more David Icke than Sheik Mansour!

Rumours abounded. We were promised multiple signings of the world's greatest players. Marco Van Basten, Ruud Gullit, Diego Maradona. All were being lined up to come and play on the hallowed pitch that I'd once graced, (before they'd got wise and dumped me). A heavenly field that I'd stolen a piece of – once upon a time. A man with more faces than the seven dwarves, and more stories than Jackanory. This thirty-nine-year-old was pleasant, polite, debonair, disarmingly charming, but ultimately, it would turn out…

Totally skint.

Knighton is one of those odd characters that football seems so full of, who yearn for the publicity that comes with owning a team – especially a top team. This would be the first (but not last) time that he came to the attention of the general public in August 1989, with his £20m takeover bid for Manchester United. This was easily, at the time, a record figure for a British football club. Michael Knighton's offer was accepted by Martin Edwards who would have trousered £10 million (bet he is so glad he didn't, by the way!) only after being promised by Knighton that he'd invest £10 million into the Old Trafford stadium (financing a new Stretford End) with plenty more money available for the world's top players. With hindsight, United and their advisers should have spotted sooner that it was too good to be true. There was a storm coming.

Before he'd even showed the colour of his money – which was imaginary – Knighton travelled over to the Cliff where all the first team squad and back room staff were asked to gather in Teresa's canteen to meet their new owner and boss. He spoke to the manager first.

'I'll give you a hundred and fifty per cent Alex,' Knighton declared grandly as they all shook hands, looking like kids in the presence of Father Christmas.

'Aye,' replied the clearly wary Ferguson – a shrewd judge of character if ever there was one! 'Just a hundred will do.'

God only knows what was going through the boss's mind at the time. Worse swiftly followed as Knighton walked along the line of players and staff, stopping at Nobby Stiles. Before shaking Nobby's hand he suddenly launched into a weird imitation of the legendary Stiles 1966 jig, whilst holding an imaginary World Cup trophy.

'Nobby,' he laughed, 'your famous jig! No front teeth.' Still he jigs. 'Russian Linesman, some of the people are on the pitch, it's amazing to meet you!'

'Pleased to meet you too Mr Knighton,' answered Nobby, trying not to laugh and apparently looking like he was being mimicked by a nutter. As Fergie, Archie Knox and all watched on, it was already apparent that something didn't ring true.

Matters hardly improved when on the opening game of the season against reigning champions Arsenal at Old Trafford on a sun-drenched Mancunian afternoon, Knighton took to the pitch before kick-off wearing a Manchester United strip, performing keepie-uppies and leathering volleys into the empty Stretford End goal. The tannoy had announced him as the club's new chairman. This was news to Edwards who almost choked on his pre-match drink in the boardroom as he heard this – because the deal had yet to be concluded. Cue huge roars for Knighton from the crowd, who seemed to have bought into their new chairman-elect's dream of world domination. Knighton took a bow and blew kisses to his adoring audience on the hallowed turf. Despite the fact that United blew away the Gunners that day with a sumptuous 4-1 demolition, their performance hardly registered. The following day's newspaper headlines spoke only of Knighton's carry-on beforehand... watched, it later emerged, by a simmering Fergie standing in the shadows in the tunnel.

'What the bloody hell is he playing at?'

A question which was very shortly to be asked by all.

Luckily for us, the whole United deal fell through. Something to do with having insufficient funds, as well as being a complete and utter 'Moon Man' who had wasted everyone's time.

Some years later, however, after finally buying a football club (Carlisle United), Knighton claimed to have been abducted by a UFO. Back on that day at the Cliff, when first introduced to the United employees, few would've been surprised at this, for they were already convinced Knighton had come from another planet.

Anyway, back on the pitch, after the impressive 4-1 victory over Arsenal, all came crashing down with one of the most humiliating days in Manchester United history. A draw and three defeats were a mere aperitif to the forthcoming nightmare. On 25th September 1989, at Maine Road, underdogs City, under Mel Machin, inflicted a crushing 5-1 defeat on the Reds that cut us to the quick like a knife. There really was no place to run in Manchester. Bitter Blues suddenly scuttled out of every nook and cranny, every crack and orifice they'd been hiding in for decades. Open any door you'd see a City fan with five fingers stuck in your face. The game itself was freakish, as everything they hit went in. We watched, faces white with shock, from the away enclosure. United fans had mingled across the entire stadium, as in every Maine Road derby back then. United fans were everywhere, including their North stand. After only a couple of minutes fierce fighting broke out, and the Reds winding up the City fans in that stand were escorted down the touchline after causing mayhem, with the game having to be paused by the ref. After a bright opening start by United, the delay cost us our momentum. As the match re-started, City unbelievably stormed into a 3-0 half-time lead. It was crazy, with unadulterated misery unfolding before our Red eyes. No one saw it coming. We were hardly anything special, but City had been hopeless up until that rotten Saturday afternoon in Moss Side. They'd not so much raised their game, but gone through the roof.

Fergie's team included a host of new signings, with West Ham midfielder Paul Ince, Southampton winger Danny Wallace and Middlesborough centre-half Gary Pallister. All were caught in the crossfire. As the goal tally mounted, and the noise and furore grew ever louder from the bouncing Kippax and elsewhere, they must've wondered what was going on. It was horrendous. The Blue side of the city dancing with joy on the terraces, gleefully enjoying rubbing it in our faces. As the second period began, Mark Hughes cracked in a typical, stunning volleyed goal back to reduce the deficit. Game on! The stage surely set for a glorious comeback and for us to ram the taunting back down Blue throats.

So went the plan.

After going a numbing 4-1 down, the fifth nail in the coffin came late on with a thunderous Andy Hinchcliffe header, and he raced off waving – yes, you guessed it – five fingers. We had truly been hammered and it was hard to take. Anger was rising with the manager. The board and Martin Edwards especially were already coming under pressure with angry letters from the fans. A sure sign things at Old Trafford weren't healthy. Imagine if social media had existed then!

The 5-1 debacle that had Fergie going home and putting his head under the pillow for the evening was a huge dose of fuel on the fire. This was Fergie's third full season and United, despite having spent a small fortune, still seemed light years behind both Liverpool and Arsenal. Thank God Liverpool's fortunes had also begun to wane.

I sensed from chats with my mates that Fergie was on a slippery slope. I'd witnessed it before with Sexton and Big Ron. Once the wolves start to howl?

For the City game, Bryan Robson was out injured and, like us, he was forced to watch from the Maine Road stands surrounded by mocking Blues. I spoke to him the next day over a few beers and he still had steam coming out of his ears. Afterwards, Hinchcliffe and other City players had really rubbed their noses in it. I just know that if Robbo had been playing no way would that result have occurred. Robbo would've shouted, screamed, threatened and cajoled those failing red shirts. Over his dead body would we be rubbished and humbled by City. Bryan Robson was a force of nature. A rare breed these days. A player who simply loved United to the core.

For the manager, matters came to a head in early December, when after a 2-1 home defeat by Crystal Palace, a flag was unfurled on the terraces by disillusioned supporter Pete Molyneux.

'3 YEARS OF EXCUSES AND IT'S STILL CRAP. TARA FERGIE.'

Open revolt had begun and the mood turned savage with the fans' anger vented onto the man from Govan. Following the Palace game, United lay in a miserable twelfth position, but come New Year's Day they'd dropped even lower to fifteenth. We'd been paired away at the City ground, with Brian Clough's Nottingham Forest in the FA Cup third round, and on the banks of the River Trent, rumour was that this was Fergie's final throw of the dice. Lose and it was all over. He'd be sacked. Officially, this was of course denied by Martin Edwards, but the pressure had become unyielding.

The 7th January 1990 was to be a date with destiny for Alex Ferguson and Manchester United. Whilst our fans had begun to doubt our ability to beat Forest, one thing was certain – the fans would be wild in their support as the Red Army regrouped and assembled to ensure that despite the baying in the TV, press and tabloids, this would not be Fergie's last stand.

Thousands travelled from Manchester without tickets in the hope they'd gain entrance, and many did so. What's always astonishing to me about my club's support, particularly the old school (this even relates to today) is that, when the Red chips are being burnt to a crisp, they rally and get behind the team even more. To the end, over the cliff if necessary. As evidence of this, I give you Denis Law's backheel that led to that tumultuous, unforgettable season in the Second Division. Not all for the right reasons, I must add!

The game against Forest, when Manchester United's team was ravaged by injuries and rabidly off form, now stands as one of those rare occasions when a match was won as much on the terraces as on the pitch. The fans willed the team to win and sucked the ball into the net! It was sheer raging defiance. I was there and it was a truly proud day on my United Road. Unsurpassed still, for many of a certain age and a Red persuasion. Nine minutes into the second half, following on from a tight opening period, the deadlock was broken when a clever, curling cross from Mark Hughes found the head of youngster Mark Robins, to stoop low and put United in front! Around me, as the ball hit the net, chaos, wonderful madness ensued! I remember screaming 'Go on lad!' I'd seen Robins since he was a kid finish those type of opportunities for fun. There was a calmness about him. A gift: Paul Scholes and Ole Gunnar Solskjaer possessed the same quality. It was something players are born with and can't be taught.

Mark Robins was to be the pivot around which Manchester United turned into what we have been ever since.

Mark was a year below me and a lovely, quiet lad from Oldham. His dad was high up in the police force and, my god, did he push him. This was often the case, and you'd see parents at the training sessions and the junior games shouting, encouraging – some more than others. One particular Saturday morning at the Cliff, we were warming up five minutes before kick-off. Some were doing short passes to each other in a triangle; others stretches or sprints, simply getting ready for the start. I suddenly heard Eric Harrison's dreaded window bang and looked over to see Mark's dad actually on the right-hand corner of the pitch crossing the ball into the box for him to practice finishing. We all watched on and knew what was coming! Out appeared Eric to hand the pitch invader a monumental mouthful, and I can assure you that Mr Robins senior never dared set foot across that white line again. Anyway, if it helped with Mark's cracking header past the Forest keeper Crossley on that bitterly cold Nottingham late afternoon, well done. A fair cop.

The final whistle blew.

'Que sera sera, whatever will be will be. We're going to Wembley. Que sera sera!' Fergie came across to acknowledge the fans, for I'm sure he knew, and I believe possibly for the first time realised just what lay at the heart of Manchester United. Not the money or the cold, calculating, commercial pulling power. Not the suits, the hangers on, or the flimsy and the fickle. It was those who sang about a scarlet ribbon and were already dreaming of Wembley.

After a nerve-wracking run to the 1990 FA Cup Final, which included a ferocious bunch of hard-fought matches at Hereford, Newcastle and Sheffield United and a scintillating double tilt against local near-rivals, Joe Royle's Oldham Athletic in the semi-finals, only Crystal Palace remained between Alex Ferguson's first trophy at Old Trafford and a chance for him to breathe. A memorable cup run had followed the victory at Forest. A late goal for a 1-0 win from Clayton Blackmore, on a pigsty of a pitch at Edgar Street. A 3-2 battle royal in the North East, in the bearpit of St James' Park, before Danny Wallace stroked home a winner. A Brian McClair header from a corner on a bright spring Sheffield afternoon in the Steel city earning a dramatic semi-final showdown with Oldham, and after a pulsating 3-3 draw on the Sunday at Maine Road, it was Mark Robins again stepping forward to settle the replay.

Come the final, on a tension-filled Wembley Mayday afternoon, another classic ensued with two life-saving goals by Mark Hughes, one in normal play, the other in extra time making it 3-3 with a late equaliser. Managed by one of my early heroes Steve Coppell, Crystal Palace fought with great tenacity all the way and by the final whistle a draw proved more than a fair result. Playing in an all-white strip, United had been far from their best, the goalkeeper Jim Leighton, especially, having a mare of a match. Unsettling and fallible to the endless crosses and power that the South Londoners launched mercilessly at us, Leighton ended the game shell-shocked. With the Eagles' powerful pairing of Ian Wright and Mark Bright, aided and abetted by any number of their teammates who were prepared to rough Leighton up, the manager had a problem. He displayed an early example of his unrivalled ability to make hard decisions. Fergie knew he had to be brutal with someone who had only ever given him wonderful service. Jim Leighton had followed Fergie from Aberdeen. If not friends, they were close. Both had been through battles together in Scotland as Aberdeen smashed apart the Old Firm. A trusted servant, Fergie now had to break Leighton's heart by dropping him for the replay. In came reserve keeper Les Sealey and Leighton's career at United was finished in an instant. Broken, but is that not what makes a great manager? The courage to make decisions, whatever the personal consequences.

Fergie knew well only bringing the FA Cup home to Manchester guaranteed more breathing space, as the burning desire to win the league drove him relentlessly on. Leighton was simply a casualty of war, amongst the first of many in Alex Ferguson's ultimate desire and challenge: to 'Knock Liverpool off their fuckin' perch.'

Whereas the previous Saturday Crystal Palace had mixed their play up a little, it swiftly became apparent that, this time around, Coppell's men had wound themselves up and were determined to try and kick United off the pitch. Back in our traditional red and full of confidence, we matched them kick for kick, elbow for elbow – and with Sealey in much more commanding form giving the defence confidence, a first-half stalemate ensued.

Now established at left back, my old mate Lee Martin earned himself a place in Manchester United folklore when, on fifty-nine minutes, he latched onto an astute Neil Webb cross-field pass and caressed it down in his stride before, in a flawless and elegant movement, lashing the ball past the Palace keeper Nigel Martyn to electrify the Mancunian enclaves of Wembley stadium and win the cup. I like to think that Lee's storming run through to score the winner was down to that long rest he had back in May 1985, beneath those same stairs, as United fans sang his name. It was a wonderful moment for the kid from Hyde who had taken his chance in the wake of my mate little Arthur Albiston's departure from Old Trafford. Among all older Reds and all more knowledgeable younger fans, Lee Martin will forever be known as the man who won Manchester United the 1990 FA Cup. No one will ever be able to take it away from him. Ever.

As for Fergie, the relief was etched on his beaming face and, as he bathed in the shadow of victory under the Wembley floodlights, no doubt already planning for the next campaign, the Red Army danced and sang along on the historic terraces where we'd won the European Cup back in 1968. By then, Wembley had become a bit of a shithole it's fair to say, but it was tinged with the magical gold dust of memories past and it had a magic that the new Wembley will probably never match. Little did we know in 1990 that this was to be the start of something quite extraordinary in the lives of all Manchester United supporters, millions who were blessed enough to witness what was set to follow.

The early 90's also saw a much needed career change for me personally. Although Welsport started well and built up momentum supplying many amateur football clubs with new team strips, I soon found out in most cases, they would make them last for years. So it was never going to be the much needed regular repeat orders for me.

There was also a UK recession at the time. Corporate handouts like golf umbrellas, give away T-shirts and the like also took a big hit as companies tightened their belts and the orders dried up.

I was now coming up to my mid twenties and needed to get serious with my life. Get on the property ladder, married, kids, the usual stuff. Something had to happen. I started to do sales work within Baza's laminate business TBS, looking after some key clients, although I could never really see this as a long term route. His two brothers were joint partners in the firm and there was in essence three families involved, including offspring so it was all a bit crowded. It was around this time I came across a new material that I thought had real potential. A rep had dropped a sample box in at reception and I got talking to him. Not many things grabbed my attention back then – United, the ladies, beer but this did. It was called Corian and like garlic bread, for me the future!

I also fancied the idea of being my own boss, rise and most likely fall off my own back which to be fair I did a few times. So that was it, I was off to conquer the world of shopfitting and interior fit out, where I indeed made a pretty good living and still do today as I write. As expected though it was never without a few serious 'Washout Walsh' moments along the way.

The following season of 1990–91 saw Manchester United become the first English club allowed back into Europe, after the Heysel ban. The irony wasn't lost on anyone at Old Trafford. God rest the souls of the thirty-nine innocent Italian victims, who in May 1985 in Brussels were only there to watch a football match. Unforgivable…

As the nineties dawned and Madchester – and later, the rest of the country – exploded in a wild kaleidoscope of ecstasy-laced free love, somehow it managed to swerve the unhinged distaste that existed between the supporters of United and Liverpool. The rivalry bitter, venomous and sufficiently poisonous to make a rattle snake bite its own tongue and say 'Whatever? Just chill a little.'

As the Happy Mondays played 'Step on it', The Stone Roses blasted out 'I am the Resurrection', and Northside asked, 'Shall we take a trip?' When Tony Wilson, God bless him, declared to the world, 'Manchester, so much to answer for.' United made it through to the European Cup Winner's Cup Final to take on Johann Cruyff's Barcelona in Rotterdam.

Beforehand, back in April, there'd been another appearance at Wembley, for Manchester United to take on former manager Ron Atkinson's Sheffield Wednesday in the League Cup Final. We had never won that cup back then, so we were up for it. My mate Moet Mason's company, Morson Group, had sponsored their suits, and as part of the arrangement, Ged had by hook and by crook manoeuvred himself virtually onto the Wednesday bench – well, at least right behind it, in full view of the television cameras. Being friends with many of the United players, this caused a few stares as they glared across, seeing him there amongst the opposition. Sensing a perfect business opportunity, Ged was wearing one of the Morson baseball caps that I'd had made through Welsport, knowing that his logo would be seen all over the world. As the footballing world bore down on the Sheffield Wednesday bench, there was Moet Mason, sat directly behind Atkinson, advertising the family firm for free. No wonder he's a millionaire so many times over! Suddenly, Big Ron turned around and clocked the cap.

'Get that off now!' he screamed. Ged swiftly did as he was ordered. Job already done. Come half time, the Wednesday manager jumped up, forgetting his camel coat, and headed off to the dressing room. Seeing this, Ged picked it up and followed him in. Being, as he now proclaims himself, 'Big Ron's official camel coat carrier' back then! Once inside, Ged watched nervously as Big Ron tore into his players, trying desperately to avoid attention and ultimately ending up hiding in the showers so he could carry on listening in. At least Moet couldn't blame this one on me!

As for the game, United never really got going, and a terrific first-half drive from Sheffield Wednesday's John Sheridan, a self-confessed Red, won the cup. Although a huge disappointment on the day, the League Cup Final was a bit of a non-event, wedged between a two-legged European Cup Winner's Cup Semi-Final against Legia Warsaw. A convincing 5-2 victory on aggregate meant the loss against Wednesday was swiftly forgotten.

For the first time since 1968, Alex Ferguson had led Manchester United into a European final and the events of Wednesday 15th May 1991 will never be forgotten by those who were there or watched on television. Around 25,000 United fans travelled across the North Sea to dance and sing in the Rotterdam rain. Being the first season back in Europe for English teams following the Heysel ban, there was much nervousness as to how the massed ranks of the Red Army would behave.

Ultimately, the authorities needn't have worried. It would be a friendly invasion. One love. After Italia '90, football's popularity soared no end and a new generation of supporter was born. This was the official reason put forward for the drop off in hooliganism. The truth was that so many lads going to the game were tripping off their heads on ecstasy and the last thing on their mind was scrapping. The smell of certain substances amongst the travelling Mancs was a big part of the trip – trip being the key word. There were probably enough drugs knocking about over those three/four days in Amsterdam and later Rotterdam to make even Pablo Escobar consider relocating to Manchester. With two-thirds of the ground draped in United flags and banners, the atmosphere was electric. It crackled and fizzed and you could taste and smell the excitement. The terraces were a living, breathing throng of Mancs and had a certain psychedelic twinge to say the least! Monty Python's hugely ironic 'Always look on the bright side of life' had been adopted by United supporters and was sung with gusto, along with other favourites by the Mondays and Roses. Baggy clothes were the dress of the day. Madchester had invaded Holland armed only with peace, good vibes, smiling faces and Manchester United Football Club.

The game itself saw a United team in all white rise to the occasion much more than their vaunted FC Barcelona counterparts and, after a first half in which we were by far the better team, on sixty-seven minutes, Bryan Robson floated in a free kick. Steve Bruce rose to head the ball goalwards and Mark Hughes (a former Barca player) was left with the simple task of poking the ball over the line. Rotterdam exploded! Shortly afterwards, Hughes latched onto another superb through ball from the magnificent Robson, rounded the goalkeeper Busquets, and drilled in a stunning drive from a tight angle to hand United a 2-0 lead! As the stadium rocked, a joyful soaking mass of Mancunian delirium, the mood suddenly changed with ten minutes remaining when the great Dutchman Ronald Koeman reduced the deficit with a free kick. The United fans quietened down – almost becoming pensive – as for the first time in the match, Cruyff's team came alive. The Catalans launched a late rally, only for a Clayton Blackmore goal line clearance to save the day and, for the first time in twenty-four years, a European trophy was on its way back to Old Trafford. There were many heroes that night. For the match winner, Sparky, this was a personal triumph after being let go by Barca. Robbo, as ever inspirational, had thrown off the years and, finally, keeper Les Sealey. Another legend who was taken from us far too soon.

As for me, the rest is a bit vague – I was rather groggy, for obvious reasons. I made the trip with our Guy, Shay and Jim. A great few days were enjoyed by all. One especially odd memory is of playing pool with the rock singer Robert Palmer in a bar after the game back in Amsterdam – he was there doing a gig.

'It was Clayton's finest moment in a red jersey,' said Fergie post-match. 'So long as there's a Manchester United, that rescue act will be remembered.' None enjoyed the victory more than our manager, who cut a wonderful sight on the pitch with his players, conducting the orchestra as the fans sang 'Always look on the bright side of life' over and over. Though they were mad, rowdy and in a mostly drug-induced stupor, the mayor of Rotterdam and his chief of police heaped praise on the United supporters. The Spanish newspapers stated 'The Red Devils came dressed in white, like angels, but were devilish United in their beating of Barcelona.'

One lovely way to end this chapter is that, as the victorious Manchester United coach arrived at the stadium with the trophy, I watched as hundreds of fans swarmed around it. As the doors opened, a hush suddenly settled on the crowds as Sir Matt Busby appeared and, like the parting of the Red Sea, they moved aside to let the great man through.

'God bless you, Sir Matt' shouted one, then another...

ADVENTURES AT THE OLD FIRM
CHAPTER TWENTY SIX

With my Irish Catholic heritage, it's no surprise that when I was younger, I supported Celtic as my second team. Though I also must admit it – Lou Macari and Rod Stewart helped loads! It always charmed me that even an all-time world-renowned rock and roll superstar like Rod, when it came to football was just like me, you or anyone else: in total awe of our idols on the pitch. In his case it was Denis Law. Even to the extent that Rod would have his hair cut and styled to resemble the King of the Stretford End.

Due to Ged Mason's links in Scotland and our good friend Andrew Fernie, who was the Morson man in the north, we started to travel up for Old Firm matches. Now, Andrew is a die-hard Rangers fan and through various connections at Rangers, including another made by Norman (Whiteside) when he was still with United, regular get-togethers were part of the Glasgow trip.

Norman had been in rehab for injury at Lillieshall Clinic at the same time as Ally McCoist and Ian Durrant, so I can only imagine how that went down – what a threesome.

On top of this, when Rangers signed Gary Stevens from Everton, the party was complete, as Andrew made contact with Gary through some mutual friends in Barrow, Gary's hometown.

Once Moet Mason had attended his first Rangers match at Ibrox he was well and truly hooked. He became a regular in the players' lounge after games and at official functions in the city. It really was a great time for the game north of the border, as the UEFA ban on English teams after Heysel meant that some top names were in Rangers blue, such as Terry Butcher, Ray Wilkins and Chris Woods.

I have to admit, when he would tell me of his ongoing involvement, I was shocked.

'What? You're a practising Catholic Moet, you can't support that lot?'

'Why not?' he'd replied 'What's religion got to do with sport? It shouldn't be anywhere near it.' I knew Ged had a good point and was probably right, but it'd been bred into me that they were the enemy. 'KILL RANGERS' scrawled on a Collyhurst wall a lifetime ago.

I tried to fight my corner whether I truly believed it or not. 'No way, I'm not having it. How can you sit there with thousands of them around you singing fuck the Pope? It's just not right, Moet.'

It didn't bother me that much if I'm honest, but one person who just couldn't for the life of him stomach this was Paddy Crerand. He'd go mad at poor Ged and was really serious about it. Paddy had been born and raised with the ferocious rivalry and the horrible stench of religious bigotry. It was real to him and on another level to what we could understand. Ged would always handle the stick well with a pinch of salt and never got upset by it, although I know for sure he was never particularly at ease with the religious songs aimed at his own catholic faith. However, there was an occasion one time when introduced to another Rangers fan who happened to be a Catholic Priest, Moet couldn't tell Paddy fast enough!

One time we travelled up with Norman Whiteside and Paul McGrath for a game. These two were best mates and the different religious backgrounds from home quite rightly never entered into their relationship. It was simply irrelevant, that was until it came to the Old Firm! For this occasion, there was a mixture of us, a concoction of both sides. We'd have a good drink beforehand, but come close to the kick off all go (including Norm and Paul) our separate ways, meeting only again once the last whistle and venomous chants and songs had faded away. Often myself and Moet would go with each other into the opposite ends in alternate seasons.

I'd get my tickets back then off Billy McNeil for the Celtic end. What a brilliant, lovely man he was. RIP Caesar - that dreaded alzheimer's again! For one particular match Billy had got hold of two tickets for us behind the goal in the away Celtic end at Ibrox. Because of certain reasons the game on Saturday 4th November 1989 had an even more frightening intensity. You could feel the staggering hatred and vitriol between the two sets of fans. It was a real living and breathing organism. United and Liverpool was a northern thing as I've said before, a footballing battle between two cities, but this was so much more dangerous. The whiff of religion gave it that smell of sulphur. It was a war based on a violent history that crossed the sea back over to Ireland. The Orange Order,

Battle of the Boyne. Up to their eyes in Fenian blood. It was outrageous, if at the same time exhilarating, to be present, witnessing and feeling it.

Just to add to the undoubted tension of this cold and bitter Glasgow afternoon, the former Celtic striker Mo Johnston had only gone and committed the unspeakable sin of signing for the Rangers. This was unheard of. For Gers manager Graeme Souness, it was a brave attempt to drag his club out of the dark ages. Good luck with that Graeme! Not just a hoops man in a Rangers shirt, but a Catholic as well? Johnston was their first major Roman Catholic signing and the highest-profile to sign for the club since the World War One era. The move antagonised and outraged both sets of supporters. Some Rangers fans burned scarves and threatened to hand in season tickets over the signing, while Celtic fans referred to Johnston as Judas. The Rangers' kitman protested by making Johnston arrange his own kit and withholding from him the chocolate bars dispensed to other players. It just had to happen when in the dying moments guess who hit the winning goal?

Mo bloody Johnston!

Never have I felt such a feeling of impending violence all around me as the Celtic end exploded in a cacophony of threats and abuse for their one-time hero. It was time to make a move. I said to Moet, 'C'mon we're off!' The plan became drive south straight back to Manchester and have a safe night out on our home turf. For Glasgow was most definitely set to erupt. We'd managed to grab hold of a complimentary car park pass for right outside the stadium and had travelled up in Moet's brand-new Lotus sports car, which was like sitting in a kid's buggy. You'd be almost sat on the ground!

We managed to drive safely out of the car park to the traffic lights before landing in the midst of a war zone! The heavy police presence and cordons outside Ibrox had smartly kept the two sets of supporters apart, but at these lights, the junction was where they could first get at each other. Well, my god, I've seen some scenes over my many years on United's Warwick Road and forecourt, on Anfield Road and outside Elland Road, but this? This was on a completely different scale. There were women fighting blokes toe to toe, kids jumping on backs. Bricks and glasses flying through the air. Myself and Moet were so low down in that car someone was getting booted and stamped on in the head right by my passenger window a foot away and I had a proper close-up view of it all. Next minute a petrol bomb landed and exploded on the pavement about ten feet away! That was enough, 'Rag it' I screamed at Moet. We were sitting ducks and what a lovely target we made in a brand spanking new, flash black sports car. Off we soared as Ged put his foot down and went like lightning through a red light and towards a slip road taking us to the relative safety of the M8 motorway and homeward bound.

On arriving back, we could afford to laugh a little, but only after a few drinks to calm down. It'd been a lucky escape through carnage resembling the battle scenes in Braveheart.

'Tell you what, Moet' I remember saying. 'It's never boring mate, is it?'

TWENTY-SIX YEARS
CHAPTER TWENTY SEVEN

Monday 3rd May 1993 (Part one)

It was only fair that when dawn finally broke over the River Irwell on that day of dreams, the boss man in the sky decreed:

That there should be sunshine. And the sun did shine.
That all beers should be drunk cold. And so it was.
That all songs should be sung loud. And so they were.
That all tears shed should be tears of joy. And they did indeed flood.
That all things worn should be red, white and black. And the world around us changed to those three colours.
And, that all those we loved should be hugged within an inch of their lives. Mother, fathers, brothers, sisters, wives and lovers. As for those no longer with us, we put a scarlet ribbon on their gravestone, so they could party too. The day had arrived and it was magnificent. A red letter day – scarlet and fierce.

For all Reds it had been an eternity. Twenty-six long, lean years while the Scousers taunted us just down the East Lancs. Now, there was a new word to be bandied around in Manchester – an old-world word snatched back from history. A word not to be used in London, Leeds, Liverpool or Birmingham, but Manchester... Manchester. The home of the Industrial Revolution. LS Lowry, Alan Turing, the first railway station, splitting the atom, the first computer. The city of the Busby Babes. Of Best, Law, Charlton. Of Baza Welsh, and now the new King – Cantona! It was Monday 3rd May 1993, and a word not sung for many moons could finally be shouted from the rooftops.

Champions!

Across a jumping, jubilant city, from Moston to Wythenshawe, Sale to Shaw. Ardwick, Ancoats, Collyhurst and Newton Heath. All points north. On the council estates of Harpurhey and Blackley they were dancing in the streets. Toasting with Strongbow, whiskey chasers and, for a change, half-decent wine in Collyhurst. The streets of Salford, that 'Dirty old town', United red throughout, simply went mad! Stretford, Urmston and Flixton were out on the roads. Stick a traffic cone down, pull out the tables, crack open a beer and drink and drink to 'Eric the King. The leader of our football team!'

From the hostelries of Altrincham to the wine bars of Hale, Bowdon and Alderley Edge they raised their glasses in the air. The red, white and black flags across Manchester not just flying high, but covering the sky. The party had begun! I'd best tell you how we got to this magical moment and what it meant to me.

One year previous…

It started with 'them' again.

You know who!

Sunday 26th April 1992

Anfield: of all teams it had to be this lot who put paid to our title challenge. After going head to head with Leeds all season we blew a gasket at the last, losing to Nottingham Forest at home, West Ham away, and then going down at Liverpool. It all ended in tears and recriminations. A 3-2 victory at Bramhall Lane earlier in the day for Howard Wilkinson's side meant that United had to win or it was all over. Alas, no rainbow's end as a home team pumped up beyond the heavens ran their hearts out to deny us, and a crowd equally excited danced on the grave of Manchester United's 1991–92 hopes in our attempt to end the twenty-five-year drought. They were deliriously happy knowing that they had ensured that our long wait would now go on. A veteran commentator for BBC Radio Merseyside stated, 'In all my years covering this club. All the trophies won. Never have I seen this stadium so fired up.'

Here, of all places, Manchester United were never going to be allowed the grace of keeping a fading dream alive. Despite three times striking the woodwork through Paul Ince, Brian McClair and Andrei Kanchelskis, it appeared the script had already been written. A game too far. Ian Rush, so deadly against any other team in Europe, not just England, finally broke a gypsy curse of never scoring against United, and at that moment we knew.

We just knew it.

All was wrapped up nicely for the Scousers in the dying moments when a Liverpool breakaway initially saw a Ray Houghton shot strike the bar, only to fall clear for winger Mark Walters, who fired home the rebound to send three-quarters of Anfield delirious with joy. Playing with all the desperation of a man being chased by a tiger, knowing he just had to keep running or else, United produced a brave last stand. A performance brimming with guts, and no lack of skill, but on a day when lady luck not so much turned her back, but spat in your face, we'd gone down. 'Always look on the bright side of life' mocked the Scousers with our own song. Another version also being belted out. 'Always look on the runway for ice.'

Neutrals shake their heads when they hear songs and chants and taunts like this, failing to understand the deep friction that exists between us. At the final whistle, as Alex Ferguson shepherded his devastated players off the pitch, a smiling Ronnie Moran sidled up to him, 'Heavy lies the crown Alex. Always in our shadow.' On leaving the ground to board the coach home to Manchester, two lads who weren't wearing any colours approached Ryan Giggs and Lee Sharpe. They handed over some paper and pens for both players' autographs and then proceeded to rip them up in their faces before throwing them on the floor. 'Fuck off Mancs,' was their taunt, delivered in a thick Scouse accent as they walked off laughing their cocks off after what was a great day for them.

Ferguson noticed this and headed over. 'Ryan, Lee, you remember what's just happened here. This is what being a Manchester United player is all about. The jealousy and hatred here is all they have left to hold onto. So, take a deep breath, close your eyes and remember their faces. Because, I promise you, one day, we won't just knock them off their perch, we'll smash it into a thousand pieces. Now, get on the coach.'

Wednesday 25th November 1992.

A drizzly, miserable, grey Mancunian afternoon loomed and United's still youthful, fifty-two-year old manager, Alex Ferguson, was sitting in his chairman Martin Edwards' office, deliberating over buying a striker. United's goals had dried up dramatically. A measly seventeen in sixteen games, stuck in a lowly eighth position and already looking out of the title race. A broken leg suffered by summer signing Dion Dublin from Cambridge and Mark Hughes and Brian McClair misfiring badly meant we had to move fast. They spoke about Sheffield Wednesday's powerful David Hirst and had already bid £3.5 million for him. Sadly, Edwards told Ferguson, Wednesday's manager Trevor Francis had no intention of selling. Others on the list included Southampton's Alan Shearer, but the word was he'd already provisionally signed up to Jack Walker's bankrolled Blackburn Rovers, now coached by Kenny Dalglish. Even United couldn't compete with what Walker was throwing around. Blackburn were the new kids on the block and they were desperate to make a mark. Everton's Peter Beardsley was another player mentioned, but again that was a deal that couldn't be pulled off. Out of the blue, Edwards' phone rang and it was Leeds United's financial Director Bill Fotherby, asking Ferguson if he'd consider selling Denis Irwin.

'They want to know if you'd consider selling them Denis Irwin?'

One look at Ferguson's face gave Edwards his answer.

He got back on the line to Fotherby. 'I'm afraid not Bill, I've got Alex here with me now.' An idea came into the United manager's head. He swiftly scribbled down a player's name and passed it to Edwards. 'Before you go off the line Bill. What's the possibility of us having Eric Cantona off you?'

Seldom has a spontaneous idea or thought delivered such incredible joy for so many people. This was a moment of genius. Historic.

The line went quiet and Edwards looked across to Ferguson. After a moment Fotherby came back on. 'Well, I know Cantona and Howard don't see eye to eye. He's a strange one is Eric. Let me have a word and I'll ring you back.'

The phone went down. A shot in the dark, Fergie's intuition – call it what you want.

The Seagull was set to land at Old Trafford.

The trawler was about to set sail.

Saturday 9th January 1993.

As the referee Mr Peck from Kendal blew to end the match, Old Trafford erupted. Manchester United 4, Tottenham Hotspur 1. All present on that day knew, on this cold and dark late January afternoon, that they'd witnessed something quite extraordinary. This was not just a performance laced with wonderful flair and three points that saw us go top of the table above Norwich City. It contained a moment of pure genius – on fifty-two minutes. The moment of bliss was conjured up by the magical right foot of our new number seven. The majestic, straight-backed Frenchman strode around the pitch like a peacock on speed. He made a pass of such sweet touch and beauty that it caused the kind of gasps from the crowd that are normally reserved for the ballet, not a simple football match. It made grown men cry. In fact, it wasn't a pass but more of a kiss. We were already a goal up through a first-half Eric Cantona header.

Our new talisman was ably abetted by a blistering supporting cast of supreme quality in Giggs, Sharpe and, late in the match, Kanchelskis. With Hughes and McClair back in equally explosive form, inspired by the French phenomenon and wreaking havoc, waves of red shirts ran riot against a shell-shocked Spurs team, who from the first minute to the last that day hadn't known what hit them. Even the full-backs Paul Parker and Denis Irwin hurtled over the halfway line at every opportunity to join in the carnage. Certain that every run would be found by Cantona's inner radar. His ability to pick out a pass sometimes verged on the supernatural, with balls not so much passed as guided by mystical power. Alex Ferguson watched on from his seat with a look of satisfaction and, like everyone else in the stadium, a sense of wonder.

Seven minutes after half-time, Cantona played a one-two with the darting Irwin that didn't so much dissect the Spurs defence as put a spell on them. A delicate, unerring chip shot collected by the Irishman who ran onto it and fired it gloriously past the diving goalkeeper Erik Thorvstedt. Old Trafford went wild! Enraptured. Even after the cheering had died down for the goal, a special whispering hush settled across the stands. One that signalled that something truly special had just occurred.

In a blink of an eye, a moment of magic, Cantona had opened every United supporter's eyes wide… Every player's too, for that matter.

Just what the hell had we got on our hands?

Saturday 10th April 1993.

An Easter miracle.

'We didn't start playing until the 90th minute.' – Alex Ferguson.

Manchester United were at home, and with just over an hour gone against Sheffield Wednesday, Old Trafford was quivering – a nervous wreck.

It was a stiflingly hot day and United's play was littered with errors. The expectant crowd groaned and moaned. After our recent blistering performances, flushed with tempo, the level of expectation meant we expected a goal fest, but it proved anything but. The title race had evolved into a straight shoot-out between United and Aston Villa. They had the edge. If they won all their remaining games then the league was theirs. It was essential that we didn't drop any points, but as the shadows danced across huge swathes of the pitch, hopes dimmed.

As the second half drifted on uneventfully, a breakthrough seemed increasingly unlikely. Our clever ball players, such as Eric Cantona and Ryan Giggs, were experiencing the kind of day that every magician dreaded. It was a day when the rabbits simply refused to emerge from the hat and the magician dies a death on the stage. A Tommy Cooper moment! As for the visitors, Trevor Francis's Sheffield Wednesday seemed content to just sit and wait for an opportunity to truly ruin our day and our season. With ex-United player Viv Anderson and my old pal, the gangling but effective Carlton Palmer defending heroically, all paths to goal were blocked off. A concerned Fergie turned to his substitute and now elder statesman Bryan Robson. Eternally cursed by injuries, Robson still played an integral part in matters of the United dressing room and, when fit, remained an important player for the manager. Respected beyond words by Fergie for his courage and leadership, Robbo's appearance as he warmed up on the touchline earned one of the loudest cheers of the day from the home supporters.

Suddenly, the referee pulled up injured and the game was halted for quite a while. Struggling badly, Ref Peck motioned that he couldn't carry on and the whistle was handed to the substitute referee/linesman Mr John Hilditch. A seven-minute stoppage. Hilditch restarted and the game continued with the clock already showing 4:30pm. Sheffield Wednesday winger Chris Waddle raced into the United penalty area. He dropped a shoulder and went to beat Paul Ince, who sent him crashing to the ground. A small pocket of South Yorkshire roared loud and Mr Hilditch pointed to the penalty spot. No argument. A blatant foul by Ince. Who stepped up? None other than a boyhood United supporter, Stretford's own John Sheridan, expected to possibly hammer a final nail into his hometown club's title challenge. Sheridan appeared cool, calm and collected. His two brothers watching on from an angst-ridden Stretford End, were the opposite.

'Please miss, our kid. Please.' Many couldn't or simply refused to watch. There was a funeral-type, strange silence around the stadium. The only voices heard were prayers and insults. Steve Bruce sidled up to Sheridan as he prepared to take the kick. 'You're a Red aren't you John?' he said smiling.

Sheridan stared hard at him. 'Not today mate.'

Up he strode to stroke the ball past Peter Schmeichel with ease and he rolled away, punching the air. Old Trafford watching on aghast. Fergie put an arm around Bryan Robson's shoulders.

'Get on and sort it out son,' Robson smiled. A battle or two remained in the old warrior yet. On he went to replace Paul Parker as the noise level rose, with the realisation hitting Old Trafford that an entire season rested on the last twenty minutes.

Immediately, Captain Marvel flew into the Wednesday players, tackling like his life depended on it. With Robbo now alongside him shouting and grimacing, Ince found a new lease of life and, after what felt like an eternity, Manchester United woke up. Led by Robson, the team roared on, fuelled by an equally desperate crowd who now knew their team needed nothing short of an Easter miracle to rescue even a point. Still Wednesday fought back, unyielding, with Anderson and Palmer standing tall. Maybe it's fate or maybe destiny's child decrees it – some things are just not meant to be. You're allowed the odd cup competition and the agony of coming second. You can't always win – and if you did then victory could never be so sweet. We'll tease you with the dream, then like water dripping through your hands, take it away and nail you to the floor. My United Road looked set to hit another huge bump – it seemed by now that I'd never see the Reds achieve the ultimate accolade of champions. I had begun to feel that that honour only belonged to London, Leeds, Liverpool and Birmingham.

With only four minutes on a clock that was ticking down quickly – strange how when you're winning it goes slowly and when you're losing it goes like a train – we won a corner. Ryan Giggs raced across to take it. The boy from Salford, a United supporter, stolen from the grasps of City as a thirteen-year-old by Fergie with his legendary powers of persuasion. The man himself watched on, eyes totally focused on Bryan Robson, who was standing on the edge of the penalty area determined to score. In came Giggs' corner and as Robson started his run, Steve Bruce met it from twelve yards and fired a guided header high past Woods into the top corner. Old Trafford erupted in sheer joy – and relief. Get in there Brucie!

The Captain was mobbed by his grateful teammates and disappeared under a sea of red. Still, Fergie's gaze never left Robson, who rushed into the goalmouth without any hesitation after Bruce's effort and ended up in the back of the net, taking two Sheffield Wednesday defenders with him. He knew how important every second was – he wasn't ready to celebrate a draw! He was a man with a mission – every cell in his body was blood red and fired up.

The pressure for a late winner became utterly relentless. The country listened on, as all the other games had finished by then. Ince spread a long raking pass wide to Ryan Giggs on the left wing and his cross almost led to an own goal by an exhausted Viv Anderson, who stabbed it inches wide of the post for yet another United corner. The clock turned five and still the game went on. Giggs sprinted across to take the corner – this time from the left. The ball was cleared but fatefully it fell back at the feet of the dancing Welshman. Looking up and scanning the scene, Giggs tried again, only for the ball to overrun and head over towards the far right-hand touchline. It reached the unlikely forward figure of Gary Pallister. His cross deflected back over the penalty area landing, heaven-sent, into the path of an on-rushing Steve Bruce, who smashed another unstoppable header past Woods, to send Old Trafford spinning wildly out of control!

No one was spared the madness and delirium that swept over the stadium, with even Alex Ferguson and Brian Kidd going momentarily crazy and becoming honorary members of the Stretford End. Ferguson charged down from the stand dancing a manic, Scottish victory jig! His face had gone to heaven and back. Kiddo ran even further past the manager onto the pitch, sliding to his knees. Arms raised, eyes to the sky. Sheer joy etched on so many faces. For this was the day. This was the hour and this was the moment. The moment we had all been waiting for. This was the moment that fate, destiny and lady luck had finally looked around this famous old ground and changed sides. Trevor Francis must have rued missing out on Cantona – who'd been offered to Wednesday and had trained with them after being retired for a while after calling each member of a disciplinary committee an idiot – one at a time.

Manchester United and Aston Villa remained within a hair's breadth of each other in the title race. An angry, disbelieving and fretful Trevor Francis slammed the amount of injury time added on by the ref, claiming, 'United got the winner on Sunday!' We now led Villa by a point at the top of the table and we were beginning to believe, for the first time in a generation, that the footballing gods were smiling upon us. Something was most definitely in the air.

Wednesday 21st April 1993.

With the title now so close you could smell the Duraglit, fifteen thousand loyal Manchester United supporters turned up at Selhurst Park for the next to last away game of the season, against Crystal Palace. Every travelling supporter was there to burst his or her lungs to roar the Reds over the line. Just as many had gathered back at Old Trafford, watching the game on a close circuit screen. On the radio, news broke that Villa were already behind at Ewood Park. A cheer went up, then another. It was 2-0! Suddenly, amongst the United supporters the noise level switched from nervous excitement to near euphoria as the realisation struck that we were almost there! Win the final two games at home to Blackburn and away, back at Selhurst Park versus Wimbledon this time and Manchester United were closing in on the title. Nothing surely – neither fate nor injuries nor fixture congestions – no amount of screaming diatribe from Leeds, Liverpool or City could halt that fact.

There was still a job to be done against Crystal Palace and, with the Eagles involved in a desperate relegation scramble, it promised to be anything but a walkover. The game began as a cagey affair. United, playing in their third strip of yellow and green shirts, the old Newton Heath colours, from the days when we were just a railway workers team – my granddad would often tell me about this and even which pub they changed in before and after matches. Yes, no changing rooms for the green and gold of Newton Heath, back in the day – wonder how Paul Pogba would feel about that now?! I digress. Anyway, United just couldn't settle that day with misplaced passes and no fluency in their play. It was obvious that the team had the jitters.

Another roar erupted from the United enclaves – Blackburn were now three up against a Villa team in meltdown. Bleedin' hell!

The passion and furore bellowing from the volcano of the away masses lifted high into the South London evening sky. On the pitch, only Eric Cantona rose above the hundred-miles-an-hour frantic football from both sides. His touch was sublime and his composure on the ball, when others around him were treating it like a hand grenade, was a sight to behold. Ironically, on an evening when calm heads amongst the Mancunians were in short supply, it was the tempestuous Frenchman with his legendary short fuse, the length of a matchstick, who was in the eye of the storm when all around were losing it. Half time arrived and Fergie rose swiftly from the visitors' bench with a look of relief. United reappeared for the second half a team reborn. Their football was now crisp and incisive. Cantona, at their very heart, was probing and setting the tempo as yellow/green shirts finally responded to his sleight of touch, deft flicks, and short but devastating passes. What a football genius we were witnessing, in his pomp and prime. On sixty-five minutes, Cantona attacked down the left and his wonderfully delivered cross found the right foot of Mark Hughes. Steadying himself, Hughes let fly a typically thunderous volley that flew like a cannonball past the Palace goalkeeper Nigel Martyn into the top corner! A magnificent Sparky strike and his 100th league goal for the club – one greeted by United supporters with scenes of utter joy. Back at Old Trafford they were also dancing in the aisles! Aston Villa had been beaten, so victory over Blackburn in five days on home turf would secure United's first title in twenty-six years. The game raged on. Only a minute remained. The ball landed at Cantona's feet. The tumult from the crowd was deafening. There were tears on the faces of United supporters.

So close. So, so close. Selhurst Park had turned into Manchester, or it certainly felt like it.

Spotting a run from Paul Ince, Cantona's astutely placed pass found him with ease. Ince took the ball in his stride and fired low past Martin to signal unbelievable riotous scenes on the United terraces! Only a collapse of biblical proportions could stop us now. A journey that had begun in a sepia Manchester, masking our old kit colours, was set to be realised in modern technicolour times with a party the likes of which this city had not witnessed since the end of World War Two! Fergie hugged Brian Kidd on the touchline. They both knew we were almost there. Almost there. If Villa didn't beat a struggling Oldham Athletic at home on the following Sunday, the title would be ours – but that was clearly asking too much.

Surely?

Sunday 2nd May 1993.

It had begun the day before. Just after 5:45pm United supporters around Manchester, England and the world were watching the dying embers of Aston Villa versus Oldham Athletic on Sky Sports – teeth gnashing, hands clasped behind heads, breathless moments. The air was tense at Villa Park because Latics were leading 1-0 with just seconds left to play. If the score stayed the same, then not only would Oldham have saved themselves from relegation, but Manchester United would be crowned champions twenty-six agonising years after their last title. It was 'squeaky bum time', in Sir Alex's own words.

The world seemed to stand still and I could hardly bear to watch. I kicked every ball away from the Latics' half and headed every ball. I was on the pitch in my head fighting against Villa for my life, screaming and shouting like a lunatic.

The final whistle blew and the whole of Manchester went mad! As for the squad who had finally ended the curse and caused most of our great city to jump into a barrel of beer – they went mental as well. Many of the players had gathered at Steve Bruce's house and they partied long and hard. What began as a small get together with close friends and neighbours swiftly grew into a full-scale celebration as team mates naturally migrated to their Captain's home. Soon all were present, and any thoughts of the next day's game disappeared. The unyielding pressure forever present in the closing months of the campaign had given way to one almighty blow out! Last orders didn't apply at the Bruce's. Tell me one United fan that didn't go out on that Sunday evening when Oldham got that result at Villa Park, or at least crack open a good few beers at home? I remember standing there with my mates at the bar with that first pint feeling a strange mixture of relief and excitement – but also disbelief. We'd finally done it.

Champions !

The word rolled easily off the tongue despite the fact that it'd been a long twenty-six years and there had been casualties on and off the pitch (including me!). Now, the carnival was set to roll – for Fergie and his boys had finally laid that ghost to rest.

Get in there my United!

CHAMPIONS
CHAPTER TWENTY EIGHT

Monday 3rd May 1993. (Part two)

'Who's the Champions now, scum? Who's the Champions now?' we all sang to the tune of tie me kangaroo down sport. Aimed at Leeds? Liverpool? Both? Take your pick. Over in Liverpool, Graham Souness must also have rued the fact that he too had failed to take up the offer of Cantona! And how did Leeds feel to have handed us the title with the sale of Le Roi!!?

The celebrations continued all the way through to the following bank holiday Monday and, as I walked down Warwick Road early afternoon ahead of an evening kick-off against Blackburn, it was already clear that the mother of all parties was under way!

I finally met Billy G and Pigeon Les across Trafford Bridge on Salford Quays, at Pier Six. There were proper hugs of relief and we all had grins wider than the Irwell. We had waited such a long, long time for this. Get the beers in!

Billy and Les had grown up together. They were closer than brothers. Whilst Billy had lived the dream and played fifty-one times for United, Les followed his own path. A path at times troubled. But nothing ever came between them.

As kids, they'd both been brought up in the shadow of Old Trafford and minded supporters' cars – for a small fee of course. Then, with the money they'd made, they'd nip off to watch the match. From their Ordsall homes, the glow from the floodlight pylons and thunderous roar of the crowd was a constant childhood companion. United lived both in the lads' backyards and in their hearts.

It was tough love growing up in Salford, but when it came to Manchester United, there was just one love. Their adventures growing up together are legendary; the tales outrageous and hilarious – but maybe better left for their own books!

What was certain for me was that I couldn't have had two finer friends to share that special day with. Now, since first going to Old Trafford as a snotty kid with my Uncle Al some eighteen years before, two of the biggest challenges were how far you could sling a bog roll onto the pitch, or whether you could get a song going. Not just your mates singing it, but the whole stand. That was the ultimate and I was, albeit out of tune most of the time, a songbird! Well, on the Quays that afternoon, myself, Les and Billy started the French anthem 'La Marseillaise' and finished it with 'Oo, ah, Cantona!' – Cantona being Marseille's finest son! The song rippled through the bar and carried outside onto the pub concourse and down Trafford Road. We sang for twenty minutes and a lot of the lads who hadn't heard it before joined in. Soon red choirs of our French anthem version of 'Ooh, ah, Cantona' rang out across the quay. We were like kids again, 'Fuckin' ell Welshy!' said Les. 'What have we started?'

'Listen to 'em,' laughed Billy. 'They're singing our song!'

As the sun split the flags on the Salford Quays, in all my years, even to this day, I've never experienced anything like what occurred in our dirty old town, back on that early, warm May day back in 1993.

When our dreams came true.

Approaching kick off with the United players nursing hangovers and sweating the booze out, Fergie was able to name a full-strength team. In the dressing room he'd gathered all his players and staff together and stood facing them. 'I want you all to look around this room because without each and every one here we could not have won this league. Now you've all done absolutely marvellous. Aye, I'm bloody proud of every single one of you.'

He focused his death stare on the players. Many of them still dog rough and desperate not to catch the manager's eye. 'Now, I'm not even going to ask what you lot got up to last night. I don't want to know.' That said, Ferguson's glance turned towards Steve Bruce, who swiftly put his head down smiling. 'I don't want this lot turning up here tonight and ruining it for everybody. Dalglish will have his players wound up and ready for a scrap, so if you're not up for it, they'll turn us over. Now, your fitness is good. Despite the rumours I've been hearing today and looking at the state of some of you. Whoever doesn't perform in the first half is coming off for Robbo in the second, so make sure you're on your game. And, finally, this is one of the few occasions where you can just go out and enjoy it. So, express yourselves. Soak it all up… But win!'

Laughter broke out around the room, but the message was clear from the manager. Defeat for Fergie on this of all nights wouldn't be tolerated.

There have been many special nights under the Old Trafford floodlights. Wonderful atmospheres, spine-chilling occasions, but as the cry on the terraces began with 'Bring on the champions,' I looked around in my daze and thought this must have been one of the best ever. Few have ever come close to matching or beating what occurred on this warm Mancunian summer's evening – the night of Monday 3rd May 1993. The United crowd had become a single singing and dancing organism – a tight-knit, deliriously happy community of mates and brothers and dads, sisters, uncles and aunts. A joyous gang of fellow souls sharing the glory and the wonder of basking as champions. At last. 'Championes Championes!!!'

Amongst the crowd, the flags, banners and scarves waving there were as many tears as smiles. Thoughts of those no longer present who didn't live to see such riches. Twenty-six years is an awful lot of funerals. United season tickets are passed down through families like their DNA. The average age of a ticket holder is about 92 because no one dares admit that they are using a ticket that has been passed on through the generations. The faces may change, even names, but the passion like Manchester United never dies.

The players, led by Steve Bruce, obviously in their red, black and white, were met by a wall of noise from the 40,447 who were fortunate to be present that night. They headed into the centre-circle to accept the acclaim of the rapturous Red Army. As Queen's anthem 'We are the champions!' blasted out, the home team broke away for a kick about. The anthems continued with a tribute to their latest hero and legend already in the making. 'Ooh, ah, Cantona' started up and it swiftly resonated around all parts of the stadium. Intoxicated with a magical cocktail of alcohol and euphoria, the ecstatic red choir began singing as one, hailing the new king from across the channel. Cantona cut a calm composed figure. The trademark shirt collar up and ready for battle. Magnifique!

As Alex Ferguson had warned his team beforehand, Blackburn, managed by an enemy in the form of Kenny Dalglish, turned up planning not just to poop on the party as to chuck a grenade into the punch bowl! To piss on our Bonnie! United started nervously, with passes going astray all over the field. No one in a red shirt seemed capable of even trapping a ball, never mind creating an opportunity. Even Cantona was affected. His first touch, normally so assured, deserted him. The Rovers, meanwhile, were fast, hard-tackling and seemingly intent on turning this Mancunian fiesta into a damp squib. On eight minutes, midfielder Jason Wilcox played a pass out wide for his full-back Nicky Marker to cross low, and Scottish international forward Kevin Gallagher lashed a sensational near-post effort past a stunned Schmeichel into the top corner. On the ball hitting the net, the roar of 'Champions' started up loudly once again from the Old Trafford terraces to rouse the team. More importantly, Fergie headed down to the touchline, his face reddening with fury, his arm gesticulating angrily. A look that said more than a thousand threats and a message that was succinct and clear: 'Step it up or else.' As though he'd pressed a switch, a light bulb switched on. United clicked in and began to resemble their true selves. The passing became swift, incisive and slick with one man at its red heart. Cantona's radar was back on.

The runs of Hughes, Giggs and Sharpe were reached with precision by the Frenchman's exocets. On twenty-one minutes Paul Ince was fouled and Ryan Giggs stepped up from nearly thirty yards to flash a left-footed free kick into the top right-hand corner past a stunned Bobby Mimms. 1-1!

Old Trafford exploded in delight at this wonderful goal by the prodigious Giggs. Fergie himself beamed widely at the supreme skill of the youngster who already had the footballing world drooling at his dancing feet. A boy wonder who was beginning to remind many older supporters of a past United legend. A local kid, but sadly for us born in Wales, as were all his forebears, whose lightning pace off the mark, bewildering dribbling and balletic grace and movement over the grass saw him illuminate countless grey Mancunian afternoons. The word on Ryan Giggs was that even George Best rated him. High praise indeed!

Half time arrived and, as promised, Ferguson introduced his talisman, Bryan Robson. The second period was one-way traffic as Manchester United played with a freedom of expression that came from the knowledge that you're the best. At their very heart – who else but Cantona.

It became a siege with the Frenchman creating havoc, no more so than when he produced a delicious sliding pass, taking out three Rovers shirts, for Paul Ince to race onto and fire low past Mimms from eight yards. A cameo of our season. The class of '93.

In the dying seconds, Cantona again danced through a host of defenders on the edge of the penalty area to set up Mark Hughes, only for him to be brought crashing to the ground. A free kick. Only one Manchester United outfield player had yet to score in the campaign and, as Old Trafford held its collective breath, Gary Pallister was called for. Smiling widely, he lumbered upfield and casually lashed a right foot shot into the net that Mimms never even saw. A perfect way to end the game. Then came the moment that all those with United in their heart had been waiting a generation for.

On a starlit Mancunian evening in front of a deafening, emotionally packed Old Trafford, Steve Bruce and Bryan Robson prepared together to hoist up high the Premiership trophy and officially signify the end of a twenty-six-year drought – well, it's probably more accurate to say that it had pissed it down for 26 years and the sunshine was just about to begin! Hysterical joy and camaraderie and an overwhelming sense of relief filled the air. The albatross disguised as a liver bird that had circled Old Trafford for a generation had had its neck wrung!

Sitting quietly near to where Bruce and Robson stood to collect the trophy was an elderly gentleman. Eight decades and three years old. Forever immortalised in the legendary Spinners' tribute song about the players lost at Munich, The Flowers of Manchester, as 'The Father of this football team.' This man had arrived at a bombed and burnt-out ground in his thirties. Manchester United was on its knees after World War Two. Along with his assistant Jimmy Murphy and with the memories of those who had been lost as buttresses, they laid the foundations of what United is today. A worldwide phenomenon.

From the blood-drenched, sleet covered runway of Munich to European Cup glory within ten years. Then he had retired and the walls of the kingdom had begun to crumble. Manchester United fell from grace... until this moment. A smiling Sir Matt Busby watched on, with tears in his eyes, but fiercely proud, as amidst a thousand flashlights, blinding and illuminating the black Manchester sky, Bruce and Robson lifted the Holy Grail of Manchester United. The chalice of our Red dreams. Old Trafford erupted and my United were back!

Immediately after the presentation on the pitch, Manchester United physio Jim McGregor walked amongst the jubilant players handing out Morson baseball caps, not forgetting made by Welsport. Billy had dropped them off at the Cliff and had asked Jim whether he would mind passing them around when the time came. Meanwhile, on honeymoon, 6791 miles away in the Philippines, watching on with a celebratory drink in hand, Ged Mason spotted the caps and almost spat out his Moet. As a lifelong United supporter, life couldn't get much sweeter for Ged than seeing his friends and heroes Bryan Robson, Steve Bruce, Ryan Giggs and co. with the world's spotlight upon them, all wearing caps with the Morson name on them as they ran round the pitch with the Premiership Trophy! That extra sweet flourish didn't last long though, because the very next day all hell broke loose when Ged received a call from back home. It was his dad. Gerry had just put the phone down after taking a call from a fuming United chairman Martin Edwards on the subject of the baseball caps. Apparently, the club's main sponsors SHARP ELECTRONICS were up in arms that the United players had been photographed wearing unofficial branded gear. Suddenly, Ged was in the dog house, not only with his dad, Edwards and the sponsors, but also soon with the players who'd worn the caps – as they all received club fines. Happily, it soon died down, and Moet Mason, like the rest of us could bask in the glory that summer singing Queen's 'We are the champions', and finally mean it.

As for myself, Billy and Les? Following the match our marathon drinking spree continued unabated. After a few more hours revelry at the Jubilee pub in the heart of the Ordsall estate and then the Oxford pub in Manchester, with Salford's shall we just say uncrowned royalty, we got word that the United players had decamped to the Amblehurst. Billy rang up from a phone behind the bar to double check. He asked to speak to Bryan Robson. Robbo came on the line and told Billy to jump in a taxi and join the party. On arrival, United's main security man Ned Kelly was on the door. He recognised us and in we went.

What a privilege to be there, in the flesh, on this of all nights. A night that would go down in Manchester United folklore. I got to drink with the lads who had made it all possible. Memories tend to blur, but I do remember Les posing in Gary Pallister's ridiculously loud jacket and getting his picture taken with some Cypriot supporters staying at the hotel, whilst claiming to be a player – beaming at the camera with teeth like Liberace's keyboard framed with his famous grin! I saw the night through the bottom of a pint pot and a whisky glass so it's hard to recall everything that happened, but the buzz and the sense of wonder has never left me.

It so happened that I was about to get married and my stag was the very next day – well, the same day by the time we'd finished, I suppose! I'd booked the United team club coach to take myself and a load of mates to Chester Races. I remember Robbo coming up and asking if he and the other players could tag along. Tag along! Fuckin' 'ell! Then, I remembered there were no seats left on the coach. What could I do? No way could I turf somebody off. It just wasn't right. 'Not a problem' replied a smiling Robbo. 'I'll book something and we'll just follow behind.'

So, it came to pass that the next day a pile of half-dead, still-pissed-up Reds filled the official United coach singing about being champions, while the champions themselves trailed behind us in a little white clapped out minibus! Utterly surreal.

Pigeon Les never made the Chester trip. He'd simply, in a metaphorical way, hit a wall. After the Amblehurst, Les somehow found himself at Smithfield market in Manchester in the early hours. He got himself a fry up breakfast and, not fancying the walk home back into Salford, 'borrowed' a flower van. Typically though, Les later rang the owner telling him, 'Your van is on Liverpool Road mate, with the key under the wheel!'

Those two days could never be recreated. Everything was simply perfect.

My enduring memory was of singing right through the night:

"We are the champions, my friends,
And we'll keep on fighting 'til the end."

UNCLE MATT (Part two)
CHAPTER TWENTY NINE

'The great Matt Busby lay there, the father of his team.
Three long months passed by before he saw his team again.'
The Flowers of Manchester

Almost every birthday, Christmas or Easter celebration, I'd meet Sir Matt. He became 'Uncle Matt' and his daughter 'Auntie Sheena', yet still I'd stare across, at the old Scot, utterly blown away that I was sitting at the same table or in the same room as one of the ultimate living legends of my football club.

Sir Matt had charisma. Anyone in his company could not fail to see that he possessed greatness.

We got on so well. Saying that, it was impossible not to.

Sir Matt had a warm and calming presence about him – an aura. A man of few words maybe, though I cherished every one that he spoke. To this day as I write, I fondly remember his laugh. Strange to say though, I never, ever, once spoke about football with him, even though I ached to. It simply never felt like the right time to mention it. I'd wait for him to start the conversation about a game or the team but – nothing. United, especially Munich, just never came up in conversation, and I had far too much respect and love for the man to even approach the subject.

If I'm honest, to me he was more Saint Matt than Uncle Matt. A superhero who loved his whiskey – in moderation of course! He'd always say, 'A nice healthy dram is good for you before you go to bed.' He was always telling me wee stories from his early days in Glasgow. On one particular night at a house party, his Mum had told him off in front of everyone! 'Matthew, you're drunk! Whatever will you be doing next?'

He laughed saying, 'Nick, I was twenty-two years of age!'

Sir Matt's son Sandy was another Busby diamond, a chip off the old block, who I also got to know well over this time. Once when Sir Alex was in our group at Haydock races, Sandy turned to me and said quietly, 'You know what Nick, it's frightening when I sit and listen to Sir Alex. It might as well be my dad talking.' When you look at both characters though, they do share some remarkable resemblances. Neither took the step straight into football. Whereas Sir Matt went down the Orbiston coal pits for a while, Sir Alex was an apprentice tool maker in the Govan shipyards. These times in their lives undoubtedly shaped them as people and I don't think they ever lost the working man's mentality and principles. Simple, old fashioned customs and values that were instilled in them both for life.

So you won't be surprised to hear me say that the only other man I've met who gives off the same aura as Sir Matt is – Sir Alex. A breed apart these Scottish men of granite, morals and huge hearts.

As anyone who knows me will tell you, I love a good sing song after a few beverages, even though they'll also tell you I'm hardly Frank bloody Sinatra. Thankfully, Uncle Matt did too, but he had just one song which he taught me off by heart. We'd often end the night singing it.

I've been wi' a few o' my cronies,
One or two pals o' my ain;
We went in a hotel,
We did very well,
Aye and then we came out once again.
And then we went into another
That is the reason I'm fu';
We had six deoch-an-doruses,
Then sang a chorus,
Just listen, I'll sing it to you!

I belong to Glasgow,
Dear old Glasgow town,
But there's something the matter with Glasgow,
For it's going round and round!
I'm only a common old workin' lad,
As anyone can see,
But when I get a couple o' drinks on a Saturday,
Glasgow belongs to me!

There's nothing in being teetotal
And saving a shilling or two.
If your money you spend,

You've nothing to lend,
Isn't that all the better for you!
There's nae harm in takin' a drappie,
It ends all your troubles and strife!
And it gives ya a feeling that, when you land home,
Well you don't care a hang for your wife!

I belong to Glasgow,
Dear old Glasgow town,
But there's something the matter with Glasgow,
For it's going round and round?
I'm only a common old workin' lad,
As anyone can see,
But when I get a couple o' drinks on a Saturday,
Glasgow belongs to me!

On Thursday 20th January 1994, Sir Matt Busby, aged 84, passed away quietly at the Alexandra hospital in Cheadle, Stockport. He was surrounded at the end by his loved ones and he would finally get to meet up with his lovely wife Jean and the lads he'd lost on that Munich runway half a lifetime ago, none of whom had ever left his heart. Though it was heart-breaking, it wasn't such a sudden shock, for we knew Uncle Matt had been very poorly for some time. Even still, there was always a part of you that thought, after what he'd endured at and after Munich and after recovering from a stroke back in 1980, that this remarkable old gentleman would live forever. Sadly, no one does, and as the news was released Manchester fell deep into mourning.

Outside Old Trafford, in the middle of winter, a quiet and shocked crowd gathered to share their grief and a sea of unseasonal flowers began to spread over the forecourt. Flags, scarves, teddy bears, private messages to the father of our football club.

Denis Law was interviewed by ITV news and broke down in tears whilst Bobby Charlton, quick to cry, simply couldn't speak because he was too choked up.

United were due to play Everton at home the following Saturday and I invited my then father-in-law Peter to attend using one of our family's season tickets. He had been one of Sir Matt's closest friends for many years and it was simply the right thing to do.

Come Saturday afternoon at ten minutes to three, a lone piper led the two teams out from the tunnel into a veil of tears. Old Trafford stood silent, the piercing wail of the mournful pipes cutting across the packed terraces, full of solemn tear-stained faces. The television cameras cut to an inconsolable George Best. He wasn't alone. Black ribbons had been placed on Sir Matt's seat. The sight of that alone was enough to break any Red heart.

After a period of silence where the only sound you could hear was of sobbing fans and hearts breaking, the referee blew his whistle and the crowd exploded in a cacophony of sound. Lungs burst and heads throbbed with emotion. There was a gigantic release of emotion that I swear could be heard above in heaven and far away on that Munich runway which had so shaped Sir Matt Busby's life, and where the souls of so many of his babes had departed this earth.

A very special mention to the Everton fans present that day. They acted with class and respected what was, for my Manchester United, in essence, a funeral without a body. We'd lost our Sir Matt…

Finally, the game began and, fittingly, United played exceptionally well. The football was free flowing with the star man undoubtedly being a young winger full of tricks, light as a feather and rapier quick. Ryan Giggs led the Everton defence a merry dance throughout and it was his headed goal that handed the Reds a 1-0 win, though in reality it could and should've been a rout. Yet, on that late, cold January afternoon under a sombre, black Mancunian sky, Giggsy had warmed the hearts of supporters and handed them the gift of being able to smile through what had been truly a sad day, as Old Trafford bade goodbye to the boss. Giggsy epitomised what Sir Matt always demanded of a United player and it was fitting that he had played so well that day, as we honoured the memory of that special man.

After the game I dropped Peter off at his house in Hale – named Lynwood after his good lady – and he asked me in for a drink. They'd a nice bar in the house that Peter had built himself. Already perched at the bar was Auntie Sheena. I walked over and gave her a huge hug.

Sheena accompanied her dad almost everywhere and she and her three daughters, unsurprisingly, were United daft. I pulled a stool up alongside her and we began to talk. I told her all about what Old Trafford had been like that afternoon as the piper appeared and the sheer emotion in and around the old place. How proud her dad would've been. She'd wanted to go, but felt it wasn't right until Sir Matt had been laid to rest.

'Can I tell you something Nick?' she asked.

'Of course,' I replied.

She then revealed to me something that left me with a tingling chill down my back – every hair on my body pricked up. Late the previous evening, Sheena's doorbell had rung and she'd gone to answer it. Standing there, ashen-faced, was the United legend Harry Gregg. He apologised for calling unannounced at such an awkward hour, but had flown in earlier that evening from his home in Ireland and just wanted to see Matt's body and pay his respects. This was no problem for Sheena and she warmly welcomed him inside. They settled down and got talking over a bottle of whiskey about a man who meant the absolute world to them both. Then, Harry started to open up. He told her, 'I've never told this story to anyone, friends, family or obviously the press, but on the night of the crash I found myself out on the runway. I looked over, and I saw your dad across the tarmac lying on his back. Now, your dad Sheena love, never swore, but he said to me, 'I've broken my bastard back, leave me be and go and check for others in that plane.' Harry stopped for a moment to regain his composure, but then continued on. 'I always did whatever your dad told me to do, we all did, so I crawled back into that burning aeroplane. Everyone always calls me a hero and that upsets me – because I was just doing what the boss, your dad, asked me to do.'

The rest is history...

I sat listening to Sheena tell this remarkable story, which was a piece of our club's amazing tapestry.

Thursday 27th January 1994 was the day of the funeral. You won't be surprised to learn that the skies above Manchester were weeping tears of rain. Endless drizzle. The service was at Our Lady and Saint John's in Chorlton. Local flower shops had run out of roses. The roads and streets that the funeral cortege would take were lined with people waiting patiently to honour the father of our Club.

On the hearse carrying Sir Matt's coffin was a huge red and white floral tribute inscribed simply with the words 'THE BOSS'.

I remember a full primary school, every age group present, standing to attention on the road in the pouring rain on our short trip from Chorlton to Old Trafford.

Thousands stood in silent tribute as the cortege stopped for a minute outside the ground, and then a miracle occurred. The rain momentarily stopped! As we headed off to Southern Cemetery people began applauding. Faces etched with tears. Again, on the return leg, the pavements remained full, yet were so deadly quiet. Heads were bowed. If such a thing was truly possible then a city's heart lay ripped. It was Manchester's equivalent of a state funeral. Our Churchill. Our leader. Our saviour. Our hero...

Later that day at Sir Matt's wake, everyone was still so solemn. Unusually for a funeral in our area and our culture, it didn't seem set to warm up. We were all so emotionally drained and obviously deeply upset. What caused me to do it, I've no idea, but I just thought Uncle Matt wouldn't want this and I began to sing. 'Hello, hello we are the Busby Boys!' Soon, everyone was joining in. I continued: 'Forever and ever' and we had a good old singsong.

Sir Matt always used to claim after a few drams that he belonged to Glasgow. Well, it also has to be said of this wonderful old man, the father of our football team – that he also belonged to us. Manchester United. We shared him.

Rest in wonderful forever peace Alexander – yes Alexander – Matthew Busby.

Postscript
Through love and despair, Manchester United Football Club have always been there. Twenty minutes remained of the 1994 FA Cup Final between United and Chelsea and we were three up. The title had already been retained and the Reds stood on the verge of our first ever double. Here in London town, the weather was typically Mancunian as the rain poured down endlessly and I was soaked to the skin. Before the match I listened to 'Abide with Me', and it reminded me of that kindly old man who had been taken from us only a few months previous. Then suddenly, thousands of United fans stood around me launched into a rousing 'There's only one Matt Busby!'

THREE HAIL MARYS AND THE TREBLE
CHAPTER THIRTY

"We went down to Wembley one fine day in May,
United supporters so merry and gay.
When it was over and when it was done,
We defeated Benfica by four goals to one."
Wembley – May 1968

Thirty-one years later... May 1999
The time was way past midnight when the last light dimmed in the Nou Camp. High above, the Barcelona skies glittered with stars. Across the city there were riotous celebrations. It was wonderful mayhem. The unmistakable tones of Mancunian accents rang out in tribute to the memory of the man known as the father of their football club. For 26th May was the birthday of Sir Matt Busby, and in his honour thousands of bleary-eyed, drunken, ecstatic United fans sang boisterous renditions of 'Happy Birthday' to Sir Matt. Many Reds were convinced that it was divine intervention on his part which finally brought the Germans of Bayern Munich to their knees. What do I think?

Well, something happened. Whatever the hell it was, I wouldn't like to speculate just yet.

How had it all begun?

Well it had been a hell of a season and... Read on while I take you back with my own memories of that special year!

'Number sixteen.'

'Manchester United.'

'Will play?'

'Number six.'

'Liverpool.'

Cue gasps of awe in the television studio as we came out of the hat to play our deadly rivals in the FA Cup fourth round at Old Trafford. Brilliant!

The Scousers at home. In the league, United were starting to motor. In recent years, it had become an annual battle between us and Arsene Wenger's formidable Arsenal. By now we had really started to hate Arsenal too, eventually getting frenzied with events like Keown screaming in Van Nistelrooy's face in 2003 and pizzagate in 2004. They were the champions in 1998, having raced past the Reds to take the title. This time around Fergie was more determined than ever to win it back.

We'd progressed well through the Champion's league qualifying group along with Bayern Munich. It wouldn't be the last time that season that the Bavarians would cross our path, but much more later.

This was a United team knitting together wonderfully. A midfield four of David Beckham, Paul Scholes, Roy Keane and Ryan Giggs. Their sublime concoction of devilry – a joy to behold. Up front Andy Cole and Dwight Yorke – devastating – whilst waiting to come off the bench if ever required, the clever and inventive Teddy Sheringham and a little Norwegian goal-scoring machine called Ole Gunnar Solskjaer. This was a kid deemed priceless by Fergie with his ability to read the game from the touchline, picking out weaknesses in opposing defenders, then coming on and destroying them.

As Prince danced and celebrated the arrival of 1999, on 24th January, Gerard Houllier's Liverpool arrived at Old Trafford. As ever, it being a cup tie, they'd brought a much larger support than for home games, which only helped to make the atmosphere bristle with even more bitterness and animosity. It just got under your skin. I was sat with Billy G and Moet Mason in the Main Executive stand behind the United dug out, and for most of the contest we'd trailed to an early Michael Owen header. As the second half wore on, the footballing gods seemed set to hand Liverpool the day as United laid siege to their goal, having shots cleared off the line, hitting both bar and post. That sinking feeling began to form in my stomach. The clock ground down and the shrill Scouse voices got louder. A seismic disappointment loomed large. Still the Reds charged. Two minutes remained. A scramble in the penalty area and Old Trafford erupted! Dwight Yorke had saved us at the last. A tap in on the line. Thank you, Uncle Al's lucky red underpants, wherever you were!

Anfield now beckoned for the replay but we couldn't care less. Bring it on. Around me – just relief! Billy and Moet were off their seats. Everyone was hugging. You just don't ever want to get beat by these Mickeys! We'd lived to fight again. With the grand old stadium now on fire, the Reds moved forward for one last time. 'Attack. Attack. Attack. Attack. Attack.'

rang round the ground. The ball fell loose in the penalty box to substitute Ole Gunnar Solskjaer and as I watched on, open-mouthed, hands on head, Ole gave David James the eyes from twelve yards and shot low and straight into the net. Cue unadulterated, shambolic scenes of grown men, women and children dancing and going crazy! A frenzied red carnival! Down at the Liverpool end, sheer desolation, but who cared? Not me. Ever since growing up as a young kid, there's nothing a proper United fan loves more than beating this lot and breaking their hearts in doing so. We'd gone berserk on our seats, bouncing, giving it the usual salutes towards them in the scoreboard end. 'Always look on the bright side of life, der dum, der dum, der dum, der dum.' Remember that in '92 you Scouse...

'Wemberley, Wemberley, we're the famous Man United and we're off to Wemberley!'

As the final whistle blew and the ground exploded in utter jubilation, the three of us stayed behind to rub it in – just a Salford thing! These were magic moments and we knew it. How often are you going to be 1-0 down with three minutes to go in as important a match as this, one that meant simply everything, then come back to win it 2-1, with virtually the last kick? God bless you Ole Gunnar Solskjaer. If you never kicked another ball for us, God bless you lad! Ole was a player capable of scoring from anywhere at any time. Priceless.

Finally, we made our way up the steps and to the back of the main stand into the exec bar. A few of our mates were already in there making hay. Dave Russell and his son Mark amongst them, great United people to the core. Dave came over to us and had a huge grin on his face. 'We saw you three stood on your seats at the end giving it everything. Let's get this right, lads. You're all in your mid-thirties yeah? Billy, you're a primary school teacher. Ged, you're a managing director of an international business, and Nick, you run a company yourself. I've never bleedin' seen owt like it!'

The three of us stared at each other suddenly realising how it must have looked. I laughed, because I knew we'd do the same thing all over again, for it really never got better than that.

Or so I thought.

The season was approaching a tumultuous climax and already the dream of a never achieved treble was being talked up – in whispers in case we jinxed it.

We'd destroyed the Scouser's dreams of a treble in 1977. Now it was our turn to start to palpitate. Though still a rainbow over a far-off mountain, it remained possible.

Manchester United had reached the semi-finals both of the Champion's league and the FA Cup whilst we were still going head to head, point for point with Arsenal.

It was remarkable stuff as every match became a must-not-lose. One mistake – a tiny blip – and it could all slip away.

In Europe, Inter Milan were despatched in the quarter finals, though at times it got more than a little hairy. One of the great saves from Peter Schmeichel in his last season at Old Trafford was an astonishing stop from the Chilean striker Ivan Zamorano that caused gasps around the San Siro. After a 2-0 victory in Manchester, the pressure from the Italians was relentless as they fought feverishly to pull back the deficit. A second-half goal from substitute Italian international Nicola Ventola, had for a period left United reeling. However, this was an impressive backs-to-the-wall performance by Fergie's team inspired by the Norwegian centre half Henning Berg, who was a rock. At times the Reds were forced to ride their luck but, ultimately, a Paul Scholes strike two minutes from time eased nerves and a place in the last four was earned. Post-match, the manager was beaming from ear to ear with the showing of his lads. 'They were fantastic. In general play I thought we were excellent – composure, the possession on the ball. I'm very, very proud of them. There have been times in the past when we haven't got the luck. Maybe that's changing?'

Maybe gaffer, maybe?

A small footnote to these memorable events in the San Siro occurred when, before the match, Pigeon Les had managed to get himself a ticket in the Inter end. As he walked across the Stadium concourse, a tasty looking mob with Milan scarfs round their faces came towards him. Immediately Les sensed trouble and, as he reached them, planning his moves, one lad pulled a scarf down from over his mouth. 'Alright Greeny!' he said with a broad Ordsall accent. It was Salford MUFC on tour, pretending to be Italians!

'Alright lads!' smiled Les, 'You had me fuckin' worried there for a minute!'

Wednesday afternoon: 14th April 1999. There was myself, Moet, Chris Wright and brother-in-law Terry on our way down the M6 to Villa Park for the FA Cup Semi-Final replay against Arsenal. The first game with the Gunners had finished goalless after the Reds had been robbed. A perfectly good Roy Keane goal had been adjudged offside by referee David Elleray. He was never my favourite referee, to put it mildly. Would've been better with a dog whistle, that one. We were chatting in the car about what team would start the replay. Could the Gaffer risk it and change the front two, replacing Cole and York with Sheringham and Solskjaer? Another problem was Giggs, who'd been badly off form. Many United supporters were starting to lose patience with him. Ryan needed to step back up – fast – to become the fantastic footballer we knew him to be.

As for the press, they were already motoring into mega-hype regarding our treble chances. Manchester United were playing OK, but by no means were they performing great. We just kept going, grinding teams down and, most importantly, winning. Many doubts remained and the feeling was that if anyone was going to derail us it'd be Wenger's mob, either in the league or the FA Cup, and there'd be nothing they'd enjoy more.

The matches between the two sides were always thunderous affairs with not a hair's breadth between them in terms of talent and commitment. Each drove the other on and the rivalry was just as intense between the managers. Surely there must've been grudging respect between Wenger and Fergie? If so, it was rarely shown. Winners to the core, both men hated losing and despised more than anything else getting beaten by the other. Another issue about that now-legendary replay was that tickets were so much easier to get hold of due to the short notice and it being played midweek. That meant proper Manchester lads and lassies would be cheering in the stands, and not the usual corporate crowd.

What a game we saw! A game that Gary Neville says was the best game that he ever played in. One that had everything – and this was the night that even I began to believe the treble was more than a pipe dream.

Against our new bitter enemy, Arsenal, and playing with a much-changed side, United took a deserved first-half lead with a cracking, well-placed shot from twenty-two yards by an on-fire Beckham, only for the Gunners to equalise with a freak Denis Bergkamp deflection early in the second half.

Roy Keane was then sent off for a second yellow and, when Phil Neville hacked down Ray Parlour in the penalty area with time almost up, it appeared that this epic contest was about to be brought to a tragic finale. Why didn't you stay on your feet Phil? What would Eric Harrison have said? He'd have crucified him, that's what. Eric wouldn't have banged on the window at the Cliff. He'd have put his foot through it. Such was our conviction that Arsenal's number ten wouldn't miss, that Ged even said, 'Let's do one and beat the traffic away from the ground and we could still make last orders in Kitty's bar back home.' Thank God we ignored him!

Up stepped the magnificent Dennis Bergkamp, and as we watched with a mouthful of Hail Marys, Peter Schmeichel leapt to his left like a cat and clawed the shot away! Yes! We were still alive! Thank you Mother Mary and thank you Schmeichel, you Danish beauty! Extra time arrived and what happened next has become part of Manchester United folklore.

Ryan Giggs had been thrown into the action to replace a tiring Jespar Blomqvist, but before Viera passed him that legendary ball, let me tell you a short tale regarding the Schmeichel penalty save.

I became friends with Jason Ferguson (son of Sir Alex), for the first time a year later on a lads' trip to Monaco, with Moet Mason, Ryan Giggs and his mate Dave Gardner. Ged had just completed a huge deal with Morson and was celebrating. Ryan and Dave had always spoken about what a great weekend trip the Grand Prix was each year, so off the four of us traipsed. I bumped into Jason at our hotel bar and clicked straight away with him. The place was full of famous faces (honestly, you'd fill a skip with all the names I could drop if I started!). Jason, I immediately clocked, was similar to me. No fan of big time Charlies, or anyone pretentious or flash. We'd both rather find a back-street pub with spit and sawdust on the floor and have a couple of pints. The problem was that the principality of Monaco wasn't exactly Oldham Road on a wet Wednesday! Simple bars were as rare as tax collectors there. Instead, we found ourselves in a lavish bar with a view of the Mediterranean and gaggles of supermodels, where the price of a drink wasn't far off your average monthly mortgage payment. Giggsy was chatting away about the previous, treble-winning year, saying that himself and the other players had all said that it could never be achieved again. Such was the last-minute drama and luck involved, 1999 had to be the all-time pinnacle that would never be bettered.

It was a conversation that maybe didn't win the treble, but went some way to ensuring a double. No surprise, there was a Ferguson involved, not his legendary old fella from Govan, but, the son, and my new mate Jason. At the time he was working for Sky Sports as their Senior Match Director. This gave Jason invaluable access to Arsenal footage, more importantly Denis Bergkamp's penalty taking. He discovered that when there was little at stake, say the Gunners were three or four up, then the mercurial Dutchman tended to hit them wherever he fancied-but, if the stakes were high? When it involved points or trophies, Bergkamp always went low to the Goalkeeper's left. This information was incredibly important, for with both sides so equally matched, just the slightest edge could prove priceless. After watching endless footage of Bergkamp's spot kicks, Jason felt confident enough to pass this information on to his dad. He told him between the two semi-finals, after the first had ended 0-0. Ferguson senior listened, took this on board, and that was where it was left. Come the fateful, Wednesday evening replay, as Bergkamp stood ready to face Peter Schmeichel in the dying moments, and surely send Arsenal to Wembley, Jason's research came to fruition, when Bergkamp shot low to Schmeichel's left, and the big Dane dived to save it! Come the final whistle, after extra time, when Giggs' wonder goal had won the day, Jason, who had watched the epic events unfold from Sky's Outside Broadcast Truck, set off to go and congratulate his dad. He swiftly came across him outside the entrance to the dressing rooms. A smiling Jason put a hand down to his left, and a proud and delighted dad burst out laughing, and went across to hug him. They make a good team those Fergusons!

I mentioned to Ryan that I remembered the night well – and him getting caught with a forearm in the face off Ray Parlour after coming on as sub. Giggsy effed and blinded to the ref, who just waved him away. 'I was fuming' replied Ryan. 'And so wound up.' A few minutes later Patrick Viera hit that misplaced pass and a legend – plus song to boot – was born. Of all the people to have gifted Giggsy the ball – it couldn't have happened to anyone better!!! With his mad up Ryan Giggs flew into the annals of Manchester United legend as he raced over the halfway line with steam coming out of his ears. Arguably the greatest defence in modern English football history stood before him. Lee Dixon, Tony Adams, Martin Keown and Nigel Winterbottom, all determined to nail down this will-of-the-wisp Red Devil, who Fergie once described when in full flow as 'Like a sheepdog chasing a crisp bag in the wind.' On went Giggs at full pelt, dancing, jinxing, ghosting and powering past the Gunners – making Viera look like a camel on a tightrope – before arriving in the penalty area populated by the other three knackered defenders and ghosting past them before sending a piercingly accurate shot past David Seaman. It flew into the net. A moment seared into United folklore! Maybe the greatest goal ever scored in the FA Cup!?

As Ryan tore through the cockneys I remember Moet shouting, 'Go on Giggsy, at em, go on Roy of the Rovers,' as he went past one and then another Arsenal shirt. 'Roy of the Rovers' and again, 'Roy of the Rovers' and then bang! 'Yesss! Roy of the fuckin' Rovers – what a goal!' Giggs didn't stop running, taking off his shirt and being mobbed by hysterical United supporters who had flooded onto the pitch. Giggsy said he noticed a few mates from school amongst them. Paul Scholes spoke mostly of the smell of beer! It was that kind of night when Manchester United overcame the most unbelievable odds to earn a place in the FA Cup Final against Newcastle. More importantly, I also think it was the night that we destroyed Arsenal's self belief. I honestly believe that if they'd beaten us they might have tipped us for the title.

Those of us there that night were truly blessed. No one loved it more than Alex Ferguson, who was obviously delighted at beating Wenger's Arsenal and reaching the final, and more so being a dad, proud that it was Jason, along with Giggsy, who had produced his own moment of magic.

Maybe it was a moment that would never be celebrated in a song, but it's a moment that the Fergie clan will rightly cherish forever.

Afterwards, on the way home, everyone was singing, many hanging out of their car windows in the crawling traffic away from the ground before finally reaching the M6. A car pulled up next to us that had a Gary Neville shirt being twirled in the air to the sound of 'Que sera sera!' As we pushed north towards the Manchester road signs, I began to think just what it would mean for United to pull off something as truly remarkable as the treble. Then again, I'd had more than my fair share of scoops that night. 'The luckiest team won,' claimed Arsene Wenger afterwards, in his typical Arsenal style. Aye, well, there's a lot to be said for luck.

Sometimes, these things are just written.

On qualifying for the Champions League knockout stages, Gary Neville, in an immediate post-match ITV interview, asked: 'Have Juventus qualified?' Neville was worried because they had been in the last three finals. Furthermore, throughout the nineties, 'La Vecchia Signora', this grand 'Old Lady' of Italian football had tormented the Reds with a series of comprehensive victories in terms of style and substance, if not scorelines. Three defeats and a single victory. The worst by far being United's first trip to the Stadio delle Alpi when we never created a single clear-cut opportunity. It was men against boys. Neville claimed he'd never encountered such a gulf in class and wouldn't again in his magnificent 602 games playing for the club.

So, after knocking out Inter Milan in the quarters, who did we draw? Yes, you know who!

On Wednesday 7th April 1999, Juventus turned up at Old Trafford for the Champions League semi final, first leg, and for forty minutes they played United off the park. Inspired by the magnificent World-Cup-winning Frenchman Zinedine Zidane (who Fergie had allegedly passed on just before Le Roi had retired) and with teammates like Deschamps, Davids and Inzaghi, the Italians were sublime. Leading 1-0 at the interval – a worrying away goal – it could've been so many more as the Zebra stripes cut a fine if painful sight across the old stadium's turf. Ultimately, after a half-time Fergie rocket, United roared back in the second half to grab a deserved last-minute equaliser from Ryan Giggs, who blasted in a close-range volley, causing Old Trafford to erupt more with relief than joy. United had given themselves a chance. Following the match, Juve's goalscorer and recent Chelsea manager Antonio Conte declared, 'This tie is already over. Manchester United must accept that we are the better team and that it will be the 'Old Lady' going to the final in Barcelona.' Talk about flicking the tail of a Red Devil.

Two weeks later in Turin the game began badly. After only 11 minutes, millions of hearts sank – all over Manchester and in the stadium. 2-0 down. 3-1 on aggregate! Caught sleeping at the back, Juve launched a blistering opening assault to leave the thousands of Reds who had travelled to the concrete hulk in northern Italy shell-shocked. The first goal hurt us after seven minutes when the majestic Zidane carried on from where he had left off in Manchester, setting up the infuriating goal poacher Filippo Inzaghi to beat Peter Schmeichel from close range. Fergie always claimed with his smart turn of phrase that this Italian hitman was 'born offside.' Never has the man from Govan uttered a truer statement. On eleven minutes, we were two down when that man again slid in and a wicked deflection off Jaap Stam beat Schmeichel once more.

Slowly, instead of losing faith, the Reds began to play their game. No panic, just patience. Keano was Fergie's rock. He would never allow anyone in his team to give in – and woe betide them if they even tried to! The ball was passed with great care and penetration – the United way. Driven relentlessly from midfield by our captain, we tore into them, taking advantage of a hint of complacency. On twenty-four minutes it was Keane who lowered the deficit to 3-2 on aggregate when, from a David Beckham corner, he leapt high to score with a glorious header past Peruzzi into the Juve goal.

Hope now burst onto the tightly packed United area of the stadium – and in patches everywhere. Not just a few had managed to sneak or jib their way in, and they were like sardines in one patch and speckles everywhere else! The songs and roars screamed from all over the terraces – suddenly tinged with Manc accents. The fans showed, like the team, that it's not in the club's DNA to stop believing. Never give up, for you're not allowed! Whether commanded to fight by Matt Busby, Jimmy Murphy, Eric Harrison, Keano or Alex Ferguson, you just didn't dare not to.

Again, United attacked. Like a pack of wolves. Relentless. It was wonderful stuff. Red shirts swarmed forward. Juve were clinging on.

Ten minutes before half time, disaster struck for Roy Keane when he was booked for a late tackle on Zidane, meaning he would miss the final should we make it. No tears though. A shrug of the shoulders and the Cork man continued to lead his teammates in magnificent style. His was an awe-inspiring Captain's performance never to be topped by anyone in a red shirt.

A minute later it's 2-2 on the night! A Beckham cross and Dwight Yorke's diving header electrified the travelling Mancunians once more.

It was heart-stopping, rip-roaring football. Manchester United had gone to Turin and were tearing it up. No team ever did this to Juventus in

Turin. No one...

The second half saw no respite for the 'Old Lady', as United continued to bomb forward with almost suicidal delight. We would never settle for a tight score back in those days – I've got to say, I really wish I hadn't had to watch some of the recent United managers rip up our tried and tested rule book!

As the score stood, we were going through. The minutes ticked furiously down. It was footballing chaos. Beautiful. Nerve-wracking. The stakes were higher than the Alps that loomed near this grand old cathedral of Italian football. More heartbreak for United occurred thirteen minutes from time when substitute Paul Scholes was carded for fouling Didier Deschamps, meaning he too would now miss the final, if we should make it. Like his Captain, Scholes shook off his initial bitter disappointment to carry on the fight. Nerves almost shot, fingernails bitten, Barcelona was five minutes away when, on a counter attack, Yorke bundled through the last line of Juve's defence before being brought down by Peruzzi. Penalty surely – but the ball fell for his best mate Andy Cole who rammed it into an empty net! 3-2 on the night for the Reds and all doubts disappeared. Manchester United were back in the European Cup Final. For me and to all Reds, it will always be these moments that we yearn for! Always!

The United dressing room post-match was a strange blend of jubilation and dejection. Sir Bobby and the chairman, Martin Edwards, had made their way down from the directors' box to thank the players, whilst Fergie gave every one of them a well-deserved hug. Nicky Butt and David Beckham posed for photos and Teddy Sheringham, David May and Peter Schmeichel chanted 'Barcelona!' The abiding image, though, was of a quiet Roy Keane sitting alone, taking the occasional swig out of a plastic water bottle, coming to terms with missing the final after what was undoubtedly his finest hour in a red shirt. Scholesy also sat alone, clearly trying hard not to let his true feelings show. The mood was mirrored among the fans, who were gutted for these two lions.

So ended a wonderful night under the Turin stars and a momentous season continued as if on the wings of angels. A thousand memories and even more heart attacks lay in wait. All was yet to unfold with the possibility of winning something that we hadn't dared to believe was even possible. The greater the chance for everlasting glory, the bigger the fall. There was a reason no English club had ever won a treble before!

Fergie's fifth Premier League title matched Sir Matt's record and it was clinched with victory at Old Trafford – the first time we'd pulled it off at home since the days of Sir Matt – on the final day of the season. It was a close and messy battle and could have gone either way, though the Spurs fans at Old Trafford were probably delighted to see Arsenal lose out.

A 2-1 win over Spurs with goals from David Beckham and Andy Cole on each side of half-time, after player of the year David Ginola had gone off injured and Spurs had taken the lead, was the final nail in Arsenal's coffin. Arsenal had also won their last game of the season – with half the ground probably checking in on what was happening at Highbury – and now we were on target to match their double from the year before.

Like all proper United fans, when you weigh it up, you have probably stood or sat in most parts of Old Trafford throughout the many years of going to the match. This particular game I got a ticket with Jersey Mick in, let's say, the old United Road paddock towards the Stretty. What it meant was that I stood and watched Andy Cole cleverly lob the keeper with a virtually perfect view. What a great finish, by the way, as was Beck's curler just before the break. The relief around the stadium was unbelievable.

As Roy Keane, to the utter delight of a delirious crowd, lifted high the Premiership trophy, thoughts turned now to completing a second double. A load of us headed on into town to celebrate long into the night and I distinctly remember a few of us walking down Deansgate in the early hours singing 'Yip Yap Stam' – the new song about our Dutchman mountain centre-back.

A week later Newcastle awaited us in the FA Cup Final. Thoughts were already turning to the Nou Camp. Fans were planning to travel to London then straight on to Barcelona for a tumultuous few days.

What was built up to be a huge challenge for the Reds turned into a relatively simple Wembley stroll as Ruud Gullit and the ever-underperforming Geordies were easily outclassed 2-0. Sheringham and Scholes sealed the cup and put yet more silverware into the United trophy room. Now, all that remained was the one that mattered most.

Barcelona and Bayern Munich were calling.

Surely it was tempting the footballing gods to hope for even more glory?

Interestingly, as I've already mentioned, the final would be played on the 26th May. Sir Matt Busby's birthday. Uncle Matt would be watching, I'm sure, with a small dram in hand. Our Glasgow guardian angel with a heavenly eye on the Nou Camp.

BARCELONA
CHAPTER THIRTY ONE

On 26th May 1999, I found myself in a taxi from home at 4:05am, going to Ringway Airport, on my own, to watch the lads play in the second European Cup Final of my lifetime. I just couldn't miss it and took up the opportunity of a ticket just days before. Due to work and family commitments I hadn't expected to be able to make it. Then I was offered a ticket through the ex-players' association. How could I possibly turn it down?

I spoke to Billy G to see if he was going, but by then Billy was a teacher at St Vincent's primary school, and the headmaster, Mr Carr, wouldn't let him take the time off. Miserable git.

My other mates were all booked on two/three-day trips.

Pigeon Les and his mob were partying in Lloret De Mar, like the Salford Vikings wreaking fun and mayhem.

So, for one of the only games ever, I went on my own! How glad I am that I did, for I wasn't alone for long! I met so many people that I knew, both at the airport and on the plane. I began by having a couple of beers with Steve Bruce, who had his teenage son Alex with him. Next I bumped into Andrew and Howard Kay, who used to sit next to myself and Uncle Al in the cantilever back in the seventies. We'd come a long way from back in 1974 and the Sunderland game in the Second Division.

Luckily, I also met up with Les, Shay, Moet and dozens of other mates on the day to begin what was to prove a truly unforgettable experience in the Catalan capital. On arrival at Ringway, I found it to be decked out in red, white and black. Thousands were preparing to make a footballing pilgrimage to Barcelona. Me amongst them. I must have said a thousand silent Hail Marys in a blatant case of holy bribery to ensure United brought that big, jug-eared beauty back home.

The Red Army hit the skies as the charter flights hurtled off the runway in the direction of Spain – and one of its jewels – Barcelona.

Already, countless Reds were descending upon Catalonia from across the continent, and indeed the world. They came in tens of thousands, drawn, as if by an invisible cord, to the Nou Comp, all with one wish only: to see their team crowned European champions. Thirty-three years was a long time to wait for a club such as ours. Sir Bobby gave forth a rallying call.

'It's time we put something on the table again.'

Expectations were huge, despite the loss of Keane and Scholes through suspension. We had decent enough replacements in Nicky Butt and Jespar Blomqvist but this was the formidable Bayern Munich. They were also on course for a historic treble. Only one of us could succeed. Game on!

Ottmar Hitzfeld had a decent record against Alex Ferguson. It was he who'd masterminded Borussia Dortmund's semi-final triumph against United two years previously. Hitzfeld felt the tactics he would employ would prove sufficient to thwart and strangle our attacking instincts. Andy Cole and Dwight Yorke would be shackled by Thomas Linke and the huge Ghanaian international, Samuel Kuffour. Wing-backs Markus Babbel and Michael Tarnat would be expected to tame the twin threat of Ryan Giggs and Jespar Blomqvist. Tidying up behind these four and still possessing the power to motor forward would be the great winner, Lothar Matthaus. During an exceptional career, thirty-eight-year-old Matthaus had achieved every honour in the game but one. Yes, the European Cup (as I still call it). Barcelona offered a last opportunity to put this right and Matthaus, they claimed, would just not let such an opportunity pass. Nothing and no one was going to stand in his way. He usually got what he wanted.

Little did Lothar realise what we had in store for him.

The night before the final, Alex Ferguson took United's last training session wearing a replica shirt of the 1968 European Cup winning team. It was a small but telling and poignant act on Fergie's part, showing his knowledge of just what this competition meant to Manchester United and their supporters. Ours was a club steeped in the history and tradition of this magnificent trophy. We'd spilt precious blood in our gallant efforts to win it and that blood will never be forgotten. The loss of Sir Matt's 'Babes' on that infamous Munich runway in Southern Germany still cuts deep into the psyche of all connected with the club. It did then and it does today. Every February 6th the hearts of the Red half of Manchester saddens. That the final was against Munich and also fell on Busby's 90th birthday meant emotions, already running high, became tinged with an almost spiritual feel. We had to do it for Sir Matt and his babes.

We just had to...

Alex Ferguson was rightly being viewed as a worthy successor to Busby. A natural inclination to give youth a fling had given his teams more than a passing resemblance to Sir Matt's teams. For Edwards, Colman, Pegg, Whelan and Charlton, read Beckham, Giggs, Butt, Scholes and Neville. The 'Busby Babes' never got the chance to win the European Cup. Fate decreed that it wasn't to be. Come kick-off in the Nou Camp, Alex Ferguson would ensure that his Manchester United were playing for more than a simple trophy. They'd be playing for their history. The loss of Keane and Scholes forced Ferguson into a tactical rethink. Beckham came in from the wing to cover his Captain's absence, whilst Giggs would switch wings and Jespar Blomqvist would play on the left. Ferguson remained convinced this team possessed sufficient firepower to counteract losing two such influential players. Though it was a huge gamble, he was sure it would pay off. Besides, if all was not going to plan, Ferguson could turn to the life-saving talents of Teddy Sheringham and a certain Ole Gunnar Solskjaer – two lifesavers to bring off the bench. The ultimate parachute plan.

Now, in the early Catalan evening, the Nou Camp, daubed three-quarters blood red with the legions of United followers, was prepared to cement his legend. Barcelona had been invaded by the Red Army – tens of thousands would never have a chance of a ticket but just had to be there. Meanwhile there seemed to be hardly any Germans – unless they were all in museums while we filled the bars and cafes? Manchester United had all but invaded and taken over Barcelona! Everywhere we went that day, bars, outside the stadium, I'd bump into familiar faces. One was a comically fuming Paddy Crerand who was ready to declare a one-man war on Catalonia after being hit with a baton by a riot cop thug in uniform. A further 5,000 mostly Guinness-hatted United supporters were forced to follow proceedings from the Nou Comp forecourt, using crowd noise and a half-sighted video screen. Surely United daren't let such raw passion and undiluted love go unrewarded. Surely we could triumph?

It made me think of when Billy was asked by Ron Atkinson back in the mid 1980s to explain to the squad of first team players of that time what United meant to the local people of Manchester and Salford. He told them that there were people who would go without food and spend their last penny to watch United. They'd travel to Newcastle on a Wednesday night when it was freezing, take the following day off and risk getting the sack. It was that message, and Billy believed strongly what he was talking about. Billy Garton had lived the dream but more importantly he was one of us. Myself, Moet Mason, Pigeon Les, big Malc, Uncle Al and Baza. All were United through and through, and all were praying under this now dark Catalan sky for the night to go well.

We had tossed a coin to see who would play in their home colours – and as a good luck charm we had won. We would be playing in red, white and black, Bayern would be in grey with maroon trim.

The pre-match entertainment laid on by FC Barcelona was surreal even to the eyes of a tremendously pissed-up Red Army. A worryingly overweight Montserrat Caballe was ferried onto the pitch on a golf buggy to perform a morbid duet with the deceased Freddie Mercury. Freddie appeared from the stars – courtesy of a gigantic video screen. Together, they belted out – unsurprisingly – their classic hit 'Barcelona', whilst deep below, in the bowels of the stadium, the teams nervously prepared. For the managers this was the worst time. Their job complete, now it was all down to the players. It came down to trust. Ferguson gathered his clan around him.

'There's not a team in the world that can beat you,' he said. 'And that's why you must not be afraid. I'm proud of you, and honoured by what you have already given me and the club. The only thing I regret is that I can't send you all out onto the pitch. Because, without exception, you all deserve it.' With that he wished them the best of luck. Now, it was down to the eleven men in red. Maybe twelve. Or even thirteen.

Ottmar Hitzfeld too gave his final instructions. His players were briefed and everyone knew what was expected of them. Hitzfeld had already been quoted in the German media as saying this would be their year. The absence of two of the greatest ever United players, Keane and Scholes, was an unexpected and monumental bonus for Bayern Munich. Their powerful midfield of Jens Jeremies and the immensely talented, if temperamental, Stefan Effenberg now more than fancied their chances against Beckham and Butt. Ferguson's surprise inclusion of Jespar Blomqvist had momentarily taken Hitzfeld aback, but he recovered swiftly to realise it mattered little. The plan wouldn't change. Babbel would mark the elusive Swedish winger and victory would be theirs. Bavarian confidence was overwhelming, Munich was already planning its victory celebrations. The lederhosen were being prepared, the beer halls filled with barrels and steins…

Led by the goalkeeping Captains Peter Schmeichel (playing in his last ever game for United) and Oliver Kahn, the two sides came into view onto the pitch.

The sheer scale of Manchester United's support swiftly became apparent. Apart from one section behind a goal, the whole of the Nou Comp's vast towering terraces were bathed red, white and black. From every one of Manchester and Salford red's pubs. From Aberdeen to Malta and beyond. Flags and banners lay draped over and across this wonderful monument to football.

I was standing, transfixed, with Terry. No more words. Neither of us had ever experienced anything like this. The reception for our boys had been thunderous and they were bathed in wonderful expectations.

Steffen Effenburg was captured on camera glancing around at the stadium as if to say, 'Where are our supporters?' Finally, the Champions League theme ended and amid rapturous cheers the players broke ranks to warm up. The noise was rising to a deafening crescendo as the highly respected Italian referee Pierluigi Collina wished both his linesmen a good game. With the 98,000 lucky spectators in the Nou Camp now verging on a collective heart attack, Collina appeared to steady himself. Even the most calm and collected of characters couldn't help but be affected by the atmosphere. Drenched in passion, both young and old.

There were those who had witnessed a similar occasion back in 1968, and others like myself, already full of excitement and anticipation, before a ball had even been kicked. The young kid who'd cried when Southampton had broken his heart back in 1976, was the same kid now – still saying his prayers to the angels and the saints. The city of Munich has and always will be synonymous with Manchester United Football Club. The forthcoming events of the night of 26th May 1999, would make Barcelona equally so.

United kicked off…

The early stages resembled a jousting match as both sides tried to settle down.

On six minutes their big bustling centre-forward Carsten Janker was brought crashing down by Ronny Johnsen, twenty-five yards from goal. As the Nou Comp held its breath, up stepped their brilliant, if somewhat arrogant, playmaker Mario Basler to fire low through the wall beating Schmeichel hands down. Bollocks!

1-0. Basler slid away on his knees, celebrating, soon to be joined by his jubilant teammates.

Once again it was apparent that United would have to do things the hard way.

Why was it always this way?

Struggling to hit back, the Reds continually ran into a grey wall of defenders.

Bayern were superbly organised, tight at the back, breaking fast and looking what they were: a potent force. Basler was bossing the midfield. Oh, for a Keane to sort him out. United were huffing and puffing, nothing more, with the Germans looking by far the more convincing team. Matthaus was simply magnificent, throwing away the years, flying across the halfway line and letting loose a tremendous effort just over the bar. Come Collina's half-time whistle, Hitzfeld's men were in total control. Around me the faith remained, but whilst you could never write off this United team, it was dawning on the Red Army that maybe this was simply a match too far?

On his way to the dressing room, Alex Ferguson was a man with an awful lot on his mind. He told the players, 'Keep your shape, keep trying to attack and a goal will come.' Just as the bell sounded to return for the second half Ferguson played his ace card. 'Lads, when you go back out there just have a look at the cup. It'll be about five yards away, but you won't be able to touch it. I want you to think about the fact that if you lose this game, you'll have been so close to it, and will hate the thought for the rest of your lives. So, you just make sure you don't lose!'

As the game restarted, the Germans continued as they'd left off. Supremely organised, confident, grimly determined and hunting down the United forwards in packs. Try as we might to cheer them on, the spark looked to have gone from our players. Something needed to change, for already the game was starting to drift. Teddy Sheringham appeared on the touchline warming up. As he stretched, an annoyed Sheringham eyed Basler, who was conducting the Bayern fans with what appeared to be early victory celebrations. He wouldn't forget this. Finally, United gained a little control in midfield with Beckham, aided by the strong running Butt starting to get on top of the ball. Bayern retreated in a clear attempt to lure the Reds on and then catch us on the break. United were creating sporadic moments of decent football, the odd half chance, but nothing of real substance. It was the Germans who remained by far the most dangerous.

Just after the hour, Basler stormed clear into our half and from a full forty yards attempted to chip Schmeichel, only to miss by a whisker. An outrageous attempt, but typical of Bayern's confidence. The clock ticked down. The tension was becoming unbearable. Twenty-three minutes remained when Sheringham was finally brought on for a terribly under par Blomqvist, who hadn't been allowed to breathe by the Munich defenders. Immediately, the clever front man began to create problems for the Germans, problems that previously hadn't existed. Still Bayern appeared the more likely to score again. Their substitute, raiding midfielder Helmut Scholl, made his presence felt immediately, setting up Stefan Effenberg, as he shot narrowly over. Ferguson checked his watch on the touchline. Fifteen minutes remained. A sloppy pass from Butt was seized upon by the Germans and this time Effenberg sent Mario Basler streaking away on the break. His astute pass found Scholl who, from twenty yards, clipped a wonderful shot over Schmeichel striking the inside of the post with the ball bouncing back into the relieved big Dane's hands. My god, it should've been all over. I noticed on the video screen that the Munich supporters were now holding their heads in their hands. On eighty minutes, Lothar Matthaus departed the scene. His exit was greeted with rapturous applause from their end. It was only Matthaus's sheer exhaustion that had caused Hitzfeld to make the change, because his Captain had been immense. He was still a class apart.

With Sheringham's astute prompting, United were straining every sinew to break through the Bayern rearguard. With only ten minutes to go, on came Solskjaer for Cole. A last throw of the dice by the Govan gambler. Despite pressurising, there still was no real flow in United's play and, littered with sloppiness, they again gave the ball away. Once more Bayern broke forward menacingly: Scholl let fly a tremendous drive that Schmeichel tipped away for a corner. Basler strolled across to take it, milking the applause of his adoring fans whilst doing so. It was becoming a pisstake. The resulting corner came to nothing and United cleared, only to see the Germans win back possession and win yet another corner. Over it came and as if in slow motion, Scholl's clever header back into the six-yard box found Janker who thundered an overhead kick against our crossbar! Jesus wept! I'm certain the shudder could've been felt back in Manchester and Munich. All those Hail Marys, someone was listening, for we were still alive!

By now it was all or nothing. Madness reigned amongst the Red hordes. Throats were hoarse. Maybe, just maybe, lady luck was wearing a devil's tattoo on her arm after all. Please God, let us score!

Six minutes remained when Solskjaer's cute back-heel saw Sheringham fire low, but straight at their goalkeeper Oliver Kahn. It was clear we'd fight to the very end and it was also noticeable that at long last the Bayern defenders were tiring. Beckham's clever cross found an unmarked Yorke's head, but it was cleared once more. United were forcing Bayern ever further back. The noise from the Red Army was reaching high into the Catalan heavens. Wet with sweat, myself and Terry watched on helplessly.

Again, we attacked. Beckham played in Neville, whose precise cross found Yorke, only for him to mishit from nine yards. A gigantic groan came from breaking Red hearts. Was that the chance? To waste a little more time Hitzfeld substituted Basler, who gestured on the way off to his supporters that it was job done. There was less than sixty-seconds remaining. The European Cup was clearly on its way to Munich. When all appeared lost I turned to prayer – Terry too. Someone right next to us had dropped to their knees to 'have a word'. Around us people could hardly bear to watch as Collina signalled that three minutes of extra time was all that remained in Barcelona.

Bayern Munich seemed dead on their feet as, for one last time, Manchester United flew forward in search of redemption. Linke was hounded by a rampaging Solskjaer and was forced to concede a throw in, level with the penalty area. Up came Gary Neville to hurl it in. The immense Kuffour managed to head clear, only for it to land at David Beckham's feet. Finding his best mate back out wide, Neville's attempted cross in the box was blocked by Effenberg, and deflected out for a corner. Hope remained. I said a little prayer to Sir Matt. If you can do anything old friend, now's the time!

The old man listened, I'm sure!

Beckham sprinted over to take it. Behind that goal was a seething, uncontrollable swarm of red humanity. 'What's he doing?' someone shouted as Schmeichel made his way over the halfway line into the German box. From the side of the pitch, Ferguson screamed at him, but the big Dane ignored him. It was now or never. Over came the corner. Schmeichel's gigantic personality and presence caused chaos amongst the Germans. A mad scramble ensued. The ball fell loose to Dwight Yorke who hooked it back into the six-yard box, only for a Bayern leg to clear to the edge of the penalty area and a waiting Ryan Giggs. Hitting it first time, Giggs screwed his shot back towards goal onto the foot of Teddy Sheringham, who pivoted and poked. 1-1! Yes! Jesus, Mary and Joseph we'd only gone and done it again! A miracle! A fully-grown Manchester United miracle.

Around me utter, wonderful, unadulterated carnage.

Mayhem.

God, I loved this club. Across the Nou Comp the explosion of noise told its own story, for the prayers of the many had outweighed those of the few. The 1999 European Cup Final was all square. Red flares exploded, sheer relief, nothing more. Now for extra time as the Germans kicked off, but do you know what? Yes you do!

We were coming again!

The flawless Denis Irwin smashed a long ball clearance down into the Bayern half. Picked up by Solskjaer, he teased and tormented his opponents into giving away yet another corner. Around me was a footballing orgy with people still writhing about on the floor celebrating the equalizer, screaming with joy at the top of their voices, hugging each other with relief, ready for another 30 minutes of agony and ecstasy. Again, Beckham prepared to deliver. For some reason my mind drifted back to Uncle Al proposing after the 1968 European Cup Final.

Over came the ball to be met perfectly by Sheringham, whose flick on found Solskjaer unmarked from six yards out. Cue absolute pandemonium! I still find it hard to explain what happened as Ole scored. It was just a sheer wall of noise and emotion. Bedlam. A moment that most United fans still, to this day, describe as the most exciting moment of their lives. Solskjaer skidding away and dropping in delight in front of disbelieving supporters. Magical, unforgettable scenes on a night that even the finest wordsmith would find hard to describe.

Put simply, my Manchester United had won the European Cup again, on Sir Matt's birthday. We had won the treble and every Bayern player lay devastated on the turf as Collina was forced to help some back to their feet.

Samuel Kuffour was broken, his face contorted in rage and tears. It'd been his job to mark Solskjaer and one second of switching off due to exhaustion meant the little Norwegian maestro had nicked away to stab home the winner. On the bench Matthaus looked like he was watching his house burn down. Such great efforts were now in vain. Never mind eh! Six seconds remained and no sooner had Bayern restarted than Collina blew to end the match!

Sheringham sought out Basler who lay slumped in the floor, clearly in shock. 'Congratulations son,' he whispered into his ear. 'You've just been Man U'd!'

Not a slogan liked, even despised by United fans, but we can forgive Teddy this one time. There could be no other explanation, amidst the wild, unadulterated scenes of fervid celebrations amongst the Red Army, something truly spellbinding had occurred in the Nou Camp.

A beaming Alex Ferguson raised high along with Peter Schmeichel the measure of our dreams, and a fragment of Manchester would forever reside in Barcelona. Amidst a blinding array of dazzling flashlights, the Nou Comp erupted in joy, as United supporters danced with tears in Red eyes, watching the spontaneous celebration started by David May of every player lifting the trophy above his head, one at a time, to the ecstatic United end.

High above, at that exact moment, I was later told by a very drunken United supporter from Wrexham that a shooting star had shot across the black Catalan sky doing a victory roll. Surely it couldn't have been. Could it?

Happy Birthday Uncle Matt!

A

B

C

D

E

F

A   1990 FA Cup Final replay in Kilburn pub - From left; Shay, me, our Guy,
      young Pat Crerand Jim, Franny

B   Lee Martin carrying cup. Sparky and Gary Palister with their new Morson caps on

C   Me and Uncle Matt

D   The lone piper for Sir Matt

E   Bergkamp save

F   Deansgate like you've never seen

THE WELSHY BABES
CHAPTER THIRTY TWO

Rock, paper, scissors and goal nets!

Life moves on.

In 2002, I went through a bitterly sad marriage break-up, and anybody that has been through such a break-up knows that it's a rotten time for everyone involved.

I'll always remember meeting Peter Docherty in the Saint Ambrose school playground a lifetime ago, when I'd moved across town to South Manchester. Peter told me that he hadn't seen his old fella (Tommy Doc) for years. Firstly, coming from a pretty strict Catholic family, I couldn't believe that a Dad could leave his actual family – but the fact that he didn't keep in touch as well was to me unimaginable?

Now, the world had turned. It was happening to me. I had totally fallen in love with someone else and my marriage was over. To say people showed their true colours was an understatement. It brought out the best and worst and I soon realised who my true friends were – and they remain so today. Those others, outsiders looking in with their own unwanted opinions and making accusations had their own reasons for letting me down. I learnt a new saying. 'Never judge a man until you've walked a mile in his boots.' It's something I've often repeated to others since and I really believe it's true. Anyway, the top and bottom was my eight-year marriage ended. I came out of it, however, with two beautiful children. My Jamie and Bella, for whom I'll always be forever grateful and truly thankful for. Again, my mind switched back to the Docherty family situation, and I told myself that whatever happened, I was going to see my kids whenever it was humanly possible.

My mate Guy Norbury was a professional tennis coach at David Lloyd's club in Cheadle and he knew a few of the Manchester City first team players who were members. He rang me one evening saying 'Do you and Jamie fancy coming to Maine Road on Saturday to watch the Blues play Spurs? I've got three main stand tickets off one of the City lads and it should be a great game.'

'Sorry mate,' I replied. 'I've something on, but thanks for the kind offer.'

'I'll take Jamie if you want?' Guy insisted. He'd been great with both my kids, and they'd known him since they were babies. Guy had even given them some free tennis coaching at times. 'Yeah OK,' I said, not thinking really and knowing my six-year-old would be fine. Jamie adored football and loved Guy to bits.

'I'll pick Jamie up at one o'clock from yours Nick.'

Walking away from the house phone it suddenly dawned on me and I rang Guy straight back. 'Hey mate I've just thought about it. City, Maine Road, Jamie's first live match. It's not happening, I can't risk that. It just wouldn't be fair on the lad. Thanks anyway!'

This got me motoring and I was straight on the phone next day to the United ticket office, where I remained friendly with a couple of members of staff. I was a member of the AFMUP (Association of Former Manchester United Players). Yes, Alan Wardle and his committee did actually let me join, even though I didn't make the obvious pass to Bobby at Bootham Cresent. I remained a little embarrassed to be in such esteemed company but, having been on a professional contract, apparently I was entitled to membership. I went to some of their events – not all by any means – mostly with Billy Garton, and was always made to feel welcome. However, once Billy moved to the States I just stopped going.

I do remember one Sportsman's Dinner at Old Trafford after a golf day when I found myself sitting next to some older gentlemen. I got chatting to them whilst having the customary soup and one in particularly was a delight and full of wonderful old tales about our great club. Alan Gowling tapped me on the shoulder. 'Do you know who that old bloke is?' I shook my head because I'd not yet found the right time or indeed courage to ask his name.

'It's Charlie Mitten,' said Alan. He pointed further down the table to another guy sat next to Charlie. 'And that's Stan Pearson.' It was truly an honour to be in such distinguished company.

Happily, our contacts in the ticket office came through with flying colours and sorted out four season tickets for myself, Jamie, Billy and Billy Jnr. Both of us made a pact that whatever happened in the future, these would remain in our families for life, and today this remains the case.

Priceless family heirlooms.

Then there was the kids' football....

Fifteen nil! How do you get yourself into these situations, Welshy? It was my own fault. I'd been watching our Jamie at his football team's training sessions and found myself chatting to the guy who organised the team, Nigel. I went as far to suggest if he ever needed a hand with the sessions, I'd be happy to help out. Cue my introduction into the wonderful, wacky and emotional rollercoaster of kids' football. 'That'd be great Nick,' he said. 'We've actually got a game next Saturday morning at Brookway school near Wythensawe if you're interested?'

'No problem' I replied. 'I'll definitely make sure I'm there.'

And with those words it began. Little did I know what I was letting myself in for. Come the day, I turned up and certainly didn't in a month of Sundays expect what happened next. I walked across the pitches to where most of the activity was taking place. It was around half nine and I'd been out the previous night and felt as rough as the proverbial dog. Nigel spotted me and came over carrying a bag of balls and another one full of poles and nets.

'You know you mentioned you'd help, Nick? Well something's come up. We've had to split the lads into two teams, and they're yours over there,' he said pointing.

I'd watched the training on a couple of occasions and the standard was hardly brilliant. You have to remember these weren't the backstreets of Salford or Langley. It was Hale Barns around the lanes of leafy Cheshire. Here they were more likely to spawn a future crooked Tory Member of Parliament than a Paul Scholes or a Ryan Giggs. I noticed straight away though that Nigel had picked the best of a bad bunch for his half, and when I looked across to my lot? Imagine the fat kid from Grange Hill, Joe '90 and the Inbetweeners at eight years of age. Plus throw in our Jamie and a young lad called Dom Kinsella, his mate from school. Jay and Dom were always kicking a ball around when I picked them up from St Vincent's primary in Altrincham, and they were clearly my only hope.

'Your team's playing on that pitch over there,' said Nigel. 'And, here's your whistle.' What, I'm refereeing as well?! Inside one of the bags that he gave me was what's called a Samba net. Now, anyone that has tried to put one of these things together will understand the difficulties. It makes a striped deckchair look a doddle. Added to that a bunch of kids who didn't even know where they were playing. 'Who's in net?' 'Can I be Captain?' Or, 'Can I go to the toilet?'

I stood there in a state of shock. I had no idea this was going to happen and no idea what to do, plus I had a hangover that Paul Gascoigne would have been proud of. One of the other dads, Kevin Kinsella, who I'd never met before came to my aid thankfully, asking if I needed a lift with putting the goal frames together. Kev went on to be my number two, and really good friend. Clough and Taylor we eventually jokingly named ourselves. Next came a tap on the shoulder as I'm kneeling on the wet turf, shaking my head in disbelief and with my best jeans already soaking wet through. My United Road had taken a downhill turn to say the least!! I had thought I might end up managing Manchester United after a glittering career – not a bunch of hapless kids!

Another tap on the shoulder, what now? I look up and there's a bloke dressed in the type of flashy, bright tracksuit that even Big Ron would have thought over the top. He held out his hand. 'Hi, I'm Tony, the manager of Wilmslow Sports Football Club. We're the opposition.' I got up off my knees and we shook hands.

'Alright mate? I'm Nick,' I replied. I looked in the background and saw his team warming up in little triangles, knocking the ball around impressively, whilst half of my 'Welshy Babes' were playing rock, paper, scissors or chatting away to each other about bleedin' Star Wars.

'Five minutes to kick off then, Nick,' added smarmy Wilmslow Tony before breaking into a 'Look at me' jog to show off his smart tracksuit and shiny boots, obviously bought for the new season ahead. I'd love to write that what happened next was a stunning opening chapter into this strange little world of mini footballers, but instead it was a nightmare as we were slaughtered 15-0. The scoreline left me traumatised. I was still in shock when knobhead Tony came across at the end to shake my hand again. 'Well done Nick – good effort. Keep your chin up, eh?'

I glared at him. Did he actually just say that? They were a decent little outfit to be fair and played the ball around really well, but talk about a mismatch? Although I'd never gone on to do anything of note in my footballing life, I wasn't a lover of getting beaten at anything and, for whatever reason, their sly yolk of a manager had really got to me. OK, I was in my jeans, sweater and fancy trainers, and didn't have a clue how to put Samba goal nets up in three minutes flat like Mr Smartarse there probably could. But I promised myself that I wouldn't forget him. Keep your chin up? If he'd had said chins, I'd have probably dropped him! My days with the Red Army had maybe been preparing me to deal with muppets like him.

I took both nets down much more easily than they went up and packed the pieces away into the bag, before carrying them back across with the balls over to Nigel. 'Oh, you keep them Nick – the league starts next week and your team's first game is away to Didsbury,' he said.

'What? I don't remember saying...' Then I saw Jamie looking up to me. He was the reason I was there. My boy. Through sickness, health, break-ups and heartache forever more. Bollocks to my ego.

'How'd you get on by the way?' inquired Nigel.

'Don't ask,' I muttered, walking away from him towards our car with the two bags and my son. My real superstar by my side, and that was how it'd stay.

After my 15-0 annihilation, our next game was away to West Didsbury, where again it was a stuffing, but this time around only 5-0. Although I was gutted again at the scale of the heavy defeat, I took solace in the fact that it was only single figures. I'd like to think this was down to my tactical rethinks, but in fact our keeper had played a blinder – as well as having had a day of unbelievable luck, since the ball hit every part of his anatomy regardless of whether he was even looking the right way! Also, despite the five goals they had netted, their forwards couldn't finish for toffee.

We'd got away without getting as big a mauling more through luck than any improvement in performance. I couldn't let this go on. I had to either change it or tell Nigel I was walking away. Ever since I'd been a young kid back in the streets of Little Hulton, or at school, either in the playground or a match I just couldn't bear to lose. I wasn't good at it. It hurt and lingered in my head, putting me in a foul mood. The only other thing that came close to it was if United lost. It was an emotionally draining aspect of my personality that I simply couldn't change, and I'd no wish to do so.

What hurt me most that second Saturday morning was when some of the lads I'd inherited signed the official referee's match card Donald Duck and Mickey Mouse, instead of their proper names. I'd noticed a few of them laughing and sniggering as it was handed around beforehand, but thought nothing more of it. Now, this was under-eight's football for God's sake, I kept having to remind myself of this, but why was I becoming so wound up?

A few months previously I'd attended the kid's school sports day at St Vinnys, and was staggered when I was told on arrival that all the events were to be non-competitive. There could be no winners or losers. No joy in victory or tears in defeat. A modern PC world gone mad. It was considered 'elitist' I was told, and not fair on those less able to compete. Everyone had to win in their way. Eric Harrison would've self-combusted if he'd have been with me that day. The words 'load of bollocks' doesn't do this kind of attitude justice. This had come to mind after I'd handed in the match card back to the referee, and he'd pointed out to me that my two dopey Disney characters had signed the card incorrectly. The referee was rightly annoyed and said it would have to be reported.

Well, that was it. A line in the sand. Twenty goals conceded in two games and half the cast of a Disney movie thinking it was all some big joke. I knew who both the kids were, in fact they were more like Goofy and Dumbo. They shouldn't be here, I thought, they were crap anyway. Let them go and muck about in a Lacrosse team, or egg chasing even. No little shits were going to ruin my beautiful game. If you didn't love it, you didn't play. I was even more angry than the previous week and poor Jamie got the brunt of it in the car going home. He was annoyed too. Jamie was a talented little player and, thankfully, he had in him that priceless 'will to win' attribute. As did his mate, little Dom Kinsella. Another great kid, but they were only two. I needed an entire team. After letting off steam I finally realised I was being totally unfair, and I shut up. A short period of awkward silence followed before I pulled the car over. Jamie looked at me with a perplexed look on his face. I had a plan. If this was going to work and myself and Jamie weren't going to spend our weekends travelling around Greater Manchester getting battered by every team under the northern skies, something had to change.

'Come on Jamie,' I said. 'There must be lads at school in the playground that can kick a ball and half know what they're doing?'

'Reece,' he replied. 'My mate Reece, he's a great player Dad, and Nathan Hardy's OK as well.'

'Well tell them and get some others along to training on Friday night. Six o'clock at Stamford Park!' He smiled. I needed proper kids who adored the game and who better to use as chief scout than my own flesh and blood.

After our chat we set off to pick up Bella from her swimming lesson at the Four Seasons gym. Whilst parked up outside waiting, I noticed a young lad nearby kicking a ball against the wall, and seemingly in his own world loving it. Something that, strangely enough, you never saw much in God's own deepest Cheshire. I'd no idea why, or what made me do it, but I got out of the car and walked across to him. There was a lady stood nearby who turned out to be his mum, Ann. I asked her how old he was, explaining about my brave new plan, and hoped I wasn't coming across as a nutter. Luckily, she didn't think so and, when told he was Jamie's age, I dropped the idea of would he like to come to the football trials? I know this sounds far-fetched, but this really was my 'Fergie finds his Roy Keane' moment. I spoke to the kid and he immediately agreed to join my gang of merry men. His name was James Walsh. Tragically, James is no longer with us after he shockingly passed away just before Christmas Eve back in 2017 at the tender age of 22. I'm telling you about him because James became the fighting soul of my beautiful little football team.

You might not be surprised to know that as time went by Baza got involved, and the kids swiftly fell in love with him! None more than James. He was mine and Dad's type of footballer. Born a Walsh, but with a Welsh's passion and fire for the game. He cared passionately about the team and, in his own way, James Walsh sits equally alongside all my Manchester United legends. As our team took off and got a little older, graduating to playing eleven-a-side football in early teenage years, James played in front of our centre-backs. He'd win the ball and pass it – simply. When he got instructions from the touchline, as and when necessary, he'd launch it long. Our heartbeat, still badly missed, and one taken from us so horribly young. RIP James. Our Keano.

So, in preparation for the training session I went and bought some new balls, cones and poles. In for a penny, in for a pound. I was determined to pass on the knowhow that had become ingrained in me from my earliest memory, starting with my Grandad Harry, Baza, Bill Hardman at Parkside, Eric Harrison, Jimmy Curran, our Nobby, even Steven Sya and his guitar!

Mostly I'd do it the United way – Hale Barns style. Football was in my blood and the most natural thing in the world to me. It's quite simple and done in the right manner, starting first of all with T.E.A.M. The most important backbone, no matter what the level. We were starting at rock bottom. Holding up the fourth division. (There were only four.) Played two, lost two. Scored none, conceded twenty. It couldn't get any worse. This would, however, prove to be the start of something that if I'm truly honest ended up being probably my finest football achievement.

Friday night came around, and there was a decent turnout with quite a few kids stood chatting together, but, somehow, they appeared more serious and eager to get going. Many had already got their boots laced up and were ready to start. Others were having a kickabout. I could just sense that a feeling of wanting to impress was in the air. A new-found desire to be like real footballers, if that made sense. Anyway, it suited me.

I set up a pitch, cones first, and then got the lads together for a short pep talk. I told them that if anyone fancied playing in the new team they could, but that the most important thing for me would be that they needed to work hard and listen. I promised to improve them as players individually, and, more importantly, they'd enjoy being in the team, as this above anything else was the most important. What I really meant to say – and hoped I'd got it across – was, 'If you don't like it, see you later and don't waste my time!' I paired everyone off with a partner and a ball and had them stand fifteen/twenty yards apart, and for the first twenty minutes they just passed the ball to each other.

'Pass the ball firmly and neatly on the floor – on your toes when receiving, look at the ball, control it, don't take your eye off it. Then head up, and neatly pass it back.' Simple really, elegant, the beautiful art.

Even today I can still hear myself saying to the boys, 'Football should be played on the floor – learn to respect your teammates, head up and pass the ball neatly back – relax, but also concentrate.' The voices in my head. Dad, Eric and the lads. My tone was firm but calm, always with a smile just a second away. Those magical two words – 'Well done' – came next, because, let me tell you, every football player, no matter how young or old ever gets sick of those two words of encouragement. It's up there, along with a sincere pat on the back. Within no time, I could already see a massive improvement amongst them and was really enjoying passing on information stored in my head from past masters onto these enthusiastic young colts.

After my professional career had ended, I'd continued to play a little, at first with Salford City when Billy Garton became player manager, and a pub team – again, which he got involved with – from Monton, Worsley, called Doughty Rangers. By this time, and it was no coincidence, my love for playing had faded in tandem with my failing fitness. It all became a case of enjoying a good night out with the lads afterwards. I began to feel that, for me, football was a bit like my dancing in that my head knew all the moves, but my body just couldn't deliver. Then, along came my own personal set of Subbuteo heroes and the passion came flooding back. We'd do a bit of shooting and finally finish the session with a six a side whilst I assessed who'd I'd be starting in the team next game. It became serious stuff for me and being bottom of division four meant, in my own head, that the pressure was already on. I wasn't going to stop until we'd reached the very top…

The Rising: so, it began.

Come the next match we earned a much deserved 2-2 draw and really should've won. What impressed me most was that it was obvious that the kids had taken on board what I'd been trying to tell them. I'd stopped the rot and more importantly they were clearly enjoying it. I could see they were laughing with a spring in their step, but come kick off they became switched on. None were happier more than my Jamie and little Dom. No longer were they fighting a lone battle.

The improvement continued unabated as the weeks went on and, even though we lost a couple, the gap in quality (and goals against!) was closing fast. When it came to the very last game of the season on a late April Friday evening, we played our other club team who were known as the 'A' team, and if we won we would actually get promotion. It happened, and my little team pulled off the result of the season. I watched on proudly as they danced and jigged around the pitch singing 'We are going up, coz we are going up!' I was loving this experience, maybe I fell into it by sheer luck, but by the grace of God I'd found my niche in the footballing world once more. More importantly, Jamie was right at its heart. Along with Bella, never far from sight and always, to quote the song, 'on my mind.' Kids eh? Bloody 'ell!

Roll on division three!

Around 2003, when all this was taking place, I came to realise, and I know it's changed since then, that just about anybody could start up and run a children's junior football team. Thankfully the paedophiles who sadly infested some junior sports teams in the 70s and 80s are now being flushed out and jailed. These bastards were around when I was a kid. My childhood had been towards the end of the era in which they appeared to operate almost out in the open. There were always rumours, nothing more, but Christ, when I look back now. I played regularly against Whitehill and Nova juniors, both of whose managers have since been found to be guilty of serious sickening abuse. Thankfully I never experienced anything myself, although lads and teammates of mine have since come out to reveal what was done to them as teenagers.

In my experience managing my Jamie's team, I was also often left gobsmacked by the overall bad attitude, aggression and foul language used by some of the other team's managers. Cheating even, such as trying to get the game called off, blaming the weather if they were being beaten. Never playing the full amount of time when one of their side was refereeing. It was an extraordinary win-at-all-costs attitude that would've put Don Revie to shame! This was something that got worse the higher we moved up in the leagues. Obviously, the overall standard of football improved, but then so did the gamesmanship, as every dirty trick in the proverbial book was used to try and snatch a result. I must admit though that when up against this it made me even more determined to beat these teams, and in hindsight perhaps I too took it a little too seriously at times. I had standards though. I'd never cheat, bully or try to intimidate anyone, whether it be the ref, the opposition coach, whoever. It was too easy to lose the respect of the kids and this was always at the back of my mind, thus causing me to bite my lip. So, so many times!

Our success continued, rising another league into division two, meaning we'd be travelling further afield from our Cheshire home to far flung, romantic places such as Salford, Stretford, Urmston and Moss Side. I'd added a few new players as the games went from seven to eleven a side and onto full size pitches. We were playing under the name Hale Barns United, so you could imagine rolling up in the car park for an away game and the other mob's comments as they stood watching.

'Here they are, the silver spoon rich kids!'

'Look at them in their posh cars!'

'We'll show 'em, won't we lads!'

The little known fact that I'd picked up half of my team on the way up from local estates Wythenshawe, Broadheath and Baguley would've surprised them no end. Especially when my boys got stuck in. Occasions like this would need a Welshy, Fergie-like mental motivation tactic with the lads in the pre-match pep talk. 'Look at them,' I'd whisper over quietly on the pitch right before kick-off. 'They think you're all little posh kids – I can tell. Go and get stuck into them and show them how tough you are, and then just move the ball about quickly like we do in training, one and two touch so they can't get near you!'

I'd love seeing the fire in their eyes. Special times. We won the league again, this time at Moorside Rangers in Swinton, virtually behind the house I was born in. A late winner by our flying little left-winger James Kirkwood with a wonder goal that Ryan Giggs would've been proud of.

Finally, Hale Barns United had reached the big time. Division one. Winning had proved to be an irrepressible habit, and wonderfully infectious too. We were on a roll and, without sounding cocky, my lads were good. Very good. Personally, what it had all meant for me was that I'd managed to keep my chin up, as once told by Tracksuit Tony of Wilmslow sports team, who we'd now play. More lads joined, and I became impressed with one new lad in particular. His Grandad had turned up to watch a pre-season friendly game against Edgerton, one Sunday afternoon in early August. Blimey, he's keen, I thought. We'd started really well, fizzing passes around at speed as usual on a lovely, ripe lush home pitch. The ball went out of play and the gentleman in question stopped it with his right foot and casually passed it back along the floor to our full-back. He picked up the ball and, before turning to take the throw-in, quickly looked up to say thanks. Next moment he'd dropped the ball out of both hands and looked in disbelief, mouth open wide at who'd kicked it just three yards back to him. None other than the greatest manager the game has ever seen. Yes, that grandad. Sir Alex Ferguson, who was there watching his grandson, Jake. Jason's son. Well, that was it. My wonderful, free-flowing footballing machine went that day from playing like Brazil to Bacup Borough! As soon as Pat, my little full-back dropped that ball it was as if someone had flicked a switch and they all changed, each and every one of them in a heartbeat. All eyes constantly turned to the legend who was smiling at what was occurring. We all know that most kids want to be a footy player. Even back in my day, as a kid there was often a rumour that would go around when playing a match that there was a scout watching from a local professional club. It could actually be just an old man walking his dog, off to pick up the Sunday papers and stopping to watch a game. 'It's him!' would go the whisper! He's obviously the man with the golden ticket you often dreamt about.

So, imagine the effect when the Manchester United manager, legend and godfather of modern-day football is there within touching distance. Could I really blame them? I nearly put myself on the right wing to show I still had it, and wouldn't give the ball away. Form is temporary – class permanent, eh boss? Enough Welshy, I told myself. Grow up! As if...

My young team as teenagers were a cracking little side and great to watch too. It was an amazing run playing the game as I feel it should be played. Cavalier, taking risks, passing and movement. Always make options, help your teammate. Play as a unit up and down the pitch, whether attacking or defending. Never be afraid to shoot, or take your man on in the right area. It's an old adage, but one that remains as true today since I first learnt it in Lower Broughton. 'If you don't buy a ticket – you don't win the raffle.'

Nothing was rocket science. Football is, for me, in essence a simple game made complicated by overthinking it. In reality, though very good, none of my young team were ever going to get invited to have a trial at Manchester United. I knew more than most what a terribly steep ladder that was to climb and what it required. Not just in talent but toughness of character. Being realistic, none were a Norman Whiteside, Ryan Giggs or Wayne Rooney, but these were kids who, with a ball at their feet, made people cheer and smile. None more than me. They were a gift and will always be an integral part of my life.

The season began well, although there was a huge difference, not just in terms of quality, but the sheer physical size of the other teams. However, we more than held our own because my lads were as tight-knit as anyone could be. Quite a few of the parents and grandparents were by now lining the touchline, none more so than a certain Glaswegian, who if not doing his day job at United was a magical, permanent fixture. Always unassuming, no different to any other, Sir Alex just loved watching the kids, and in particular, Jake, play. However, circumstances forced me into having an embarrassing but polite chat with my good mate Jason, explaining that the lads melted when his old fella was present. 'In the nicest possible way could your old man perhaps stand over the other side of the pitch near the hedges, so they don't know he has turned up to watch?' It was astonishing if one of them spotted him, for the word went around like wildfire and from that moment we couldn't pass water! Other times some of the lads turned into Cristiano Ronaldo, taking on the opposition players single-handedly, and shooting from anywhere, which drove me nuts! This was their chance to impress the United manager, and by God did some of them try and make the most of it! The truth of the matter was that Sir Alex was there like any other family member, simply enjoying cheering on his offspring Jake – who I might say was a lovely little player who could ghost around defenders, and had a natural football brain. Happily, it all worked a treat! When November came around, we were up there in the top three. Next up was Wilmslow at home and I couldn't wait. My old adversaries.

By this time, Dad Baza was well involved in helping the training along with another two lads Gary Kirkwood, who knew his stuff after having played football at a decent level, and Paul Woolley, who kept us all organised with the admin side, which was a great help. We were all up for this particular match, and halfway through the second half it was 2-1 for us, when our centre midfielder and leader, Sol Webber, limped off on the other side of the pitch. Clearly hurting. Now, Sol was a tough lad, a proper athlete with one of the best attitudes you could ever want in a young player. I'd never seen him get injured and he was the nearest thing as a tackler (a dying trade, in my opinion) I'd seen for someone of that age to a young Bryan Robson. His timing, technique and strength were simply outstanding. Sol had been playing brilliantly and with there being nothing between the teams I thought to myself, if he's done for, we're in trouble here. I looked over to the far side as he crouched down, obviously in pain, when suddenly I saw someone in a dark coat and baseball cap talking over him. A familiar figure! Within ten seconds Sol had raced back into the centre of the pitch like an Olympic sprinter, rolled his sleeves up to immediately face a dead ball coming off their goalkeeper. I looked at Baza in amazement?

Five minutes later Sol smashed home a fantastic volley from a free kick to make it 3-1, and sprinted back over to celebrate with his new mate on the touchline! The game finished 4-1 with the finest performance I'd yet seen us give. Best way to describe it was Manchester United away to Juventus back in 1999. Quality, sheer grit and power all rolled into one. By then we'd started to use the rugby changing rooms next door on our Clay Lane pitch, which meant we the parents had access to the club bar post-match for a pint or two!

Everyone was in great spirits; our lads were flying in this league and nothing was going to stop us. It honestly felt that day like a Cup Final as I went around hugging each player until finally reaching Sol.

'Great finish,' I said. 'What happened to your leg? I saw you go off over on the far side and thought you were done for, mate?'

He pointed down to just below his kneecap and one hell of a gash.

'What did Sir Alex say?' I asked. 'I saw him standing over you.'

Sol smiled widely. 'He came over to check I was alright and asked what was wrong. I pointed to the gash and he said, "Oh yeah, does it hurt when you touch it?" I touched it and said yes. He said, "Well, just don't bloody touch it then and get back on out there!' So I did as I was told!'

Amazing, but I suppose if Sir Alex Ferguson tells you to do something on a cold, damp, November afternoon, you do it! As for Tony, the smartarse in the fancy tracksuit? I never bothered to lower myself. Chin up eh!

On 7th May 2007, I took charge of my last ever game at home, against Broadheath Central, and even though we got hammered 5-0 on that early summer morning, for the first time in forty-five years, Hale Barns United still won the league!

From the lower stables of division four to the heavens of division one. Pound for pound, Broadheath were probably the best team in the division. We'd beaten them away earlier in the season with a smash and grab win coming from two set pieces practiced to precision. Something I prided myself on. They were a huge and powerful outfit for their age and honestly appeared two years older compared to my lot in terms of height and development.

Also, that day there was a massive increase in turnout at Clay Lane, as the touchline was full of family and friends, and I think this all added to my little team's nerves. Midway through the first half, I was pacing up and down the touchline as usual, trying to throw words of encouragement to the lads, when suddenly I heard a familiar voice behind me. Uncle Al. Never one normally to turn out for Sunday morning games, but this was a special occasion, and he was stood next to Jake's Grandad. Always first to cut to the chase, Al said, 'Come on Nicky, get 'em going will ya!'

We'd started shocking after conceding two early goals, and could hardly get the ball out of our own half. 'No chance Al,' I replied. 'Looks like they've bottled it with all the people watching. Also, this lot are just that little bit too big and good.'

Then, it happened. I felt a firm grasp on my left wrist and glanced to my side as Sir Alex stared right at me. 'Goals change games, Nick!' he said firmly. That one moment looking into his eyes, I saw the fires burning brighter than ever. Well, talk about inspirational. He was so right, I thought. How do you think United for years turned so many games miraculously around under his Braveheart leadership? Sheffield

Wednesday at home in '93 – go on Brucie son! Do you think we'd have won on that famous night in the Nou Camp with an 'Ah, it's just not our day' attitude? Not a chance! I stared back and nodded slowly thinking to myself, you're so right boss. You're so right! C'mon Welshy, sort it!

I walked with a headwind back to the halfway line where my subs were standing, repeating to myself, 'Goals change games Nicky, goals change games.' I'd never felt more motivated in my life. We were allowed five changes that day and I was going to use them all. I told them to get warmed up, whilst I decided how I was set to go down as the finest 'Tinkerman' coach in the history of the Timperley & District Junior Football League. Three minutes later, when the ball went out of play, I raised my right arm, 'Ref, subs!' On they went. I brought a full-back off to go three at the back and four up top, including two attacking-minded wingers who lived in the opponent's half. Come on, let's do this, I thought. Game on! This moment now being where I proved what an amazing manager I was to all present. One in particular. My Nou Comp would be here on Clay Lane. Fifteen minutes later when the half time whistle blew, we were 4-0 down, and for the rest of the match I was too embarrassed to walk down the line towards Uncle Al and Sir Alex. Blimey Welshy, you've only gone and done it again.

Happily, come the end, it mattered little for we were champions! Tracksuit Tony and his Wilmslow team had lost their away match at Wythenshawe Amateurs that very same morning. I was extremely proud watching the kids celebrate. These little fellas had kept me sane during a turbulent time in my personal life. I couldn't thank them enough, but it was time to move on from the 'Welshy Babes!' That same day Manchester United also won the title, after Chelsea had failed to beat Arsenal, and in an interview at Carrington, Sir Alex, when asked if he was on the golf course again, when the news came through answered, 'No, I was watching my grandson's team play. They won their league too by the way!' Thankfully, and typical of Sir Alex, he never mentioned the scoreline!

I learned a lot in my time managing Hale Barns Juniors. About myself, my son, people generally – including the joy of being the underdog and proving people wrong. I guess that for me that journey began when my Doc's Red Army United were in the old Second Division – and I can at least see why it's possible to support and enjoy following a team that isn't necessarily at the top of the tree.

A lovely way to wrap up this particular hugely enjoyable time in my life is to recall a game against Ashton on Mersey. It'd kicked off at the end of the match between all the kids, and even some of the parents joined in! Handbags really, but a few Cheshire punches were thrown. Always a sight and a half. Hardly pay per view! The following Thursday I was at a sportsman's dinner with Ged Mason at Old Trafford, and Sir Alex came right up behind me at the table, put his hand on my shoulder and said 'Keep control of your players, would you!'

Luckily I was on it, turned to look up at him, shrugged and replied, 'I blame the grandparents.'

Happily, the great man laughed!

BILLY'S BOOTS

CHAPTER THIRTY THREE

Let me tell you a little more about my top, top mate William Francis Garton. Now, his life is a book in the waiting. A movie even. Raised in the dirty old town on the Ordsall Estate by the docks. In fact, for what we know, Billy G remains the player born closest to Old Trafford to have adorned the cherished red shirt, beating the great Eddie Colman who was tragically killed in the Munich air disaster, by a Salford stone's throw.

As a kid, through his open kitchen window he could hear if United had scored – outside in the street that the floodlight's glare lit up, across the Irwell. A Field of Dreams, though Billy's is a true story. I'm as proud as he is to say that Billy actually played fifty-one times for the Reds under Ron Atkinson and Sir Alex Ferguson. Though unless you pushed him, he'd never tell anyone.

You'd go around Ordsall back in the mid-eighties and his picture adorned a prime spot behind every bar. For one of their own to play for United was truly unique, and for someone like him to be so unassuming made such an honour even more special.

Big Ron handed Billy his United debut in 1984 against Burnley at Old Trafford, and he travelled to the ground on the bus with boots in a bag over his shoulder. Across the forecourt Billy walked, no airs or graces. Just a Salford lad about to see his dream become real. After Atkinson was sacked two years later, Billy then worked under Sir Alex from 1986–89, before sadly having to retire due to ME – an illness which I witnessed at first hand as his pal, and it was heart breaking to see him suffer...

When I started full time at the Cliff in 1983, we got on straight from the off. Billy was sharp, his Salford wit hilarious, swift and cutting. He was clued up and knew the script. At United there would be sixteen-year-old apprentice lads starting off their football careers coming from Glasgow,

Belfast, Dublin and London, upping sticks from their hometown, moving to Manchester and located in their designated digs.

Unsurprisingly, a few apart, most of the new lads were a little lost and a bit wet behind the ears when they first arrived. They were transported into an altogether new town and environment. Manchester was a different place back then, cold and harder, not so diverse or welcoming to strangers and to walk down the wrong street or venture inside the wrong area, you'd quickly find yourself in trouble. This was where myself and Billy came in. Being local lads, we knew the score and the city like the back of our hands. Where to go and not to, be it pubs or clubs. The best shops to buy the latest clobber. Where to catch the bus, find a taxi rank. Even stuff like match tickets, which was something that if not handled correctly could see you turfed out of Old Trafford faster than a Scouser with a flare gun back then. We'd advise them on all this and more, for in time they quickly became our friends, as well as workmates.

United was like being at school where you tended to look up to the older lads. Billy was two years above me and was part of a great youth team including Norman Whiteside, Mark Hughes, Graeme Hogg, Mark Dempsey and Clayton Blackmore. They almost won the youth cup in 1982, going down 7-6 on aggregate to Watford, a final now widely regarded as one of the greats. They talk a lot about the 'Class of 92', but I really do believe that the 1982 youth team would've definitely given them a game. They had special players who were equally brilliant like Norman, who was simply on another level. Sparky was also an explosive talent who'd go on to achieve great deeds in a red shirt. I actually used to think that too of Billy. I was convinced that one day he'd play for England. I'd tell everyone Billy Garton was top class. A true footballing centre-half, a thoroughbred and a superb reader of the game. What happened with the ME killed his dream, but happily, despite dark times early on, never his spirit. One of my favourite sayings is, 'A day without laughter is a day wasted', and I can certainly say I've never had one wasted being in Billy G's company.

Following his departure from United, Billy was in fact due to possibly sign for City, but his illness was flagged up on the medical, suggesting that something was dreadfully amiss. It was the not knowing that broke his heart and drained Billy's strength to go on. Being totally honest, I'm not sure how I'd have felt about seeing him play in a sky-blue shirt. We used to joke as kids that it was instilled in us all by our Mams to 'Stay away from the Maine Road.' This of course was when it was City before the Sheikh landed in Ardwick and changed the Manchester footballing landscape, albeit hopefully temporarily. Back then the days of Peter Swales, Francis

Lee and his toilet rolls. Helen in the North Stand with her bell, inflatable bananas, Moss Side terraced houses surrounding Maine Road and the rickety, broken down Kippax Street. Not our Billy that.

He did get me back involved, playing again at Salford City after taking over the player manager's job. Those were good times, though mostly for the Saturday night out following the matches. Billy drafted in some talented local lads and, when firing on all cylinders, we weren't a bad outfit. As good as gold, when asked to help raise Salford City some money and lift our profile, Sir Alex sent a team down to play us and we battered them 4-0! I can't tell you how wound up some of us were beforehand to try and win that match, although it felt very strange for me trying to beat my very own Manchester United in Salford City's orange and black kit. A few of the class of 92 turned out – Nicky Butt, Ben Thornley, as did Lee Sharpe, Mike Phelan, Gary Walsh and Lee Martin. My own cousin Kieran Toal played too that afternoon for the Reds at Moor Lane as we played them off the park.

He was a good manager and coach to be fair, Billy, although it was quite strange at times for me when he did occasionally get upset and angry in the dressing room – having one of your best mates as your gaffer.

One really funny time was when he decided to substitute me midway through the second half of an away game. He shouted loudly to me across the pitch, 'Welshy – get warmed up – you're coming off!' I was having a stinker to be fair, but how we have laughed about this since over the years…

After his professional career ended, Billy often went over to California each summer to coach kid's football, something he excelled at. After being offered an opportunity to work there permanently, Billy, wife Francine and their two young children decided to make the brave decision to emigrate and begin a new life. It was the right move for them as a family but being honest, selfishly, I was gutted. I'd miss him badly and who was I going to watch United with now?

Luckily, our Jamie was growing up and, like me at his age, became addicted to watching the Reds, so it became a ritual for us, one that we still follow today at every opportunity.

Before the move stateside we were both out and about in town one night having a few beers after a home game and I thought, sod it! 'Hey Billy, can I ask you something?'

'Course you can mate.'

'Do you ever have a dream that you're back playing for the Reds?'

Billy started to laugh. 'Funny you should ask that Nicko,' he said.

It turned out he had! Billy's recurring dream took place in the United car park. He'd pull up outside the ground and whilst walking over the forecourt, Fergie would appear from a top window near the Munich clock shouting down, 'Hey Billy, have you got your boots with you? We've a few of the lads down with a bug and I need you back son!'

My own dreams – I'd been having them for years!

They were always different and many times I was on the subs' bench, for obvious reasons! Luckily, though, I'd often get on to play the last fifteen, twenty minutes. One night in particular was pretty spectacular. I must have been out that evening to the Hacienda or somewhere similar, because as I remember in the dream the grass was over long and on a really steep slope over by the scoreboard paddock there were a couple of sheep and a cow grazing on the pitch itself!

I was in good company.

Myself and Billy had even reached the stage with our dreams on this subject that when staying over at each other's houses, we'd leave an old United shirt out on the bed pillow in whichever spare room one or the other would be kipping. The 'dream shirt,' we called it!

This went on for years until one night again we were out and about, only this time with Big Norman. Safe to say, we three were pretty relaxed and just about still standing. Norm was at the bar when suddenly I had a brainstorm. 'Eh Billo, should we ask Normski if he's ever had the dream?' Billy wasn't sure and to be honest neither was I. All quite stupid really, but I thought sod it why not, so, as Norm returned with the beers, I went in two-footed.

'Eh Normski, do you ever have a dream that you are back playing for United again?'

All went quiet and I began to think, oh, no, what have I said? Norm stared at us like we were both mad. Like a cow gazing at you over a gate.

'Dream?' he replied, almost in disdain. 'I did it!'

There was really no answer to that!

Norman Whiteside achieved great things in a wonderful career. He'd even taken the record off Pelé for the World Cup's youngest player for God's sake! Not to mention hitting the winner in an FA Cup Final, scoring in two other finals, semis, the lot. Not to mention the digging he gave Steve McMahon at Anfield in 1988. A proper Red mentioned in dispatches moment that's up there with anyone, though Norm never thought much of it. A true Manchester United legend, and then there was me? Welshy with the ultimate conversation stopper.

Big sigh…

A couple of years later I received a phone call off Norm. This itself was nothing strange, but what the big fella told me was! 'You're never gonna believe this Nicky !'

'What's up?' I asked.

'I've had the dream the last three nights running now that United offer to pay back my insurance money and the manager wants me to play again!'

By this time Billy had moved to San Diego and, despite the different time zones, as soon as Norm went off the line, I just had to ring him!

'Hiya Billy, sorry it's late but just had to let you know. You'll never guess who's just had the dream?!'

'Brilliant!' Came the reply, 'We're all mad!'

Whether we are, who knows? For my United Road I really don't know a better way to end this chapter. Good and bad, I'm still living the dream.

And I never want it to end.

DARK SIDE OF THE ROAD
CHAPTER THIRTY FOUR

My own little career path in business was going well enough and I had ventured into new areas of refurbishments such as fast food counter tops for many of the high street popular chains. I found that I really enjoyed working with architects and designers coming up with innovative ideas and solutions in Corian. A million miles away from football of course, although we did refurbish the Maine Road boardroom whilst Francis Lee took charge of Manchester City.

I had a good laugh as we fitted out the trophy room. I remember seeing the initial architect's drawings of the shelves that were well oversized and never realistically to be filled. All I ever saw in there was a mop, bucket and a washing basket full of kit. Those were the days.

I did, however, in March 2005 end up in Manchester Magistrates Court over a dispute with a former business associate. Baza got involved as he knew both families and made an agreement shaking hands on my behalf and everything had seemed fine. But as ever, there was to be a twist. The fact they went back on it afterwards was totally unacceptable, particularly as business and monetary transactions were exchanged from my side, as per dad's handshake.

I spoke to my good friend Kevin Philbin, who is a lawyer to get his thoughts. Although Kevin is essentially against anyone going to court and the legal costs that go with it, he insisted this was a nailed on case for us. They had reneged on what had been agreed. 'Just get Baza to stand up in court and say what actually happened'.

A no brainer really. What could possibly go wrong? Well let me tell you. It was a Spring morning and Baza's turn to stand in the dock to give his evidence. Suddenly, it all turned into the movie – Invasion Of The Body Snatchers.

Dad began to start inexplicably arguing with the judge! 'How dare you question me? I've created jobs for people in this town for over 30 years and paid my taxes. Who do you think you are!' Baza had totally lost it and at the time we had no idea why? He never even mentioned the gentleman's agreement and shaking hands on the deal with the other side.

Even worse for me, when we left the courtroom that afternoon and spilled outside onto Deansgate, he actually went over to our court rivals and shook hands with them. A smiling Baza even patted one of them on the back would you believe! I was in such a state of shock. To calm down and try to figure out what had gone on with him we called in The Nags Head pub. I got us a couple of pints in and then it just came flooding out. "What the bleedin' 'ell were you playing at Dad? Letting on to them was bad enough, but shaking hands and doing the best mates thing? After all they've done'?

Dad had no explanation, nothing. Ultimately, we lost the case and my £12,000.00 life's savings (which was all that was left after my divorce), wasn't enough to cover both sides of court costs. It was 'on your arse time' for me, literally. Those who have been there know the feeling. It is horrid and I would never wish it on anyone but you actually realize, you know what – it really can't get any worse than this....

A year or so later it became apparent that Dad's actions in court were totally down to his undiagnosed dementia issues which on reflection were so obvious and there is no way he should have ever been put in that position of going on the witness stand.

I didn't take him back with me the next morning to hear the judge read out his verdict. 'I found Mr Barry Welsh to be totally untrustworthy' was one memorable line the judge used. I remember saying to my mate afterwards, 'Imagine what Baza would have done if I he had heard that?'

'Time...!' came the reply.

The simple truth being Baza wasn't well, and me? I was a fiver away from buying a mouth organ, a dog and setting up a spot on Market Street.

LEARJET REDS
CHAPTER THIRTY FIVE

The ball crashed between us over our shoulders, and every glass and drink on the table in front went flying left, right, centre and in the air!

'What have I told you two about playing football on the plane?!' Yelled a Manc voice. Myself and Norman Whiteside just looked at each other in disbelief. Did he really just say that? We burst out laughing with Moet Mason staring at us both like we'd lost the plot.

'What?' he said, not understanding. Now, we've all heard it said growing up, probably off your mum: 'What have I told you about playing football in the house?!' But, on a plane?

You couldn't make it up.

After following the Reds away from a kid in everything from car, transit van, train, tube, coach – lorry even – I'd now taken to the skies as we travelled to Cardiff to watch the Manchester United v Millwall FA Cup Final in 2004, in a private Learjet, would you believe? It belonged to our good family friend from Bury, Ronnie Wood.

Ronnie first met my dad back in the early seventies in Little Hulton, when they did business together. We had a newsagents at the time and Ron came into the shop with a box full of end of line cards he'd bought from the cash and carry, and sold them to Dad at a reduced price. Ron and Baza hit it off straight away: a mutual love of United helped greatly. Dad remembers too on a couple of occasions having to bump start Ronnie's clapped out Ford Cortina. The boot was weighed down with boxes of cards. Needless to say, in time Ronnie did pretty well for himself. His Birthdays business later became a high street sensation and he eventually sold out for a very princely sum.

Great to see for this one-time Stretford-Ender, who still maintains that the church hymn 'We shall overcome' was often sang on our famous terrace back in the 1960s.

It was the season after the 1998 World Cup Finals in France and a few days before Manchester United's early league fixture away at West Ham. David Beckham had infamously been sent off for England against Argentina that summer and was subsequently blamed by the little Englanders for England being knocked out. Our number seven had become public enemy number one, and with none more so than the Upton Park lynch mobs, some of whom had even hung an effigy of Beckham outside the ground. Charming lot, God bless the queen mum, jellied eels, those lovely EastEnder folk!

I received a phone call. 'Hi Nicky, it's Ronnie. How do you and your old fella fancy going to watch United on Saturday?'

'Brilliant,' I said. 'Love to, mate.' I'd never turn down the chance of watching my team.

'Great,' replied Ronnie. 'Be at the bar next to the Hilton at Manchester Airport for 1pm, and we'll have a few drinks before the game.'

'Cheers Ron.'

He'd surely got confused? 'I think you've made a mistake mate, it's away in London, not at Old Trafford.'

'I know that,' said Ron. 'I've just brought an eight-seater Learjet, and it only takes thirty minutes to reach Biggins Hill.'

Like most things in life, what you never have you never miss. This became the same with Ron's plane, for as time went by, we kind of got used to the flying. He even had it registered in true glorious Red style, large letters on the side: RGW – MUFC – OK. Why not, we're Man United aren't we? We do what we want!

We'd get on, crack open the beers on our tables and get the playing cards out as the jet prepared for take-off. We'd start our new song off by banging on the tables!

Then, as we left the tarmac and took to the skies everyone would cheer! All very surreal: I remember saying to Ronnie on one journey, 'A bit different this Ron to having your Ford Cortina bump started in Little Hulton, eh?'

Before long, we were landing at Biggins Hill, south of Bromley in Kent. Ronnie was new to all this malarkey and it was the nearest airport he could get an OK to land at. From there it was an hour-long minibus ride around the M25, back up to Upton Park. We arrived just before kick-off and were dropped off at the bottom of Green Street, by the infamous Boleyn pub on the corner. This was memory lane for me. I'd been down this road many times previously in another, slightly less salubrious, guise. One trip that sticks out more than most took place back in 1982, when I was just fourteen years old, with my mates. I distinctly remember how frightening it was walking up the steps from the tube. Everywhere you looked, scrapping, screaming, police with dogs, sirens blaring, a 'WANTED FOR MURDER' poster had been pasted onto the station entrance walls. An Arsenal fan had been killed the week previous, which showed you how dangerous football violence had become in the early eighties.

Not forgetting the famous chicken run – those who know will remember!

West Ham and Manchester United, both home and away, was always lively both inside and outside the stadium, and that day, with the Beckham scenario hyped to the hilt by the media, remains amongst the worst. All of us had tickets in different parts of the ground and the minibus driver was told to meet us back on the corner where he had dropped us off, by the pub. It was agreed we'd leave with five minutes to go. Manchester United drew 0-0 that day, but David Beckham was magnificent. The abuse he received was off the scale, vile and sick, but that boy just rose above it. In the Upton Park tunnel beforehand, I was later told that even his fellow United players were booing him to try and relieve a little bit of the tension.

We all got there as planned and were waiting for the minibus, which annoyingly had not arrived, when suddenly around fifty lads came marching along the road towards us. I spotted them early and said to our group, 'Come on in here,' and we stepped back inside a bus shelter. I knew what was happening. After being at so many away matches there, you could smell it. This lot were here for serious trouble and probably hadn't even been to the match. Next minute Mike McGrath, son of Paddy, shouted out 'Hey Coco!' It was United's firm. The men in black. I spotted 'One punch Doyley' – so aptly named because he could drop a tree with... yes, one punch. They smiled across at us and they carried on marching past. Their day was just beginning and the next moment all hell broke loose as they ran into West Ham's firm about a hundred yards further down the road. Luckily, the minibus finally showed up and our lot swiftly boarded and we headed off to the airport. It was definitely two worlds apart, which made the journey home on Ron's new toy even more surreal!

Learjet Reds! It was never boring.

Once, I asked the pilot before going to an away game if we could possibly put a red, white and black United scarf out of the plane door, but unfortunately he refused due to safety concerns, scratching his head and obviously thinking I'd lost the plot.

Another time, going up to Glasgow to watch the Reds play Celtic, we ended up staying much later than planned. It'd all got a little messy as we partied away the evening on the razzle! Ron decided to ring the pilot. 'We've found a cracking boozer and are going to stay a few more hours, what's the latest we can get clearance to leave?' It was that simple. When you got back on board you'd close your eyes and be home faster than catching a black cab home from Manchester.

In 2009, we set off to Rome for the European Cup Final against FC Barcelona, and stopped off to refuel in Switzerland. Stretching our legs and banned from playing on the jet, myself and Big Norman decided to have a kickabout. His left foot was as majestic as ever. What a talent. He'd often shout whilst clipping a pass, always unerringly long and precise, 'Don't move!' Then, as the ball arrived under orders at my feet, I'd hear in that lovely thick Irish brogue, 'Ledge!'

None of us watching on in admiration were ever going to argue.

The actual game turned out to be a disappointing damp squib, where apart from the first ten minutes, United never turned up and the true highlight of the trip took place earlier that same Roman May afternoon. Amongst our group was the Salford tenor Russell Watson and his dad. We'd all gone for a lovely pre-match meal. The restaurant was huge, its vast ceiling decorated by wonderful, ancient mosaics with majestic pillars across the main hall reaching high. It was jaw-droppingly beautiful. A tenor was performing, though to be brutally honest he wasn't up to much, tuneless really, and hardly in the same breathtaking class as our mate. So, we chided Russell until in the end he gave up and took to the stage to sing Nessun Dorma. To say he took our breath away was an understatement, for you could hear a pin drop when the Salford lad finished, and the entire room burst into huge applause. There were even people present who'd heard him on the outside passing and came in to listen. Sadly, whilst Russell Watson captured Italian hearts, the Reds that same evening on the field failed to contain Messi and his mob, as they turned us over 2-0 for our first European Cup Final defeat. A trip that was memorable for everything but the football.

Another time we'd all met up as requested in the bar next to the Hilton. The usual suspects were present. Uncle Al, who let's just say is quite careful with his money, seemed a little giddy as he asked what everyone wanted to drink on arrival. 'Eight beers,' went the cry. Someone also suggested bacon baps were in order and these were added to Al's bill. His face was a picture.

The next minute, Mike McGrath walked through the door into the bar, and I heard Ronnie next to me say quietly, 'Oh, bloody 'ell?!'

It turned out he'd miscalculated the numbers and had just realised there were nine of us for his eight-seater silver bird in the sky. Someone had to go. Ronnie would be forced to break the news. His eyes turning to Al, whose hangdog expression meant he knew exactly what was coming. It was sadly a case of him being last asked and unfortunately grounded first. Out. His lovely wife, my Auntie Annie still tells the story of Al turning up back at their front door in Altrincham at a quarter to two looking gutted. 'What are you doing here?' she asked. 'I thought you were going down to the match in London?'

'So, did I,' he sighed heavily in reply. 'So did I, but there was a mix up with the numbers, and it cost me £96.57!'

Learjet Reds, wooah!

Sadly for us hangers on, Ronnie finally decided to sell the jet. Maybe I'll get a jet with my royalties from this book eh? An Airfix one :)

FROM RUSSIA WITH LOVE: MOSCOW 2008

CHAPTER THIRTY SIX

Moscow. Luzhniki Stadium. Wednesday 21st May 2008. As the rain came down almost Mancunian style in its ferocity, I watched with Pigeon Les alongside as Cristiano Ronaldo stepped forward to take his penalty. I checked my watch: time was short. 'Don't fuckin' miss, Ronnie!' someone shouted behind us, and then he did. I turned to Les, who looked devastated, close to tears.

'I have to go mate.'

'Nicky, you can't man, its...'

And I was gone. From Russia with love and no regrets.

One month previous.

Old Trafford: Manchester United were playing Barcelona in the European Cup Semi-Final second leg, and it was threatening to be one of those mad glory, glory nights down Sir Matt Busby Way, when your heart filled your mouth for the full ninety minutes. After a battling, if dull and dreary, 0-0 first-leg in the Nou Comp, battle resumed with a full house at the old place demanding that United show their true colours. But it was Barca who impressed early, none more so than their little genius Lionel Messi, who even sent me the wrong way in the stand a few times. What a player. I never saw George play, but if he was better than this little guy? My god! Then, on fourteen minutes our ginger prince from Langley created his own magic act. Breaking clear, Cristiano Ronaldo sped like lightning over the halfway line, only to be mugged by a crowd of yellow Barca shirts. The ball fell loose and from a full twenty-five yards Scholesy let fly a magnificent drive that simply thundered into the top corner! Cue one almighty roar!

From that moment on the Catalans laid siege to us, with Messi darting about looking for a hole in our wall. The minutes ticked down slowly while the crowd grew louder, begging, pleading for it to be over. Heart-attack stuff. Finally the referee blew and Manchester United had made it to a third European Cup Final! Moscow awaited! Scholesy what a star! He had an unparalleled ability to see passes through an extra eye somewhere on his ginger head that others could only dream about. Sublime technique with an uncanny eye for goal, whether from near or far. Arguably the finest English player of his generation and a streetwise temper that made him fearless against any odds. Sir Alex's dream of a second European Cup loomed large and I was determined to make it to the shadows of Red Square.

The following evening, Chelsea edged out Liverpool 4-3 in the other semi-final on aggregate to clinch their own place, thus denying us a confrontation against the old enemy. Maybe not a bad thing, because I don't think many hearts on both sides could've handled it. Two Red Armies congregating in Red Square could have filled Moscow's prisons for a decade!

An ecstatic Pigeon Les rang me within minutes of the final whistle after Barca. 'You up for Moscow then, Welshy?' were his first words on my mobile. 'Our Rick has got a deal on a package, there and back in the day.' Les' brother Rick was high up in the travel game with Thomas Cook, and part of his remit was to organise fans' transportation to the final in Russia.

For us this was heaven sent. Lady luck was a Red, with a beautiful red scarlet ribbon on! If life was only that simple – for at the time I'd just about got back onto my feet financially. I was slowly turning things around. I'd worked like hell to engineer the chance of a big contract at Westfield shopping centre, which was under construction in London, which would, in all honestly, be life-changing for me. It was almost in the bag, but their buyer had insisted on an 8am meeting in Shepherd's Bush the morning after the final. By hook or by crook I just had to be there.

I spoke to Rick about it and felt torn. This contract meant everything and it was essential for me to make the meeting as nobody else could cover it. I'd promised my girl Jen that I wouldn't let her down. It made me realise that maybe some things in life are occasionally even more important than Manchester United – despite being in their third European Cup Final. Rick tried to assure me. 'You'll be fine, Nick, if you make one of the first five planes flying back to Manchester after the final itself. Whichever team loses, though, are being given priority from air traffic control, so keep that in mind.'

What the hell. Win or lose, I'd make sure I was on one of those planes.

Early on the morning of the final, four of us flew out on one of Thomas Cook's planes. Myself, Les, Rick and Mike, another mate from Salford. We landed at 8:30am Russian time at Moscow airport. Rather than be herded like cattle onto the waiting buses, we immediately jumped into a cab and asked to be taken into the city centre. Rick had suggested that the best place to head to was the Ritz Carlton hotel close to Red Square. I thought we'd never get past the security guards on the door, but typically Les wouldn't let such a minor problem stand in our way. 'Just be confident lads, as if you live there!' In we went swaggering, acting like Oligarchs, and it did the trick! What a place. To describe it as merely opulent wouldn't do it justice. The hotel foyer simply dripped with gold. It was like being inside an enormous Fabergé egg.

The Chelsea team and their club's top brass – well, except for their owner and his family – were staying there, and during the day on some of our ale-fuelled visits to the gilded toilets, I remember having a piss next to Andrei Shevchenko, whilst Les shared a gold-plated urinal with none other than Chelsea coach Avram Grant!

'£27 a bleedin' pint!' I exclaimed when buying a round at the bar. As I turned to speak to Les, he'd spotted former Manchester United, and now Chelsea, CEO Peter Kenyon. This was like a red rag to a bull. Off went Les in a rage to confront him and get it all off his chest.

'Judas' roared Les into a startled Kenyon's face. Any United fan worth his salt knows the story with him and his supposed Red allegiances. Supposedly he had once been a Stretford Ender and all that bollocks, yet soon as Roman Abramovich waved his cheque book, off he sneaked, taking with him United's detailed transfer plans for the next eighteen months, ready to hijack the best signings. Anyway, Les said his piece and that was put to bed. Certainly, I don't think Peter quite expected one of Salford's finest in his face in that palace of baroque as he had his morning croissant and coffee, but there you go, such is life.

One of the defining images of that night, which is still imprinted on my mind, was the sight, at the end, of Peter Kenyon going up the stadium stairs in the pouring rain to represent Chelsea whilst Sir Bobby did the honours for the Reds. The opposite ends of the spectrum of football team representatives. You can't buy class.

As for Salford on tour, the four of us left the Ritz Carlton around midday and headed over to a highly exclusive Manchester United, executive-type luncheon to which, courtesy of our own Pigeon Les, we somehow had invites (platinum passes). He is a man with more contacts than the yellow pages. At the lunch I recognised many familiar faces as the place was brimming with players' relatives and most of the Old Trafford hierarchy. We ended up settling in a small side room that seated around a dozen people with Sheena and Janey Gibson, and a few others we knew from home. I always loved singing old United Busby songs when we got together, as did Sheena, so when we'd finished our food, washed down with some nice, local liquor, both of us got the room on its feet with a full back catalogue of United terrace classics from down the years. It's not every day that you're in Moscow building up to Manchester United playing for the biggest trophy in Europe, first sought after all those years ago by Sheena's amazing Father. My Uncle Matt.

"A day to remember, a day to recall,
as Manchester United are the best team of all!"

So, to the game. At the back of my mind was the niggling worry that I had to be on one of those first five planes out of Moscow and home, no matter what, to get to London by the next morning. A ferocious 1-1 had been fought out over the 90 minutes, with nothing between United and Chelsea as we moved into extra time. So evenly matched, it was a dogfight enriched every now and again by moments of pure skill from the likes of Cristiano Ronaldo and Didier Drogba. Then came Drogba's sending off, but still there was no breakthrough. As the Moscow rain increased in ever heavier torrents, it was now heading to a penalty shootout. I checked my watch. Oh, just get on with it! Here I was on the verge of maybe seeing the Reds win a third European Cup, whilst knowing that I had to get moving. The penalties kicked in, none were missed and then Ronaldo hit the ball straight at Petr Cech. My heart was breaking, but that was a signal. I hugged Les and was gone.

Fuckin ell' Welshy, this has to be the most grown up thing you've ever done in your life. I'd been gone two minutes walking across the stadium forecourt in the torrential rain, when I heard a huge roar go up from the United end. What the? Give me strength. Hail Mary full of grace... Let me see us either win or lose this thing. United was an integral part of my life and I decided that I could afford a few moments more. I raced back to try to get back in, but despite having my ticket, the soldiers – all armed to the teeth – wouldn't let me return onto the terraces and were definitely not of the ilk to try and blag or jib. Around me were fellow Reds who had also been too nervous to watch and had left their seats. One lad caught my eye – a Manc. We got chatting and then, the most gigantic, thunderous explosion of sound from our end that could have meant only one thing. Manchester United had won a third European Cup! John Terry had missed, and 'Viva John Terry' was born! It couldn't have happened to a...

Fergie had beaten the plaything of Roman Abramovich, who had spent the final watching on his golden throne, in his own backyard! I hugged my new mate and danced like a maniac. Finally, the security relaxed a little and I got to see us lift the trophy before heading off. Outside, I was lucky enough to flag down a taxi that took me Ayrton-Senna-style to the airport. I made the plane thank God! Homeward bound. Next morning, I drove down to London in a terrible knackered state, I must admit. Somehow, on meeting the buyer, and despite my head being still in a far-off place bathed in red, we shook hands and did the deal.

Priceless!

I'd kept my promise to Jen, and that, even on such a memorable day, was what mattered most of all.

Just a few words about my Jeno, the love of my life. Jen really is my soul mate and I wouldn't have written this book without her. She's been the making of me. We had similar upbringings. Jen grew up in Bredbury, Stockport and thankfully is Red, not Blue. Blessed like me to come from a beautiful close-knit family and surrounded by real heartfelt love. Heartfelt love that we are now so fortunate to share with our own special blended family of four wonderful kids: Jaymo, Bella, Mike and Mell.

With my Jen it really was – as Edwin dived to save Anelka's penalty and I legged it to that airport to get home to fulfil my promise – a true case of 'From Russia with Love'.

A

B

C

D

E

F

G

A   Disney originals - Jamie and Dom either side of the keeper
B   Me and Jaymo
C   Never forgetting Bella of course
D   Umbro tournament with the lads
E   Jake with grandad
F   Baza with grandson
G   Winning is a habit you could never get tired of

A

B

C

D

E

F

G

H

A   Shay and me
B   From left; Moet, me, Billy G, Les, Dave G
C   Ged, Sir Alex, me
D   Me and Jason - West Brom
E   Me and KP
F   Ged's 50th - From left; me, Moet, Norm, Billy G
G   Me and Jeno x
H   My best team

BAZA! 'GET STUCK IN'
CHAPTER THIRTY SEVEN

My Uncle Al still insists that 'If there was one man you could trust with your life, it was Barry Welsh. Once you met him, you just loved him.'

That was my old man.

My Dad, 'Peter Barry Welsh', was born on 14th June 1942, in Ancoats Hospital, the middle of three brothers, between Tony and Stephen. Baza, as he's affectionately known by all, had three loves in his life. First and foremost, wife Eileen and kids; second, the family business TBS, which he created and drove forward with his brothers back in the early seventies; thirdly, last but arguably not least, Baza's enduring love affair for the beautiful game.

One of my earliest memories is of us all driving out of Manchester on a Saturday lunchtime, going past Rabbit Hills pitches close to Irlam O' Th' Heights, and Dad stopping the car to watch some obscure, local amateur match being played. I was delighted because it meant I could get my ball out and have a kick around, whilst Jane, who could read on a clothes line, would pull out her Enid Blyton book. After a few minutes, once he'd sussed out the game, Dad started shouting encouragement to the winger on his side of the pitch. 'Go get at him, go on take him on,' I'd heard him call out! 'You've got the beating of this full-back!'

Travelling back home after the match had finished, I remember asking him,

'Who were the teams, Dad, and who were you shouting at?'

'Oh, I'm not sure,' he replied smiling wide. 'But it was a good game, wasn't it son?!'

See, he didn't have a clue and didn't care who the teams were, or know anyone playing – Baza just loved football. Anyone who knew him well prior to his illness could so relate to this story. Even in later years watching his own grandsons, if it was half time and there was another game still playing, he'd be off watching the other game. As for coaching kids, they simply adored him. 'Get stuck in' was always one of his favourite sayings whilst wearing his legendary orange socks!

'Get stuck in lads'...

He loved to tell me stories about the Red Rec, and the red and black shale pitches everyone grew up playing on in north Manchester, and how you'd have to nail leather bars on the bottom of your boots in order to get some tread, particularly if it was wet. His toecaps were made of compressed cardboard in those days! The only time you'd ever get to play on grass was in a final, or if you had an away game on the south side of Manchester! 'The soft side,' he'd jokingly call it. Later in life he told me about learning from Tommy Taylor how to head a ball – by hanging in the air – and, if you got your timing right, sometimes getting up before the defender and using him as leverage.

He was fast and tough, which went with the territory back then, but his finest attribute by far was heading. Absolutely deadly in the air. I asked him once about his best ever goal, and he told me a bullet header into the top corner of the net from outside the box for Blackburn Rovers reserves against Sheffield Wednesday! This going up the slight Hillsborough slope towards the Leppings Lane terrace. The Rovers winger had driven a brilliant hard cross and Dad, at just the right height, running straight onto it, never had to leave the ground.

'It was harder than a shot' he said. 'And I'll probably never head one better than that in my life.'

John Donoghue is a lifelong friend of Baza and always compared him to Roy Keane. 'Barry was as hard as nails.' recalls John. 'He was obsessed with football.'

Years later, when Dad was first diagnosed with Alzheimer's, he told me that those old casey balls couldn't have done him any good, especially when they were wet.

'It was like heading a brick with laces on for ninety minutes, Nicky.'

Heading a brick....!!!!!

After being released by Manchester United in 1961 (I can imagine that really hurt), Dad signed professional forms at Blackburn Rovers. The season he became full-time was a really harsh winter, with snow and ice ruining the fixture list, causing most of the second half after Christmas to be cancelled. This put a lot of financial pressure onto all professional football clubs and there were many casualties, including Dad.

Baza never gave up and eventually he ended up agreeing a semi-pro contract at Wigan Athletic the following season and continued to play at that level for the rest of his career.

A story I'll never forgot occurred in the mid-seventies. I'd gone to watch him play for Stalybridge Celtic and, pre-kick-off, I wandered off, bored stiff, up in the hills by the ground and the lovely scenic landscape that surrounded it. After a bit of tree climbing, I noticed from my high vantage point that the teams were out and warming up, so I decided to get back to the ground and watch Dad. However, I'd ventured a little further than I'd realised. By the time I got back through the turnstiles the match was already well underway. I looked out for the Stalybridge Celtic number nine but couldn't see him? That's strange, I thought. I politely asked one of the older gentleman regulars who stood down at the rails at the front by the pitch. 'Excuse me, is Barry Welsh not playing today?' He looked at me, seemingly not impressed and shaking his head.

'Not now,' he said. 'Bloody sent off after just four minutes!' I also shook my head, as if I didn't know him. Blimy, I thought. Someone must have really wound him up!

Dad had started to help grandad Harry's 'The George' pub team, who had a great rivalry with another Crumpsall hostelry called The Joiners, run by Jimmy Dempsey, whose lads Mark and Glenn I'd get to know later when they played for Manchester United's junior teams. There was nothing to choose between the two pub sides, but such did beating the other matter that both called in ringers from the semi-professional leagues around Greater Manchester to try and gain a slight advantage. It was serious stuff. Cue Barry Welsh's sudden appearance in The George's ranks! It just so happened that the Joiners' own ringer, their centre-half, was the one and same who had clashed with Baza only weeks previously before the Stalybridge match. Whilst I was still climbing a tree this guy caught my Dad clean in the face with his elbow in the first few minutes.

'What else was I supposed to do, thank him?' he said to me in the car on the way home that day. I was probably moaning that I'd travelled across town and didn't get to see him play. I loved watching Dad score a goal. I don't remember many tap-ins from him. Headers, volleys and one-on-ones were more the norm from the Welsh powerhouse. Not surprisingly after the El Crumpsall derby, where it had all stemmed from weeks before. A Salford kiss was in order and worth a sending off, all day long in Baza's eyes, so long as justice was seen to have been served!

Different days I know, and certainly a time when football was much more a contact sport. Before Dad got ill, he'd go berserk about players ducking out of a challenge, not getting stuck in or faking injury. 'Even if they caught and hurt me, I'd never show it. Now they pretend they've been hurt and nothing's bloody wrong with them. Bloody soft arses' game now with a bunch of frauds. Wouldn't have lasted two minutes in my day!'

It was never boring going to the match with Dad. His love for football often going well beyond what colour shirt they had on. He was true to his self, said what he thought, spoke from the hip and knew what he liked, and if anyone didn't like it, tough! Their problem. A more straightforward man you'll never meet. Baza was also quick thinking when needed at the match. One time at Maine Road we were in the middle of the City main stand with Lol Gee and a few other Reds when Andy Cole went through and scored for United by the Platt Lane end.

Immediately, he jumped up with his right fist raised shouting 'Yesss!' Quickly remembering where he was located, he pointed, shouting 'Offside ref!' Genius – we couldn't keep our faces straight.

In 1983, my first month at United, we played a pre-season friendly against one of Dad's old teams, Radcliffe Borough. Their big 'Desperate Dan' centre-half had kicked lumps out of me throughout the game, as was often the case when the lower clubs met United. Baza was stood behind one of the goals. I can still see him now as I write this. Around ten minutes remained and their said centre-back took the ball down to the side of their goal, quite close to where Baza was, and readied himself for an ale house clearance up field. I'd had enough by then, saw my opportunity and launched at him, catching very little of the ball with my studs, but plenty of old Desperate. As the ref came across to book me, I just happened to glance across at my old fella for some reason, and I'd never seen him happier in his life. It was as if he'd seen me score the winning goal in a Wembley Cup Final against Liverpool!

Baza had the look for once of a really proud dad.

He was probably thinking, 'Well son you've obviously brought a whole new meaning to the word average today with your performance, been kicked from pillar to post all afternoon, but at least you've given him something to remember you by.' Baza seldom praised me, but that look...

That look on his face was priceless to me that day, it really was – and it still is.

On the memory one, it was strange really with Baza. Little things which you sort of put down to wear and tear I suppose at first, getting older, forgetting where he had put his keys and just getting simple facts mixed up.

I remember one time though we actually caught him supporting Liverpool as he was watching a live match on the box at home?! Something was definitely amiss!!!

Mum sent him to the doctors to have his memory checked but he came back and said that all was well and there was nothing at all to worry about.

It was over six months later. He was definitely getting worse and forgetting a lot more things on a regular basis, so Mum decided to go to see the Doctor with him on something else and whilst there she asked was everything OK with his memory following on from his previous visit?

Either Baza had decided he wasn't going to tell Mum or he had genuinely forgot, we will never know I suppose, but the doctor rang Mum later that day to say Baza definitely had serious memory issues and that he could now discuss it with her openly as it wasn't breaking any confidentiality terms.

We quickly got him on medication, which was a blessing I suppose. This was in Spring 2006 and over the years he has also took part in various clinical trials.

He continued to work for a while. He was always the first in at TBS, his beloved company, and always the last to leave and lock up. He got to the point, however, that he couldn't even remember the alarm code – it was obviously time to ease him out.

One night I had called around to Mum and Dad's house quite late to collect some clothes, as I had lived back there for a few weeks let's say, between houses.

It was around 9:30pm and as I walked through the back door into the kitchen, I immediately knew Mum was not a happy bunny, and to be honest I knew why. I had seen it a million times over.

'Your Dad's just got in from work drunk,' she said, making her way to the oven with the pot towel triple wrapped to get what was left of his shrivelled-up tea which should have been eaten three hours earlier.

'I've only had a couple, needed to chat a few important things through on the work front,' said Baza.

I sat down at the table, really just to give him a little bit of moral support if I'm honest. I'd heard it all before so many times – whether he was cross-eyed drunk or maybe had just had three. It was always the same. 'I've only had a couple Eileen…' Lessons in life eh lads?!

Mum slammed his plate down on the hardwood table in front of him. It looked shocking, but Baza made a heroic start as he knew he was in trouble enough.

'I'm going bed,' she said, placing two tablets firmly on the table next to the plate and adding sternly, 'And don't forget to take your tablets.'

'Tablets? What do I need tablets for?' Dad replied slowly.

'Tablets for your bloody Alzheimer's!' She declared, losing her patience big time. I'll never forget his puzzled look across the table at me before saying:

'I don't remember getting Alzheimer's, when was that…?!'

He was so serious and I just couldn't help roaring with laughter, Mum even started laughing hysterically and Dad joined in, probably not knowing why.

A few years later in early 2017, it was Matthew Ged's lad's 18th birthday at Mere Golf and Country Club, Knutsford, and Ged quite rightly wanted to celebrate it in style with both family and friends alike. Dad's dementia had become quite bad by then, to the point that I didn't think it was right to take him out socially anymore as his behaviour had become totally unpredictable as he entered the latter stages of this horrible disease.

Moet however insisted he should attend – as with all my mates, he loved and missed him. 'It doesn't matter how he behaves, Nick. It's all the people who know he's ill and they will be totally understanding. I would really like him there for sure.'

I still wasn't convinced – my old dad was such a proud man and he would have hated others to see how he had deteriorated significantly in so many ways. I could even almost hear him say, 'If I ever get like that bloody shoot me, put me down or get me to the knacker's yard.'

On the night of the party, as I half expected, Baz got so overexcited on seeing everybody that his behaviour became more and more erratic, to the point that one of his old football mates pulled me to one side and said 'Get him home, Nick – it's not right.' My worst fears had been confirmed and I was annoyed at myself – I knew I should have gone with my original gut instinct.

I went over to tell Mum we needed to get going and get Dad home. She was just finishing her food from the buffet, so I got chatting briefly to Jason and his dad who were on the next table. Suddenly, next to me was Baza, bright as a button.

'Hey Sir Matt – how are you?' he says, putting his left arm around Sir Alex, who was totally fine with it. A number of his close friends had suffered with dementia so he fully understood the situation and what was going on.

'I'm fine Barry, how are you?' he replied warmly, smiling and shaking Dad's hand.

'Have you got the team in for training tomorrow morning, Matt? And do you need me in?' Sir Alex had retired himself only three years previously, but kindly went along with the conversation.

'Yes Barry, 10am at the Cliff Broughton.'

'Great,' replied Dad enthusiastically, 'I'll get there at 9:30 and get the lads warmed up first and we'll get a good morning session done with them.'

With that, he shakes hands and says no problem on for it and goes over to Mum saying 'Come on, let's get going Eileen. Me and Matt have the lads in for full training in the morning.'

He even shouts and waves across the room, 'See you in the morning Matt,' with Sir Alex waving back over.

Mum said she had never seen him so happy in years for that short winter car journey back home to Altrincham in the belief that first thing the next morning he was taking a United training session with the original father of our magnificent football club, Sir Matt Busby.

Take me home - United Road...

UNITED AGAINST ALZHEIMER'S
CHAPTER THIRTY EIGHT

Eric Harrison's Funeral: 26th February 2019

As Eric Harrison's daughter Vicky stood on the pulpit of Halifax's Minster Cathedral and read out a poem about Alzheimer's, by Owen Darnell, relating to her own father, I thought of Baza.

'Do not ask me to remember,
Don't try to make me understand,
Let me rest and know you're with me,
Kiss my cheek and hold my hand.

I'm confused beyond your concept,
I am sad and sick and lost.
All I know is that I need you
To be with me at all cost.

Do not lose your patience with me,
Do not scold or curse or cry.
I can't help the way I'm acting,
Can't be different though I try.

Just remember that I need you,
That the best of me is gone,
Please don't fail to stand beside me,
Love me 'til my life is done.'

Sitting next to me was my old friend Paul McGuiness. A pal from youth team days and, looking at him, I knew immediately that we were thinking the same thing. Whilst Eric's agony was over, Paul's dad Wilf was also suffering this dreadful disease and, like Baza, was still here. At home, living and breathing, yet, in many ways, both had already left us. When another pal Worthy (Gary Worthington) originally texted me to inform me of Eric's passing it was a strange feeling. Privately we all knew he was very poorly, though when the reality hit that Eric was no longer with us? This man who played such a huge influence on our lives growing up from thirteen to eighteen/nineteen years of age. Who we were so scared of. If he said jump, we'd say 'how high?' But there was also so much respect and, looking back now, so much fondness. These many years past now, I've never really heard anyone say a bad word about him. He taught us well and I'm not just talking about football, but more importantly lessons in life as a person.

I wasn't alone in this. It was confirmed by the people in the pews across the cathedral. Next to me was Garty. We'd travelled over to Yorkshire together. Big Norman, with his good lady Denise, in front with Kevin Moran. Eric used to say Norm was the best young player he'd ever worked with. Others sat next to me included Tony Whelan and Cliff Butler, great United people. Les Kershaw and Jimmy Ryan. Mike Phelan behind sat next to a caretaker manager called Ole Gunnar Solskjaer, for whom just forty-eight hours previous, both myself, Billy and our two lads had stood and sang in the Stretford End upper tier, chanting his name non-stop for a full thirty minutes. Something about being at a wheel!

Also sitting in front were many of Eric's old pre-United teammates. An entire row of ex-Halifax players, some in club blazers and all most probably in their 80s. I'd have loved to have watched Eric play. I'm pretty certain he took no prisoners and, like Baza, probably got his retaliation in first!

Later, when the service had concluded, we stood outside the church, hunched in small groups, shaking hands and trying to cheer each other up. Painted smiles like at any funeral. It was a sad service but also a wonderful celebration of this man who meant so much to so many. It was nice to see Clayton Blackmore, Mark Hughes and Mark Dempsey again. The talk was dementia – a seemingly spiralling illness. One of the other lads said 'My dad's got it I think – but we've not diagnosed it properly yet. Anyone know how I'd go about this?'

We were quick with advice. Worthy spoke about his Uncle Frank and how he couldn't leave the house now. His goal is one of my favourite ever by a non-Red. Frank Worthington's sublime effort for Bolton against Ipswich at Burnden Park, when he flicked the ball up and over the defender's heads before turning to smash a volley into the net!

Truly magnificent!

Dementia, however, cares little about such magic. It destroys memories and takes away the spirit.

I mention at the beginning of the book about 'heading one ball too many'. Baza, Nobby, Wilf, Eric – would any of them have believed back in the day when they bravely went up 'to win the first ball' that as they got older it may return to haunt them?

Alzheimer's isn't just a word, it is a curse – one far too prevalent these days. Unfortunately it is now too late for Baza and all the other great footballing warriors of his generation, but if this defiant illness can be prevented for today's and tomorrow's future young footballers, surely it is imperative we do so.

With Alzheimer's there is no pattern, no rhyme or reason to it, and as it currently stands it has no cure. A silent, harrowing disease that needs to be backed with infinitely more money and certainly more research to get the answers we need…

NICKY

CHAPTER THIRTY NINE

My Beautiful United Road

I'll never forget that moment in 1974 turning the corner at the Trafford Pub and walking down the Warwick Road for my very first ever Manchester United game. That same feeling even now never leaves me, almost half a century later. The butterflies of anticipation, even somehow a gratefulness that I've been given the opportunity to actually make the journey down the 250-yard brew, past John the Greeks, and onto that famous forecourt, before finally entering our magnificent footballing ground called Old Trafford.

What these money men seem to forget is that this is actually our local football team. One that for generations families have been supporting through triumph, tragedy and heartbreak. We're not a brand either. We're not Sainsbury's or Adidas. A faceless corporate organisation. See that crest with a ship sailing on it? That's got history. There's a reason it's on there and the devil below. Eric Cantona once said, 'You can change your wife, but you can't change your football team.' How true. I've been asked by mates to go to FC United of Manchester, but no thanks. To me that's like wearing a snide T-shirt. I want the real McCoy on my chest. The one established in a Newton Heath railyard back in 1878. My Grandad's United, my Dad Baza's, Uncle Al's, now mine and my son Jamie's.

In the mid-seventies we'd landed at Alicante airport en route to Benidorm. Our family's first ever time on a plane and the air hostesses actually took individual photographs of every passenger walking down the steps. The snaps were then pinned onto a notice board in the arrivals hall for sale at 100 pesetas each. The cheek of it. Dad bought them all though. Probably so no one else could. Typical!

When we'd eventually gathered our luggage and found a taxi,

I remember the driver saying to Baza, 'Ah English – Manchester United. Nobby Stiles!' We'd travelled all this way and as a seven-year-old, I remember thinking: How does he know about my team? Our Nobby? Had he been hanging around like me outside 9:30 mass at St Pat's in Collyhurst, in order to try and catch a glimpse of our United legend? If he had, I'd never seen him.

From my very earliest memory, when asked 'What are you going to do or be when you grow up?', my cousins, mates and school friends always came out with either a pop star, astronaut, fireman, racing driver. My mate Peter Dunne used to say a bin man (always adding every time 'good money on the bins, ya know').

Me? I always had the same reply and the thing is I truly believed it. I just knew it was going to happen, never a shred of doubt. I was going to play for the Reds!

'A footballer you mean then Nicky?' they'd ask again.

'No,' I'd reply. 'Just play for Manchester United. Nobody else matters.'

It was a simple enough answer to what was, for me, not a very difficult question.

I was lucky, blessed even. No story of poverty and neglect here. No broken home or abuse. Just hard-working, loving parents that created in me unassuming, down-to-earth, basic family values and goals. Oh yes, one more important thing I have to mention. I was baptised, dipped in a church font with a rather out of place Red Devil crest upon it, ensuring I supported one club forever and ever.

MANCHESTER UNITED.

Everyone from my generation I'm sure has an old family heirloom box under the bed, or stuck gathering dust in the back of a wardrobe. We were no different. Ours was a hand-made wooden piece passed down from Grandad Harry. There were mostly photographs, tattered black and white snapshots of people I didn't recognise. There was also a football programme in there – not just any, it was a Manchester United Football Club programme dated 1961. I always remember it was purposely folded over on the reserves and junior match analysis page, and as I got older, I realised why it was there, and opened always onto that particular report of a Manchester United v Blackpool A-team game that the Reds won 3-1. The second goal read even better the older I got.

'George Best beat his man and crossed for Welsh to score.' My dad. Barry 'Baza' Welsh. My hero.

If I've read it once, I must have done so a thousand times, and I used to dream, telling myself that could be me too, wearing that shirt one day and scoring for Grandad's, Dad's and now my Manchester United.

My childhood dream obviously never turned out quite how I anticipated, but I still feel extremely privileged to have once worn that red shirt, however briefly. It was a brilliant experience.

Like most hardcore Manchester United supporters, we have a unique affiliation for the club's youth policy, built initially by Sir Matt and Jimmy Murphy and then resurrected once more by Sir Alex from the very beginning of his United reign.

Most people don't realise that Manchester United have an unrivalled record of a home-grown junior or youth team player in every first team match day squad since 1937, a run of well over 4,000 consecutive games.

When we experienced that amazing win in Paris at PSG, it wasn't just the result that filled me with joy. It was watching Scott McTominay drive on the midfield, Tahith Chong and Mason Greenwood coming on as subs and then Fletcher Moss's very own Marcus Rashford smash home his last gasp penalty.

This proves the next time you go past a local park and see a small-sided junior game, somewhere amongst them there might be a future Duncan Edwards, Bobby Charlton, Ryan Giggs or just another young kid like I used to be, playing footy with a pocket full of dreams.

What I'm certain of is that this United Road of ours, please God, for generations to come will continue to create priceless home-grown talent. This is still, and always should be, the real heart and soul of our amazing football club.

Well there goes the full-time whistle and for once I didn't even get subbed!

I sincerely hope you've enjoyed the journey...

Nick

My Dad (Baza)

June 1942 - October 2020

Rest in Peace Baza
You truly were a legend and missed by so many x

ACKNOWLEDGEMENTS

First of all, I would like to sincerely thank the talented John Ludden for helping me to achieve my goal, and finally finish this book. When I first approached him by email, he never came back to me for a few months, and it wasn't until I received a call one Saturday morning, when John explained that it had gone to an old email, that I realised he simply hadn't seen it. John was interested, and really liked the idea of the story. 'It's so different,' he said, but more importantly we hit it off straight away, and he's someone I very much now class as a good mate. I remember saying to him if we make people laugh every few pages that would be great. I hope John has helped in achieving this...

Thank you also to my very good friend Kevin Philbin. I sat with Kevin and his lads in the heart of the Stretford End for three seasons. We would have been exactly where the legendary, or indeed imaginary, Johnny 'One Eye' and all the mad heads stood in that famous cage back in the day. Kevin's seats are now unfortunately executive tickets. The amount of times the lads got told to sit down and keep the noise down because it was distracting others from the game was extraordinary. Please don't ever stop being the boisterous, colourful characters you all are.

Anthony certainly wouldn't want you to do that for sure...

How United got away with doing this I will never understand, but unfortunately like everything else it's a sign of the times, and prawn sandwich money talks. If I was running United (imagine that!), I'd move the singing sections back down around the pitch as the old paddock areas used to be – it would be like a goal start every game!

Anyway, enough of that. I've been lucky enough to both stand and sit with many mates, mates of mates even, family of course over the many years, so I've decided to start with my first ever match to present everyone I can recall being with and next to, watching our famous team. Apologies to anyone who I might have unintentionally left out.

Starting, of course, with Uncle Al in the cantilever where I got introduced to Arthur Jones, Jack Trickett, Tilly the Fish, Howard and Andrew Kay, amongst others. From – now in no particular order – Keith from Bothwell Road, Bernard White, Grandad Harry, Baza of course, and Shaba our Guy, Nicky Shenton, David Baker, Peter Dunne, Blacky, Darren and Bill Hardman, and, of course, the one and only Wilkie.

Little Duncan and Pat Connelly RIP. Eyes right song on the Stretty!

Our Jane. Remember Leeds in their KKK hoods? You were scared to death at your first ever game! L B son, Jim Mc, Gezbo, Pat Riley and Robbo, not forgetting Parrafin Pete in the Scoreboard. Neil Riley and Hamy. I last seen you at Highbury, after Choccy's penalty miss, enough said.

Tony Ford, Ian Verity. Mark Owens, Mark Ellison. The United Youth lads stood at the back of D stand. Worthy, Jof Hardy, Russ, Andy Math, Andy Robbo, Ken Scott, Rob Philpot and Fraser. Not forgetting Drew McBride, who taught me some classic Celtic numbers. Billy G, Les Green (Pigeon Les), Hunty, Cranky, Dave Garton. Rick and Mike. Moscow Reds!

Lol and Damian Gee, Jersey Mick and Sean Goodwin. Boothy – thanks for looking after our Jamie at the back, who was only twelve when the coppers came in smashing heads in Rome.

Terry O'D, Chris Wright, Barry Kilroe and Chris May. Dodging the tear gas in Porto getting in! Mike McGrath, Ged Finneran and big Wes watching Cantona's Kung-Fu kick at Palace. Billy Cullis, Joseph and John Craig from Glasgow. Mikey and Jaymo, jibbin' in the back of a French lorry so we didn't miss kick off. Moet, Peter, Vinnie Dunne, Big Al and all the lads from the Albion in Montpelier. Pat and Dom Mcguinness watching probably the most unbelievable last-minute United moment in the Nou Camp. John Duffy on the way back to the airport. Billy McCarthy R.I.P, with Ro and little Billy watching Tevez warm up against West Ham. Joe O'D Cantona's volley vs Arsenal. Ged Murphy and the lads in the United-filled executive box at the Etihad, when Scholsey scored his last-minute header! Jason Ferg, West Brom away and Fellani's equaliser, 'United Affro, United Affro... allo allo!'

Sean Collins sat watching John O'Shea's last-minute winner at the Kop end. Sue C and Linda v West Ham.7-1, sorry! Kevin Kinsella and the boys, Josh and Paul, Blue Nose! Fleury, Chelsea away. Big Norm, Russell and his old fella at the Rome final. Pop Junior and Kieran.

Guy Norbury disgusted with me for applauding Keane off the pitch after the Harland challenge! Andy Fernie, Simon Platt, Billy the Bad

Magician. Bernie from George's. Big Gordon and Joe Jordan. The Goodison semi-final '85. The scenes beyond belief before kick-off. Jeno, West Ham away, the Rooney hat-trick. West Ham again, Jaymo-Rashford's bender. Dave Toal, Highfield Road. Ron and Stevie Wood. Pete Done. Big Malc, Paul Mc and the Jamiesons in the box against Liverpool. The League Cup Final. Matt and Georgie Mason, any Nani goal. Ged Couser, Frankie Garton and Phil Olsen. Dermott and Archie Craven. Mick Cookson, Lindsay Walsh. Paul Walker, Paul Goulden and Stanley, Chef, Mell, and our Bel. Joe and Dessie Scanlon.

And, last but not least, Millwall's own Joe 'the boy' Toner. The 1990 Charity Shield. There's probably so many more, but the road just goes on and on....

Thanks to all my family and friends...... UTFRs x

*Old Trafford June 2020
From left; Big Malc, Uncle Al, me,
Baza, Jaymo, Moet, Pigeon Les*

Printed in Great Britain
by Amazon